GEHRING
LOST
& FOUND

11/29/22

To Dr. Ulrich—

All My best,

Frontispiece: Charlie Chaplin in *Shoulder Arms* (1918).

GEHRING
LOST
& FOUND:

Selected Essays

by Wes D. Gehring

BearManor Media

2019

Gehring Lost & Found: Selected Essays

For information, address:

BearManor Media
4700 Millenia Blvd.
Suite 175 PMB 90497
Orlando, FL 32839

bearmanormedia.com

Typesetting and layout by John Teehan

Cover photo: The author in his first BSU office (circa 1978).

Published in the USA by BearManor Media

ISBN—978-1-62933-481-3

To Sue

TABLE OF CONTENTS

PART TWO: FILM/LITERATURE HUMOR

PART THREE: CONTROVERSIAL AND/OR TRAGIC

PART FOUR: GENRES AND/OR DIRECTORS

PART FIVE: DECODING THE DETAILS

PART SIX: THE LIGHTER SIDE

"FILM COMEDY IS ..."

laughing at this "cockeyed
caravan" instead of
turning on the gas,

realizing the "boy genius" was
no genius when it came to
homogenizing the Marxes,

wondering if a reference
to Carmen Miranda should
have occurred in "Brazil,"

hurting your sides instead
of those people talking
during Charlie's "Oceana Roll,"

knowing the "Great Stone Face"
still managed an Oscar load
of expression with those eyes.

(Originally appeared in *Literature/Film Quarterly*, Vol.
23, No. 2, 1995; Wes D. Gehring copyright.)

ACKNOWLEDGEMENTS

I WISH TO EXPRESS MY GRATITUDE to BearManor Media for their interest in publishing a selection of my essays stretching back to when the world was young. Individual thank yous would necessitate an accompanying Stephen King length volume covering 40 years of names and libraries. However, a few people were present for much of this long adventure. Janet Warrner has been there from the start with editorial and proofing assistance. Kris Scott has performed multiple computer tasks in the preparation of many books and essays—with a special thank you to her student staff in assisting on the preparation of this text: Isabella Fuller, Kristen Rice, Riley Beall, and Maddie Hershberger. Ball State emeritus professors David L. Smith and Conrad Lane were frequent sounding boards through the years, as were Los Angeles friends Anthony Slide (who doubled as a long distance mentor), and Joe & Maria Pacino. Plus, my family provided so much support, especially my daughters Sarah and Emily. With a dad for a film professor, they have also grown into long-time movie assistants.

The many libraries are scattered over several countries. Yet, there were always four constants: the New York Public Library's main branch at Fifth Avenue and Forty-Second Street (guarded by the lions "Patience" and "Fortitude"), New York's Performing Arts Library at Lincoln Center, the Academy of Motion Picture Arts and Sciences' Margaret Herrick Library (Beverly Hills), and my home base Ball State University Bracken Library (especially its tireless interlibrary loan staff).

These essays have been drawn from a number of publications whose interest made this text possible. A major thank you to: *Film Classics Reclassified*, *The Forum* (Ball State University), *HUMOR: The International Journal of Humor Research* , *The Indiana Magazine of History*, *The Journal of Popular Film & Television*, *Literature/Film Quarterly*, *The Muncie Star Press*, *SCIO: Journal of Philosophy* (Spain's San Vicente Mártir Catholic

University of Valencia), *Studies in American Humor, THALIA: Studies in Literary Humor* (Canada's University of Ottawa), *TRACES of Indiana and Midwestern History*, and *USA Today Magazine*.

I own the copyright on all the essays, save those for *USA Today Magazine*. Thus, I owe a special thank you to the magazine's Publisher and Editor-in-Chief, Wayne M. Barrett, for facilitating copyright permission from the "Society for the Advancement of Education, Inc. All Rights Reserved." I am primarily a freelance writer, which means I retain copyright, unless I had signed a contract. However, at *USA Today Magazine* I wear several hats: Associate Media Editor, columnist, and an occasional essayist. Thus, it is their copyright.

For consistency, some reformatting has been done concerning the different style sheets used by scholarly and mainstream publications over a forty-year period. Footnotes have been standardized for the scholarly pieces. However, the "casuals" (essays), such as for *USA Today Magazine*, retain in text references.

AUTHOR'S PREFACE

> In order to laugh at something, it is necessary (1) to know *what* you are laughing at, (2) to know *why* you are laughing, (3) to ask some people why *they* think you are laughing, (4) to jot down a few notes, (5) to laugh. Even then, the thing may not be cleared up for days.
> – Robert Benchley (from *After 1903—What?*)

I HAVE BEEN A FILM PROFESSOR for 40 years, and this book contains a few of the essays which best define me and my work. It has helped that I always wanted to be a writer. Moreover, it has been a blessing that my favorite pastime has also helped my career. How about that? I use the phrase "define myself" but writing is really a Rosetta Stone to discovering who you are. Ideally this sometimes taps into common elements to a larger audience—what a biographer calls "the universal in the particular." It just might be what moves the needle.

The following pieces cover many topics, but my greatest niche has addressed film and/or humor. A key early catalyst was comedy theorist Jim Leach's comment, "a genre which encompasses the visions of Jerry Lewis *and* Ernst Lubitsch is already in trouble." He went on to request a more ambitious examination of comedy genres, noting what many film comedy enthusiasts have long felt—"if a genre is defined too loosely (as with comedy), it ceases to be of any value as a critical tool." Much of my career has addressed that request. Still, all of what is here honors that ancient axiom, "That the unexamined life is not worth living." Thus, the essays touch on many other topics, including my fascination with both biography and deconstructing art. And writing is my most winning means for self-discovery. I am a firm believer in Vonnegut's mantra on writing and not letting one's hat size get larger in the interim "[It allows] mediocre people who are patient and industrious to revise their stupidity, to edit themselves into something like intelligence ... [writing] also allows lunatics to seem saner than some."

Of course, there is autobiography in all forms of writing. Thus, my father loves film and/or comedy and is quick with a quip. Presto—here is a selection of his son's essays on film and/or comedy which attempts to be entertainingly insightful. *However*, one cannot forget the subtler D. H. Lawrence observation on one's self and the arts, "Trust the tale, not the teller." The interpretation of art should start with you. How did you first react to the creative work? This step comes before the artist's definition or the perspective of any given critic. However, this does not then preclude exploring what the artist and others explicate from the object. Weighing and discussing these varied evaluations are what make one an educated individual. Liberal arts is about being exposed to a diversity of ideas and/ or people. And recognizing that diversity stimulates the human spirit and a greater capacity for self-realization. Consequently, my career as a writer/ professor can be summed up by Robert Frost's observation, "I am not a teacher; I am an awakener."

Paradoxically, who you are and where you are in the script of your life actually perform that metamorphosis on a more personalized subliminal level, too. I am reminded of that ephemeral fact from an early comment in Steve Martin's memoir, *Born Standing Up*, "[I'm] writing about someone I used to know." I often had a similar feeling in sorting through scores of essays written over four decades. The pieces were frequently of a slightly different me. This is like Vonnegut's novel *Slaughterhouse-Five*, which pitched the premise that one does not die, but rather randomly surfaces in another period of said life. As I made my selections I did feel a bit as if I were pinballing through my own past.

The above thought also provides a segue to a second aspect of this anthology. It is something of a rescue mission. Like Edgar Allen Poe, I have often felt that frequently the best writing is something that can be read at a single setting ... rather like the length of a movie. Writing in the compressed form of an essay can often be exhilarating ... even to the point of experiencing one of those fleeting moments of clarity when life makes sense.

Maybe it is as simple as that most basic writing axiom—"less is more." As much as I enjoy writing books, this long form has sometimes made me feel like the director Francois Truffaut played in his film within a film, 1973's *Day For Night*, "Shooting a movie is like a stagecoach trip in the old West. At first you hope for a nice ride. Then you just hope to reach your destination." I have never felt that way writing a succinct essay.

So what is the rescue mission? My desire to become a writer has always been driven by a longing to join that army of voices preserved between book covers—a time-tripping escape into another world of friends and ideas. My aspiration is a cross between a sort of immortality of words, and a punched time card proving I was briefly here in this "rough cut" existence. And yes, given that my philosophy of life is "cling to the wreckage," I know nothing is forever. However, books endure longer than the journal essay that quickly joins yesterday's newspaper in the recycling bin.

Be that as it may, in the final analysis, the following "pieces of time" *attempt* to provide a personal modicum of lucidity to two delightful distractions in life—humor and/or film. If *Annie Hall* (1977) suggests "art is where we attempt to get it right," criticism merely helps us find our own personal right ... or left, because there are no guard rails in life.

– Wes D. Gehring

COMEDIANS

CHARLIE CHAPLIN & BUSTER KEATON:

Comic Antihero Extremes During the 1920s

> In pantomime, strolling players use incomprehensible language … not for what it means but for the sake of life. [writer, actor, director Leon] Chancerel is quite right to insist upon the importance of mime. The body is the theatre ….[1]

ONE CANNOT FIND two more either unique or different antiheroic types in American cinema than Charlie Chaplin (1889-1977) and Buster Keaton (1895-1966) during the 1920s. However, before addressing this remarkable duo, beyond their pointedly different perspectives, one must footnote the decade with pioneering film critic James Agee's 1949 essay, "Comedy's Greatest Era."[2] This critique jump-started the serious study of silent comedy and created a 1920's pantheon of four: Chaplin, Keaton, Harold Lloyd (1893-1971), and Harry Langdon (1884-1944). Besides being a boon to a then neglected era of film comedy study, it began the overdue resurrection of the tragically neglected Keaton—the Lincolnesque "Great Stone Face." As notable as the essay was, it did, however, almost imply a parity among the four in many subsequent works. Nothing could have been further from the truth. Chaplin and Keaton were true auteurs, starring in and directing their films, though Keaton did not always take a credit. Moreover, the subtext to their cinema embraced pivotal philosophical perspectives about modern man.

In contrast, Lloyd was a comic by committee, creating reels of diverting mind candy. Ironically, nonetheless, he was the decade's comedy box office champion for several reasons. While Chaplin let years pass between productions, Lloyd was the most prolific funnyman in the business. In addition, his cinema was the most gag-saturated of the group—created by his army of writers. Moreover, his persona of an underdog mama's boy who eventually makes good unintentionally matched the satire-drenched world of contemporary novelist Sinclair Lewis' "Babbitt" bourgeoisie— what critic H. L. Mencken called "booboisie" America. Now, while still amusing, it seems more like a comic era preserved in amber. However, while he did not have the brilliant comic intuition of Chaplin and Keaton, Lloyd had a firm handle on the innate boundaries of his screen alter ego, which is obvious in his 1928 memoir, *An American Comedy*.[3] This is no small accomplishment, because it is not enough to just be funny. Consistency allows the comedian to create a singularity viewers come to expect and return to see again and again in a variation of the same pattern.

Indeed, this lack of an undeviating constancy was what contributed to the decline of Harry Langdon even before the coming of sound. Plus, Langdon was so late to the feature-length comedy table, he should never have been invited to sit with the aforementioned trio. Chaplin and Keaton were capable of wearing several creative hats (in fact, the creator of the Tramp was a whole haberdashery), and Lloyd was good at delegating authority to his clown posse. However, Langdon caught what film historians have come to call "the Chaplin disease." That is, after Frank Capra helped create a very successful baby persona who survived only by the grace of God (with a template drawing from the literary persona of Jaroslav Hasek's novel *The Good Soldier Schwejk*, 1921-1923), the comedian egotistically failed his attempt to go it alone even before sound.[4] With the then sudden end to his "A" picture career, Langdon returned to vaudeville and later met a comedian on his way up, Bob Hope. In one of Hope's many later memoirs, 1977's *The Road to Hollywood*, he shared:

> One day between shows, Langdon told me: "Young man,
> if you ever go out to Hollywood and become a star—and
> I think you could—don't make my mistake. Don't try to
> convince yourself that you're a genius."[5]

Keaton, paradoxically, now considered Chaplin's only artistic rival in the 1920s, was popular then, but he was neither credited with reaching the aesthetic heights of Charlie's iconic Tramp, nor the period turnstile magic of Lloyd, despite the "Great Stone Face" being equally productive during the 1920s, too. Fittingly, for the tale which is about to be told, Keaton's reviews were sometimes even cultish, such as when he falls in love with "Brown Eyes" the cow in *Go West* (1926). In contrast, a typical Lloyd review often opened along the lines of, "I don't know why I'm even critiquing this picture, his films are always funny." Still, at the time, Chaplin was essentially a cinema god. For example, the title of a 1924 *Los Angeles Times* article worshipfully says it all: "Chaplin Shows [the] Art of Pictures [a] Century Hence."[6] (In fact, Chaplin's ability to write, direct, perform, produce and compose the music for one groundbreaking picture after another over 50-plus years remains unprecedented.)

So what were the 1920s' extreme differences between Chaplin and Keaton's anti-heroes, and how has the latter artist come roaring back to rival this genius? Chaplin's antihero is a mix of comedy and pathos, a moving exercise in secular humanism—trying to make sense of life's emotional and/or intellectual experience. For the Tramp, the key human action is sacrifice, even when that means letting go of love because it is the right thing to do, such as in the close of 1928's *The Circus*. There was pain but also resiliency, as he shook it off and proceeded to shuffle away with what poet Carl Sandburg christened those "east-west feet." Moreover, that sacrifice never plays as a lesson. Maybe this is Chaplin's greatest gift— what the later *New Yorker* critic Anthony Lane called the challenge the comedian most relished—"How to make an adventure out of a sermon?"[7] In the 1920s, Chaplin's antihero still embraced optimism. And even if a twist in life seems either impossible to comprehend, or inconceivable to accomplish, such as raising an abandoned baby in 1921's *The Kid*, it still behooves one to try.

In a big picture perspective on art there are basically two views, which one might call clarity and chaos. Chaplin, at least during the 1920s, embraced the first. That is, life is messy and ambiguous. The individual constantly feels rudderless. The clarity perspective, to paraphrase Woody Allen's antiheroic stage director near the close of 1977's *Annie Hall* says, "Art is where you get it right." You make sense of it, if only for the length of a movie. There is comfort in that … whether it is true or not. That is Chaplin in the Jazz Age.

The chaos perspective, in film terms, says life is a rough cut which will end with sudden unfinished finality. There is no comfort in this, and art should remind people that life is chaos, not an attempt to comfort them with a lie about clarity. This is the antihero world of 1920s Keaton. A signature sequence along these lines for the Great Stone Face occurs in *Daydreams* (1922). In this metaphor for the treadmill nature of life, Keaton is caught in a whirling riverboat paddle, and walks ever faster to avoid becoming a victim. It is life in an eternal holding pattern, like the two clowns forever killing time in *Waiting for Godot*, or Lewis Carroll's Alice running faster and faster to just stay put in *Wonderland*. In anticipating the Theatre of the Absurd, Keaton's antihero is about questioning, not comforting, the mind. He invites a cerebral pondering of existence itself. Keaton is the essence of dark comedy absurdity, in which his contemporary Kafka embraces the same mantra, "The meaning of life is you die." Even more to the point, to paraphrase Albert Camus, "one needs to be pulled out of our happy barbarism."

Keaton's most famous nickname fits this dark worldview perfectly— the "Great Stone Face." In a dangerous world it is not safe to reveal one's emotion. A poker face represents security, as does another basic rule— avoid involvement. The humanistic sacrifice of Chaplin's Tramp, who also goes by the interactively friendly nickname of "Charlot," only invites possible pain ... and even potential harm for whomever one attempts to help. Keaton's nihilism has also invited other nicknames, such as Spain's somewhat softening of this dark philosophy by calling him "Pamlinas"— nonsense. Of course, I have always associated that twilight tag with a darker American expression of the 1920s: "a whole lot of nothing." Certainly, that axiom jells with Keaton's more common period nickname in various European countries—"Zero."

Maybe more coherence can be showcased by a broader example involving a shared goal with humanist Chaplin and the paint-by-number Lloyd—the theme of love. For Chaplin there is the promise of love at the close of *The Kid*, when he is reunited with Jackie Coogan's title character, after the cop brings him to the boy's new home—with his biological mother Edna Purviance. Chaplin's "Little Fellow" seems embraced not only by Edna and Jackie but metaphorically by the entrance of the home itself. It is reminiscent of the part one conclusion of *Birth of Nation* (1915, a film which Chaplin had seen repeatedly when it opened). The sequence in question has the "Little Colonel" (Henry B. Walthall) returning from the Civil War and also metaphorically being embraced by house and household.

Moving on to *The Gold Rush*, the Tramp eventually wins the love of the saloon girl Georgia (Georgia Hale) by sheer persistence. And though she is a more worldly woman than Chaplin's norm, it is her streetwise maturity which eventually succumbs to his child-like devotion. And while

The Buster Keaton surrealism of *The Frozen North* (1922) is the type of material which makes him so resonate with modern viewers.

he does not get the girl in *The Circus*, he gives her up as an act of love, almost like a parent—knowing intuitively what is best for her. Charlie even orchestrates the girl's marriage and then leaves the circus in which the young woman and her new husband are performing, wisely recognizing it would be too awkward. *The Kid*, *The Gold Rush*, and *The Circus* all show the Tramp pointed towards either the hope of future happiness or at least a demonstration of sacrificial love for another's happiness. With a Lloyd scenario it is always a telegraphed ending of love and happiness, such as the concluding stroll with his screen bride-to-be (Mildred Davis) in *Safety Last* (1923). Indeed, it was such a given for Lloyd, that leading lady Davis even became the comedian's wife in real life. Again, it is pleasant mind candy escapism, without the nuances of emotions emulating from the Tramp.

In contrast, the hollowness of relationships for Keaton's "Zero" character is best illustrated by the concluding of *College* (1927), which seems to follow a pattern not that different from many 1920s university comedies, such as Lloyd's *The Freshman* (1925). That is, both comedians fail at athletic events until a miraculous finale which allows them to win the day. Thus, *College* seems to end like a Lloyd template, with Keaton and leading lady Anne Cornwall happily leaving a church after a marriage ceremony.

This would be the cheery close to any number of Lloyd pictures, and one expects as much here, since Keaton had seemingly been following his fellow comedian's formula. However, Keaton had been losing control of his career at this point, and *College* had not been something he wanted to do. Thus, one has several reels of funny yet not typically inspired Keaton shtick until that surprising close, in which he cuts off all that budding happiness at the knees. That is, one dissolves from a happily married couple, to a more than frustrated pair of parents overwhelmed by their children. Next, one dissolves to them as an old arguing couple. Finally, one has a concluding dissolve of two tombstones. This is a visit to Samuel Beckett-like existentialism years before 1953's *Godot*.

Moreover, life's pointlessness for Keaton is hardly limited to *College*. It is peppered throughout his filmography, such as his tombstone conclusion to *Cops* (1922). In this latter film he gives himself up to death with as little emotion as the title character in Albert Camus' *The Stranger* (1942). Indeed, if the central paradox for Camus is that even a passible life is rendered meaningless by death, Keaton's films frequently showcase an absurd life which is only amusingly relevant for *viewers*—not Mr. "Zero." In fact, Camus might later have been speaking for both himself *and* Keaton when he said of his personal and professional life:

> I have only ever been happy and at peace when engaged in a ... task ... And my work is solitary. I must accept that ... But I cannot avoid a sense of melancholy when I find myself with those who are happy with what they are doing.[8]

It is hardly coincidental that while Agee's essay put Keaton's antihero back in play, it was not until the 1960s that film critics were putting him on a par with Chaplin's Tramp. Why was this? Though many factors led to this less than serendipitous event, one might boil them down to the release of Stanley Kubrick's *Dr. Strangelove: Or How I Learned to Stop Worrying and Love the Bomb* (1964). While black humor had always existed, this is the film which made it acceptable fodder to be drawn to center stage American cinema.[9]

Therefore, with dark comedy and absurdity being Keaton's antihero MO, his work was suddenly being seen as timely, while Chaplin's Dickenesque 1920s antihero, drawn from a true Dickenesque childhood, had the creator of the Tramp seeming more derivative of the past.

The irony here is that Chaplin's "Little Fellow" had entered a progressively darker world in the 1930s and 1940s, which had helped make way for *Dr. Strangelove*.[10] Indeed, even with *Shoulder Arms* (1918) and *The Gold Rush*, Chaplin's Tramp had dealt with war and the threat of cannibalism. But his broad humor mixed with poignant pieces of time, like *The Gold Rush*'s "Dance of the Dinner Rolls," or sacrificing love for the greater good, had made his screen alter ego Teflon Tramp—able to avoid controversy. In contrast, Keaton's "Zero" had always been based in parody, and by the time of *Go West* and *The General* (1927), the comedian was embracing what is called "reaffirmation parody."[11] Spoofs of this type are not so obvious. They are often confused with the genre being undercut. This could be exemplified by 1969's *Butch Cassidy and the Sundance Kid*. A Western, yes, but …. Paul Newman's likable outlaw had never killed anyone, always had run from "high noon" type shootouts and could not even shoo away the tethered horses of the posse chasing them.

Reaffirmation parody risked this more subtle form of burlesque going over an audience's head. Thus, the humor of Buster's cow-loving antihero in *Go West* was missed by much of its original audience, such as *Photoplay*'s period review of the film: "Hardly a comedy because hardly a laugh. Yet the picture is very interesting."[12] Moreover, the reception of Keaton's antiheroic train engineer in *The General* leaned even further on reaffirmation parody. Though now often considered the comedian's most significant film, the seriousness with which he often played his part made it seem more like a straight adventure film. Worse yet for its 1920s audiences, Buster's dark comedy often negated sympathy for his antihero. For instance, at one point Keaton pulls out his sword, and the saber portion separates from the handle and shish kabobs an enemy sniper.

Death on screen for 1920s comedy did not go over well, especially when it involved America's most traumatic war, with some veterans still alive. Thus, with regard to *The General*, even Keaton's most perceptive period critic, Robert Sherwood, said in his 1927 *LIFE* review, "… someone should have told Buster that it is difficult to derive laughter from the sight of men being killed in battle.[13] *Photoplay*'s closing comment was even more biting, "We mustn't neglect to add that the basic incidents of 'The General' actually happened."[14] Naturally, the modern viewer wants to shout, "That's the point of dark comedy!" Regardless, one should add that Keaton's trademark minimalist face would only have made the veiled seriousness of the comedian's period "reaffirmation parody" seem all the more somber. Moreover, even when Chaplin later completely embraced dark comedy in 1940's *The Great Dictator*, playing both the Hitler-inspired title character and the Tramp-like little Jewish barber, one still never saw anyone die on screen.

While the dark comedy of Keaton's *The General* proved to be too far ahead of its time, one aspect of his antihero was quite contemporary with the literary humorists of his ilk, such as James Thurber, Robert Benchley, and S. J. Perelman—the battle of the sexes. These antihero writers could only play at being rough, à la Thurber's later "The Secret Life of Walter Mitty." In contrast, Keaton had no difficulty, at least in this film, of using his heroine as a prop, or worse. This comedian was nowhere near Chaplin's Victorian romantic rule of idealizing his 1920s heroine. Thus, one aspect of *The General* enjoyed by the period *New Yorker* critic was Keaton's rough and tumble ways with his leading lady, Marian Mack:

> She is terribly inefficient, and her attempts to be of service during emergencies are all dismal failures ... but on top of that departure from the standard, the girl is subjected to a mass of indignities. She is tied in a sack and put where stevedores [manual laborers] throw barrels and packing cases on top of her. The hero chokes her after one of her little blunders, and when she perpetuates an act of considerable stupidity he hurls a log of wood at her.[15]

Though Keaton's *General* unruly behavior towards women was atypical for his antihero, traditional plot-driven heroines were seldom significant to his "Zero" figure. After all, his screen alter ego cared more for *Go West*'s cow, just as he preferred the title character locomotive of *The General*. Yet, even if he had always been heroine rough, the absurdity to be found in his films, either violent or otherwise, would have been consistent with the vaudeville act in which he had grown up. The seemingly indestructible "Buster" had been used by parents—primarily his dad—in the most physically brutal of turns, like The Three Stooges on steroids. There was much hitting and breaking of objects, particularly furniture, between father and son. However, the pièce de résistance core of "The Three Keatons" involved throwing the boy about, with the key to the program's humor being young Keaton maintaining that seemingly unnatural resistance to pain symbolized by that stone face. This forerunner to the theatre of the absurd environment is best explained in a 1927 *Photoplay* article by the comedian's father:

> His mother and I had a burlesque acrobatic set in which my wife and I threw Buster about the stage like a human medicine ball. [This sometimes involved literally tossing him into the crowd, especially if there was a heckler. One night in Syracuse, New York, father Joe told Buster:] "Stiffen yourself, son. Catching him by a valise-handle-like contraption we had fastened between his shoulders, I gave him a fling. The next instance Buster's hip pocket flattened the nose of that troublemaker in the front row."[16]

As a footnote to this tall tale-sounding article, an attached handle with which to throw a person, albeit a small one, at other people might sound like a fabrication. Yet, in American college football of the late 19th and early 20th century, quarterbacks were also outfitted with handles with which to gain yardage by being thrown over the line of scrimmage. (The forward pass had yetw to be invented—or had it?) Regardless, it was not until President Theodore Roosevelt convened a 1905 White House conference on college football to address the rising number of gridiron *deaths* that the "handle" practice was phased out. However, this ban did not apply to vaudeville, and the undersized Buster would continue to be a human projectile for another decade. This living missile was truly a "clockwork orange," part human and part machine.

Keaton later poo-poohed much subtextual thought being put into his antiheroic films. However, the comedian's memoir (whose very title acts as a misdirection, *My Wonderful World of Slapstick*), and other 1920s quotes suggest at least an intuitive anticipation of existentialism.[17] For example, in a November 25, 1922, interview with Great Britain's *Picture Show* magazine, Keaton observed, "If you want to make people laugh you must weep, or at least be in enough trouble to make you entitled to weep." Keep in mind that in Albert Camus' later existentialistic primer, *The Plague* (1948, with its title acting as a modern metaphor for the individual isolation of man), the novelist/philosopher wrote that with this isolation, "no one had hitherto been seen to smile in public."[18]

Along similar subtextual lines Keaton appears headed towards a comically whimsical tone in a 1926 *Ladies Home Journal* article chronicling some of the worldwide nicknames attached to his screen persona. Yet, then comes the existentialistic-like pay-off:

> No one as yet has given me authentic translations [for my figure's nicknames] but I imagine that most of these [character] names of endearment signify null and void, and their combined meaning, if totaled up, would equal zero.[19]

Boom! There it is. Keaton's feelings/curiosity towards his persona were as emotionless as his *dead*pan face. In Camus' *The Stranger* (a name which could be applied to sphinx-like Keaton), the novelist's title character is executed not so much for having killed someone but rather for having shown no sentiment. One is immediately reminded of Keaton's seemingly heartless murder of a cowboy early in *The Frozen North* (1922), his short subject parody of Western star William S. Hart. This is especially apt here, because it is not readily apparent the killing is a dream-driven spoof. In contrast to Keaton embracing this "Zero" perspective, think about Chaplin affectionately referencing his antihero as "The Little Fellow" in the voice-over for his tweaked 1942 re-issuing of *The Gold Rush*. This Chaplin moniker for the Tramp is an emotional "heart on his sleeve" drawing love as much as he projects it. As *Photoplay*'s January 1928 review of Chaplin's *The Circus* observed, "[Comedy is] a gag, of course, but a typical Chaplin gag [is] touched with humor and humanness ... that is the secret of [his] human interest plot, which will hold your attention to the end of the story."[20] Thus, if Chaplin's antihero emotionally speaks to one's idealized better half, Keaton's "Zero" targets the reality of cerebral cynicism—clasping an antihero as a cipher is fundamental existentialism.

This is why trains are so central to Keaton's art, whether in the delightfully absurd-looking (yet based in reality) *Our Hospitality* (1923) locomotive which begs to be called a children's "choo choo," or the title-billed iron horse of *The General*. For Keaton and comedy, trains and/or the mechanical object in general, provide a greater insight into his comedy. In Luis Buñuel's 1927 review of *College*, the surrealist perceptively wrote, "Keaton arrives at comedy through direct harmony with objects."[21] This meshes with Buster Keaton's other-worldly minimalist face. Keaton has an organic connection with mechanical props, especially large ones. Grounded in a childhood in which he was used as a "human mop," his antiheroic persona is grounded in human beings as undependable, whereas a cared-for mechanical object is stable and unfailing. Like the neglected period paintings of Gerald Murphy, such as the *Watch* (1925, which fittingly for Keaton shows the interior workings of a *railroad* pocket watch), mechanically-connected subjects suggest a sanctuary from human hurt—for an individual damaged through failed personal relationships.

In contrast, the rare mechanical object in Chaplin showcases comic human frustration, failure and easy relatability to the viewer, such as his taking apart a broken alarm clock in the early short subject, *The Pawnshop* (1916). Before ultimately reducing it to a pile of seemingly unrelated metal objects, he creates a metamorphic magic show for this doomed-from-the-start "operation." Indeed, his first act is along medical lines. He produces a stethoscope to check for a heart rate. Along the way he will drill into the clock as if it is a safe, subject it to a can opener as if preparing beans for supper, and eventually examine the scrambled insides with something resembling a jeweler's magnifying eye-piece—either for a solution, or to discover something of value. He then returns it to the customer with an expression that, if verbalized, would best borrow a phrase from Dudley Moore's antiheroic title role in 1981's *Arthur*, after also failing to fix something—"It's a goner." Of course, if one then flashes forward twenty years to 1936's *Modern Times*, Chaplin's antihero is quite literally swallowed by a giant machine and has a nervous breakdown. This attack on the dehumanization of a mechanized world, inspired by Henry Ford's creation of the first mass assembly line, again puts Chaplin and Keaton in different antiheroic camps.

While Keaton was busy growing up as "Zero," Chaplin's equally persona-producing childhood was also an act of survival. But while Buster's was an apprenticeship in existentialistic absurdity, which was a box office hit, Chaplin's was often as a street kid in search of love, whose father had abandoned the family and whose mother (Hannah) was slowly losing her mind. But in her periods of lucidity she was a loving parent to Chaplin and his older half-brother Sydney.

Hannah was once a London music hall singer. But when her career ground to a halt, she attempted to support her boys as a seamstress and part-time nurse. Though they were barely getting by, Hannah attempted to maintain a happy front for the children. Besides playfully reviving romanticized shtick from her days on the stage, she could perfectly mimic the passing parade of people viewed from their tenement garret window (the address changed often as they could afford less and less). Regardless, these ongoing comic tutorials provided invaluable lessons for the future films of cinema's greatest pantomime artist. Chaplin was later most generous in crediting his talent and general mindset to his mother:

> I learned from her everything I know. She was the most
> astounding mimic I had ever saw [sic] … It was in
> watching and observing her that I learned not only to
> translate motions with my hands and features but also to
> study mankind.[22]

(Though now often forgotten, Sydney was also a successful silent film comedian.)

When Chaplin was barely six, Hannah began suffering bouts of mental instability, which necessitated a sort of revolving door relationship with mental institutions. This sometimes meant the boys had to work at parenting their mother, as well as just getting by. For Hannah, what had begun with severe headaches reached chronic psychotic dimensions by 1898, when she was admitted to London's Lambeth Infirmary. In a horribly ironic twist upon being a praised mimic, she was eventually diagnosed with "the great mimic" disorder—that era's phrase for syphilis before the Wasserman test was developed.[23] (The medical aphorism came from the fact that the disease could imitate other medical problems.) How she contracted syphilis will probably never be known, though the need to provide for her children might have pushed her into part-time prostitution, the Victorian era fate of approximately twenty to twenty-five percent of London's female population.

Already like a child from a Dickens novel, young Charlie would now become more familiar with a series of institutions programmed to care for orphaned or abandoned children. The boys even experienced the wrath of fairy tale literature's proverbial wicked stepmother when Charlie and Sydney briefly stayed with Charles Sr. and his mistress—who, with a child of her own and an increasingly alcoholic mate, had no time or inclination for extra duties. Even then, Charlie seldom saw his father, with prominent entertainer Charles Sr. coming home late, if at all, after a music hall night of performing and drinking with the customers—an unfortunate practice strongly encouraged by management.

No wonder Chaplin would observe late in his life, "… to judge the morals of our family by commonplace standards would be as erroneous as putting a thermometer in boiling water."[24] Sympathetic fallen women are often a fixture in Chaplin's movies, including the post-Tramp picture *Monsieur Verdoux* (1947, with Marilyn Nash playing the streetwalker).

Needless to say, however, Chaplin's antiheroic films of the 1920s and for much of his career in general, are full of idealized sympathetic women often in need of the Tramp's help—a stark contrast with the often less than understanding Keaton cinema counterparts.

Consequently, like Dickens' writings, Chaplin's antiheroic Tramp films, especially *The Kid*, are infused with a social conscience and a stylized realism. In many ways "The Little Fellow" continued to highlight the important social issues of the novelist's heyday, most specifically keying upon poverty and all its related ills, such as the abused and/or neglected child, things Chaplin had experienced first hand. After all, the comedian's antiheroic character was that of a Tramp, who rescued the abandoned baby of *The Kid*, or the mistreated and abused young heroine of *The Circus*. (One should also remember that even Dickens created the empathetic prostitute Nancy of *Oliver Twist*, 1837-1839, a serialized novel.)

Given all these factors, especially the tragic and complex nature of Chaplin's relationship with his beloved mother, is it any wonder that the antiheroic yet often child-like Tramp often assumes a parental nature with a needy supporting player? The range is immense, from the aforementioned baby, to the blind flower girl of *City Lights* (1931, a production started in 1927). Plus, given the multi-faceted, often *rags to riches* nature of the Dickensian world, here was another factor which was true of Chaplin's real life, his films frequently had unlikely happy endings. Though Chaplin's movies will become progressively darker after 1930, his Tramp antiheroes will usually continue to use comedy to fight for progressive social issues. Given this humanistic agenda for change, Chaplin's screen alter ego during the silent era has at least one foot in a stylized realism.

Consequently, Chaplin's 1920s world view provides another difference between his antihero and that of Keaton's. With the latter figure's "Zero" stuck in a Theatre of the Absurd world, surrealistic events are a common experience, such as his tired *Sherlock, Jr.* (1924) projectionist falling asleep and entering the film within the film. Years later, this inspired Woody Allen to reverse the process and have Mia Farrow's screen hero exit another movie within a movie during 1985's *Purple Rose of Cairo*. However, even Buster's cinema "reality" is often surrealistic, and one is not just speaking of entering movies, or *Go West*'s cow entanglement. In *The Navigator* (1924) he dons a spaceman-like diving suit and has the most amazing adventure. A particularly impressed period reviewer for the *Los Angeles Times* observed:

> Down there Buster uses one swordfish as a weapon to fight
> a duel with another swordfish … He puts up a sign …
> "Dangerous, Men at Work." When the job is done, while
> he is still at the bottom …, he fills a bucket with water and
> washes his hands—and then empties the bucket! He uses
> a lobster which catches his leg to cut a wire, and he does
> other things equally funny … And there's an eerie minute
> full of thrills when he has a fight with an octopus ….[25]

However, the signature scene for this swashbuckling underwater Douglas Fairbanks is when he must walk out of the ocean. Buster's antihero suddenly surfacing in his seaweed-adorned diving suit is like a cross between a soggy extraterrestrial and *The Creature From the Black Lagoon* (1954).

As a brief addendum, this whole sequence no doubt was the catalyst for the Keaton-loving Salvador Dali to wear a deep sea diving suit, just like Buster's, at London's 1936 "International Exhibition of Surrealism." There have been past tangential references sometimes vaguely linking Keaton's film and Dali's stunt—but it had to have been *this* bizarre exit from the sea which caused Dali to also attempt a lecture in such a suit at the conference. Indeed, even Dali's 1936 artwork seems to second this hypothesis, such as his *Lobster Telephone* from that year—which was a box cradle and a lobster for a receiver. Of course, as a whimsical tongue-in-cheek observation from a student of the absurd, maybe lobsters open-for-comic-transformation make them a subtextual existentialistic basic. For example, when Jean-Paul Sartre tried mescaline, he believed he was being followed by lobster-like beings.

The surrealist world of Keaton's antihero is often dependent upon formalist filmmaking tricks, such as seemingly entering a movie screen, or the equally unique short subject *The Playhouse* (1921), in which Buster's "Zero" plays every character in the picture. Through an elaborate masking of the camera lens into narrow slits, and the countless backwinding of the film to expose film footage of a different Buster by a *hand-cranked* camera, he is able to play a nine-man minstrel show, the pit musicians, and the entire audience! It will take a much more technically savvy Hollywood to match it when Oscar Levant plays all the parts in a Gershwin gala from *An American in Paris* (1951), or John Malkovich goes through a portal into his own mind and arrives at a chic café where he also plays everyone in the aptly named *Being John Malkovich* (1999). Ironically these exercises in multiplicity diminish the uniqueness of the individual and make the "Zero" moniker all the more appropriate for Keaton, or these other figures.

Chaplin the filmmaker is much more interested in testing his antihero in the real world of long takes and full shots, which emphasize he is indeed doing what he seems to be doing. The most pivotal statement on this remains Andre Bazin's essay, "The Virtures and Limitations of Montage," in which he rescues Chaplin from being considered a technically limited artist. Thus, the close to this piece remains the seminal statement on how less was more for Chaplin's antihero:

> ... his gags derived from a comedy of space, from the relation of man to things and to the surrounding world. In *The Circus*, Chaplin is truly in the lion's cage and both are enclosed within the framework of the screen.[26]

Traditional editing or special effects would have distracted from the amazing mime of Chaplin. For that same reason, Fred Astaire used long takes and full shots to underline that he and his celebrated partner Ginger Rogers were actually doing it all—no "montage musical" here, à la later pictures like 1983's *Flashdance*, in which Jennifer Beal's dancing was largely created via editing and a body double.

Finally, the antiheroes of Chaplin and Keaton struggled along on canvases of a radically different size. Keaton was more than capable of scaled-down pantomime, such as his gifted ability to reproduce every tick of both a baseball pitcher and a batter in *The Cameraman* (1928). Yet, even here, the giant backdrop of an empty Yankee Stadium ultimately sells the sequence. Consequently, Keaton's antihero uses the world as his often dangerous backdrop, whether it is playing dodgeball with an avalanche of rocks in *Seven Chances* (1925), or fighting a tornado and a flood in 1928's *Steamboat Bill, Jr.*—with his immortal gravity-defying walk into a gale.

Such a large milieu often necessitated sizeable props, from his ever-present trains, especially in *Our Hospitality* and *The General*, to the diverse ships of *The Navigator* and *Steamboat, Jr.*—able to tackle either an ocean, or the giant Mississippi. And with the world as a backdrop, full of mammoth mechanical objects, or massive living stampedes of women (*Seven Chances*) or cattle (*Go West*), Keaton's long-shot, full-figure antihero was often reduced to his mesmerizing "Zero." And if one did see that "Great Stone Face," that same number still came to mind.

In contrast, Chaplin's antihero played to a small room, such as the aforementioned *Pawnshop* alarm clock, or the delightful dance of the dinner rolls in *The Gold Rush*. But there are so many other examples to choose from, such as the torn bedcover which the Tramp so naturally transforms into a robe in *The Kid*, and the same film showing a quick check of Jackie Coogan's hygiene before eating, or coaching him in the boxing sequence. *The Gold Rush* seems to pile on one after another: dancing while being accidently tied to a dog, his joyful feather pillow-bursting sequence, pretending to be frozen stiff as a board, attempting to stay balanced in a cabin tilting over an abyss, and so on. And *The Circus*, while not his greatest film, is certainly his most amusing: the various fun house mirror scenes, pretending to be a mechanical figure, ruining the various magic acts by accidently revealing the tricks, and trying to balance on a tightrope with a monkey's tail in your mouth.

These then are the two antiheroic visions of Chaplin and Keaton, which again reflect the spirit of their characters. With the Tramp there is the emotional intimacy of a small space which begs for love. With Keaton it seems more about survival in an oversized world and the paradox that mechanical things are more dependable than people, or as critic Alexis Soloski said of a David Monet play, "… there is longtime distrust of the human heart and human institution …."[27]

Who knows, maybe the differences just spring from early settings for two struggling children. Chaplin savors the precious fleeting moments with an entertaining mother at a garret window, while Keaton bemoans parents who used him as a "human mop" as he looks out a train window while going to an endless list of abusive vaudeville bookings.

(Originally appeared in Spain's *SCIO: Journal of Philosophy*, San Vincente Catholic University of Valencia, November 2017; Wes D. Gehring copyright.)

NOTES

1. Albert Camus (trans. Philip Thody), *Notebooks: 1935-1942* (1962; rpt. Chicago: Ivan R. Dee, 2010), 199.
2. James Agee, "Comedy's Greatest Era," *LIFE* (a pictorial magazine not be confused with an earlier humor publication with the same name), September 3, 1949.
3. Harold Lloyd (with Wesley W. Stout), *An American Comedy* (1928; rpt. New York: Dover Publications, Inc., 1971).

4. See Frank Capra's *Frank Capra: The Name Above the Title* (New York: Macmillian, 1971); In conversations and correspondence with the author, particularly a letter dated December 10, 1979, in which Capra reframes the influence of Schwejk on Langdon from the director's memoir. (The spelling of Schwejk sometimes appears as Svejk).

5. Bob Hope and Bob Thomas, *The Road to Hollywood* (Garden City, New York: Doubleday & Co., Inc., 1977), 12.

6. "Chaplin Shows [The] Art of Pictures [a] Century Hence," *Los Angeles Times*, February 3, 1924.

7. Anthony Lane, "Looking For Heroes," *The New Yorker*, June 6, 2005, 106.

8. Edward J. Hughes, *Albert Camus: Critical Lives* (London: Reaktion Books, 2015), 124.

9. See the author's *American Dark Comedy: Beyond Satire* (Westport, Connecticut: Greenwood Press, 1976).

10. See the author's award-winning book *CHAPLIN'S WAR TRILOGY: An Evolving Lens in Three Dark Comedies, 1918-1947* (Jefferson, North Carolina: McFarland Press, 2014). *Huffington Post* selected it as one of the Best Film Books of 2014.

11. See the author's *Parody as Film Genre* (Westport, Connecticut: Greenwood Press, 1999).

12. " 'Go West'—Metro-Goldwyn," *Photoplay*, May 1926.

13. Robert Sherwood, "The Silent Drama: 'The General,'" (*LIFE* was the satirical rival to *The New Yorker*, and should not be confused with the later pictorial *LIFE* in which James Agee's "Comedy's Greatest Era" appeared. See footnote 2.)

14. "'The General'—United Artists," *Photoplay*, March 1927.

15. "The Current Cinema: 'The General,'" *The New Yorker*, February 12, 1927, 51.

16. Joe Keaton, "The Cyclone Baby," *Photoplay*, May 1927, 124.

17. Buster Keaton (with Charles Samuels), *My Wonderful World of Slapstick* (Garden City, New York: Doubleday & Co., 1960).

18. Albert Camus, *The Plague* (1948; rpt. New York: Vintage Books, 1975), 271.

19. Buster Keaton, "Why I Never Smile," *Ladies Home Journal*, June 1926, 174.

20. *Photoplay*, "The Shadow Stage: 'The Circus,'" January 1928, 45.

21. Luis Buñuel, "Buster Keaton's 'College,'" in Francisco Aranda's *Luis Buñuel: A Critical Biography*, trans. and edited by David Robinson (1975; rpt. New York: Da Capo Press, Inc., 1976), 273.

22. R. J. Minney, *Chaplin: The Immortal Tramp* (London: George Newness, 1954), 6.

23. See both Stephen M. Weissman's essay "Charlie Chaplin's Film Heroines," *Film History* (Indiana University Press), Vol. 8, No. 4, as well as Weissman's book *Chaplin: A Life* (New York: Arcade Publishing, 2008), which includes an Introduction by the comedian's daughter, Geraldine Chaplin.

24. Weissman, "Charlie Chaplin's Film Heroines," 75.

25. Grace Kingsley, " 'Navigator' Great," *Los Angeles Times*, October 6, 1924, Part 1:7.

26. André Bazin, "The Virtues and Limitations of Montage in *What Is Cinema?*. *Vol. 1*, selected and trans. Hugh Gray (1958; rpt. Los Angeles: University of California Press, 1967), 52.

27. Alexis Soloski, "As Battered as Job, He Bills by the Hour," *New York Times*, February 28, 2017, C-5.

JOHN BUNNY & BUSTER KEATON:

Beyond Just Bookends To Silent Film Comedy

THE ROTUND 260-POUND John Bunny (1863-1915) was America's first international cinema comedy star. A former prominent stage performer, he entered the fledgling film industry when it was largely based in New York City (1910). Working for Brookyln's pioneering Vitagraph Studio, after a lengthy stage career, he quickly became an iconic cinema star, before his untimely death from Bright's disease (a kidney disorder). Beloved around the globe, his *London Times* (April 29, 1915) obituary stated:

> [He] enjoyed remarkable popularity during the last four years, and it is said that the people of five continents have laughed at his face.

In fact, the previous year London's *Saturday Review* (April 1914) observed, "Not to know Mr. Bunny argues oneself unknown… Mr. Bunny is a universal friend, and the most famous man in the world." That same year *American Magazine* (August 1914) said, "In Paris they called him 'Monsieur' [which for them meant Mr. Cinema itself], in Germany he was nicknamed "kintop," affectionate slang for "the movies," and in Russia he was "Pockson," which was vaguely meant then as "the underdog."

Bunny's persona could be called a template for W.C. Fields' (1879-1946) later screen character, since both entertainers had a gift for playing the henpecked husband, such as the latter comedian's inspired picture *It's a Gift* (1934) and *The Bank Dick* 1940, a film in which Fields' title character

John Bunny: Fat, Funny, and Forgotten.

even claims to have known Bunny). A comparable Bunny marital dilemma would be a *Cure for Pokeritus* (1912), in which he attempted a secret boy's night out of smoking, drinking, and playing poker, only to run afoul of his dominatingly Olive Oyl-thin wife Flora Finch (1869-1940). Their frequent teaming as a visually funny fat-skinny duo came to be known as a "Bunnyfincher," as well as establishing a screen tradition of physically mismatched comedy twosomes. Also, the popularity of Finch's controlling wife anticipated George McManus' classic period newspaper comic strip *Bringing Up Father*, which first appeared in 1913 and was later known as *Jiggs and Maggie*, with the latter figure often wielding a rolling pin.

While Bunny helped inaugurate the silent screen clown, Buster Keaton (1895-1966) later became the only real artistic rival to Charlie Chaplin's (1889-1977) alter ego Tramp. However, by that time, the coming of sound became a contributing factor (with the loss of Keaton's creative control) to ending his short silent feature film heyday (1923-1929). Nevertheless, Keaton's signature "Great Stone Face" had eyes which registered every nonsensical detail under that pancake porkpie hat. Consequently, his silent films remain timely by way of a *Waiting for Godot* (1953) absurdity, arguably best represented by Keaton's *Sherlock Jr.* (1924). In this movie the comedian manages to enter a film within a film, solve a mystery, and then return to what Albert Camus' existentialist *The Stranger* (1943) would call "the gentle indifference of the world."

Sherlock Jr. has remained such a touchstone movie in cinema history that it was the inspiration for Woody Allen's acclaimed *The Purple Rose of Cairo* (1985), in which Keaton and Chaplin's greatest total auteur successor (writer, director, actor) reverses the screen magic by having a character step out of the movie within the movie. Only in this postmodernism period, his extraordinary action cannot produce a *Sherlock Jr.* superficial happy ending. Regardless, the exalted nature of *Cairo* might best be measured by an Allen admission in a recent *Rolling Stone* (May 13, 2016) interview. The modest existentialistic artist confessed one could erase most of his illustrious nearly fifty-movie filmography, save for a handful of pictures starting with *Cairo*.

Be that as it may, how are Bunny and Buster more than bookends to a time when movies did not talk? One might begin with some lesser parallels before embracing a genuine cinema discovery. First, poor Bunny, who might now be called "fat, funny, and forgotten," was then much praised for having the 1910 foresight to see a better future in switching from the stage to the screen. In a composite interview from the 1913 magazine

Motion Picture Acting, and a 1914 *Pictures and the Picturegoer* essay, the journal *Cinema* (May 16, 1915) recycled Bunny's first thoughts on the subject:

> I wanted to be with the "shooters" [filmmakers] … so I cancelled my 30-week contract with the Shuberts [a major vaudeville theatre chain] … and frankly told them I wanted to work in pictures. I offered to work in my first picture for nothing … it seemed to me that the cinema— in America at least—was to be a great thing of the future.

Today Keaton also receives kudos for refusing a well-paying 1917 part in a Broadway musical in order to embrace a low-paying film opportunity. It was a wise choice but hardly as groundbreaking as Bunny's decision seven years earlier. Keep in mind that in the early 1910s many Americans still felt viewing movies was an unrefined activity. For instance, in groundbreaking critic James Agee's Pulitzer Prize-winning autobiographical novel *A Death in the Family* (1957), he describes how Chaplin's 1915 Tramp "flicked hold of the straight end of his cane, and with the crooked end, hooked up … [a woman's … skirt] … in exactly the way that disgusted Mama."

A second parallel was that Keaton's film mentor was a new comedy darling of the masses who, with Chaplin, was now surpassing Bunny— Fatty Arbuckle. Anyone teamed with this larger version of Bunny, as the diminutive-sized Keaton immediately was, found himself in another fat-skinny comedy contrast. However, while the older Bunny was largely sedimentary in his laughable contrasts with Finch, rather like she was posing with a beached whale, the giant Arbuckle was an amusing study in almost dainty motion. Though Keaton would only elevate himself to greatness after Arbuckle moved on, this comic contradiction was his introduction to film.

Third, while 1917 Hollywood was fast becoming the world's motion picture capital, numerous movie productions remained in New York. Thus, while Bunny had been in Brooklyn, Fatty and Buster were toiling away at the fancy sounding Colony Studio—which was merely a former Manhattan warehouse on East 48th Street. However, Colony would soon move uptown to a Bronx studio on 176th Street.

Maybe because New York had three major league teams, or simply because baseball was still the "national game," it was very important to Bunny and Keaton (and his guru Arbuckle). Moreover, Colony Studio's new location put it in close proximity to the city's dominant New York Giants' famed Polo Grounds, which also doubled as the home field of the New York Yankees from 1913-1922. (The Yankees, formerly known as the Highlanders, had previously played at the nearby Hilltop Park.) Besides these 1913 Yankee name and location changes, the year was also memorable for the Brooklyn Dodgers. After playing in several different parks, the team moved to the now celebrated Ebbets Field. Consequently, baseball was a pivotal part of Bunny's and Keaton's lives, surfacing in assorted ways. For example, Bunny was a fan of both the Giants and the Dodgers, and at least one of his movies, *Hearts and Diamonds* (1914), featured several period stars. The most prominent player caught on film was the amazing Giants pitcher Christy Mathewson (1880-1925)—"The Gentleman Hurler" posthumously elected (1936) into the Baseball Hall of Fame as one of its first five inaugural members. Having Bunny get away from Finch for a baseball game was a perfect scenario for his antiheroic screen relationship, and undoubtedly other such "Bunnyfinches" once existed. However, the comedian's filmography is incomplete, with many missing titles. (Besides the passage of time, early nitrate films were often recycled to save on costs.) Moreover, Bunny also enjoyed the adulation he received as a celebrity sports star at the Polo Grounds, or Ebbets Field. For instance, during a 1914 Giants game against the Boston Braves:

> at which fully 20,000 people attended, where dozens of men famous in political, civic [and] literary affairs inspired but passing comment as they entered the grandstand, thousands of people rose and cheered when Bunny made his appearance (*Indianapolis Star*, January 10, 1915).

In contrast, one of the shy Yankee fan Keaton's most memorable movie sequences occurs when he impeccably pantomimes being a pitcher, and then a hitter, in the empty Yankee Stadium of *The Cameraman* (1928). Baseball was so important to Keaton that a major factor in working for him was baseball skills. That is, whenever he was stuck for a comic idea during a film shoot, everything stopped and the company played baseball until the boss had an inspiration. Though he was a gifted player, Keaton is exceptionally funny failing to make the baseball team in *College* (1927), as well as several other sports. Plus, he did not have to be the best player on his production teams. For example, former Philadelphia Athletes and St. Louis Browns pitcher Byron Houck was a cameraman on *Sherlock, Jr.*, and a few years later one of Keaton's prop men was St. Louis Cardinal slugger Ernie Orsatti. (Houck later pitched on a Pacific Coast League team owned by Arbuckle. This is where Keaton no doubt made his connection with the player.)

Beyond these random if ever noted parallels between Bunny and Buster comes the pièce de resistance link. A 1914-1915 theatrical roadshow by the former comedian, *Bunny in Funnyland*, seems to have been the inspiration for Keaton's much honored entry into the screen within the screen during *Sherlock, Jr.* Without taking anything away from the extended nuances Keaton later brought to the phenomenal sequence, credit for this comic revelation has always rested upon the younger comedian. Of course, as Paul Murray Kendall noted in his *Art of the Biography* (1965):

> The biographer can only answer that biographical truth is not and can never be absolute truth … what he engages to tell is the best truth he can find, to the best of his abilities.

Yet, *Bunny in Funnyland* seems to provide the "best truth" possible. In other words, as the French would say, here is a "concours de constances"—a confluence of circumstances.

First, *Bunny in Funnyland* was a hit multimedia stage production at a time when Keaton was still appearing in vaudeville. It would have been most improbable for the young comedian, a real student of all stage acts, to not be aware of Bunny's touring three-hour epic—seemingly a precursor cross between the zany disjointed Olsen & Johnson's *Hellzapoppin* (1941) and television's *Rowan & Martin's Laugh-In* (1968-1973). For example, when Bunny's mega-hit show made its first Indianapolis appearance it "played to the biggest three days' business of any similar attraction that has ever appeared … [here, and] hundreds were turned away at every performance" (*Indianapolis Star*, January 15, 1915).

The *Star* went on to observe, "the opening of the performance shows the famous comedian in moving pictures. This gives way and the comedian himself steps out of the frame [screen] and then the fun begins." The sketches which follow include a reproduction of Bunny's Vitograph studio, and presumably more movie/magic chicanery. However, period newspaper accounts are sketchy, such as the *Chicago Tribune* (October 11, 1914) praising Bunny's participation as an "actor, singer, dancer, raconteur, mimic, and celebrity." Some accounts, however, suggest a close which has Bunny doing a final film flimflam by either entering or exiting a movie screen.

Second, Keaton often borrowed screen shenanigans from his stage career, and the comedian's description of how the "Sherlock Jr." film to film hoax was conceived would have been a bit of comic trickery known to a theatrical veteran like Bunny:

> We built a stage into that frame but lit it in such a way that it looked like a motion picture being projected on a screen ... the lighting gave us the [movie] illusion, so I could go out of semi-darkness into that well-lit screen (David Robinson's *Buster Keaton*, 1969).

Again, Keaton did so much more than Bunny with his screen shell game. Yet, history is made not only by major players but also by those who time seems to have forgotten. Moreover, if film scholars do not peer into shadowy corners, a sense of historical continuity is lost, and one puts art into an intellectual coma.

A third potential link between the crafty screen stratagem of Bunny's *Funnyland* being known to Keaton involves his sister-in-law—1920s silent film star Norma Talmadge (1894-1957). Her first modest contract part came in John Bunny's *Neighboring Kingdom* (1911). While the comedian's filmography is incomplete, the one compiled by historian Sam Gill (*Silent Picture*, Summer 1972) has Talmadge surfacing in at least two other Bunny pictures—*The Troublesome Stepdaughters* and *Lovesick Maidens of Cuddleton* (both 1912). Plus, the Talmadge family was close to Bunny. And Norma's younger sister, Constance, also a later silent star, was said to do a very entertaining imitation of Flora Finch. This is not exactly a smoking gun but paired with the proceeding factors, one has at least an added reason to re-examine and/or just remember the faded film pioneer John Bunny.

One might draw an analogy from the aforementioned Chaplin and Arbuckle. Probably Chaplin's most charming sketch is *The Gold Rush*'s "Oceana Roll" (1925), when those fanciful dinner rolls suddenly become the delightful dancing feet of a foreshortened Tramp. Yet, Arbuckle had done the routine in *The Rough House* (1918). Still, Chaplin essentially owns the sketch, because his version is simply inspired, topped off with pathos. Yet, Arbuckle deserves some recognition, both for continuity's sake, and creative recognition. Bunny has been largely forgotten, while Arbuckle is now remembered for a scandal of which he was innocent. History, like art, is where we should constantly attempt to get things right.

THE MARX OF TIME

The only tradition in our family was our lack of tradition.[1]
– Harpo on the childhood of
the Marx Brothers.

HOW DOES ONE DESCRIBE the influence of the Marx Brothers? Their impact upon American humor and upon American popular culture in general has been immense, and one should mention in particular their significance as cultural icons, their richly ambitious influence upon schools of comedy, their impact upon modern entertainment, and their easing of the transition from silent to sound comedy. Moreover, their comedy has made a distinct imprint upon western culture itself—lofty stuff for a comedy team that struggled for years in the lower level of vaudeville. This cultural Marx Brothers metamorphosis is also ironic, since the most distinctive characteristic of their comedy has always been its iconoclastic nature. Thus, while in *Horse Feathers* (1932) the Brothers comically dismantle the university life, today's university dissects *Horse Feathers* for educational purposes. But before examining the more philosophical ramifications of their work, permit me to relate a personal story which nicely showcases the ongoing impact of the Marx Brothers upon our culture.

In doing research on a Marx Brothers book (Greenwood Press, 1987), one must, of course, visit archives scattered across the country. Away from family and after long hours in some special collections library, one naturally searches for a diversion. For the student of film, as for many others, this often means going to a movie. Thus, on one Marx Brothers research trip I managed to take in two then current commercial theater releases: the highly praised Woody Allen film *Hannah and Her Sisters* (1986) and Terry Gilliam's *Brazil* (1985). Though both are comedies in

29

the broadest sense of the word, they are radically different. The former film, like so much of Allen's work, fluctuates between humor based upon the problems of a strongly defined personality comedian (Allen) and a romantic comedy that frequently parodies love itself. But unlike the guarded optimism which sometimes closes Allen's films, *Hannah and Her Sisters* ends upon a decidedly upbeat note. The film even manages to include the two most archetypal elements of comedy's classic formula for a happy ending—the new beginnings symbolized by both a marriage and a child's birth. In contrast, *Brazil* is the blackest of comedies. Gilliam, best known as the only American member of the British comedy troupe Monty Python, has fashioned a film without hope—a nightmare comedy of the future. Like a slapstick *1984*, *Brazil* offers the standard black comedy message: not only is the individual insignificant, he is forever fated to continue to his own demise.

Both of these very different films, however, utilized the Marx Brothers as cultural symbols of equally different things. In *Brazil* the anti-establishment heroine watches *The Cocoanuts* (1929) on television. In this case the Marxes represent two things: an iconoclastic ideal for a radical, and comic prophets who recognized early inherent pointlessness of the modern world. One should also add, the "saturation" comedy style of *Brazil* (á la Monty Python) has indirect roots in the Marxes' own comically complex presentation. In *Hannah and Her Sisters* a suicidal Allen wanders into a screening of *Duck Soup* (1933). Prior to this he had been asking himself: if the world is without reason, why go on living? But slowly the comedy magic of the Marxes envelopes him. Here the Marxes symbolize pure comedy, those random moments of joy which make life worth living. Allen leaves the theater completely revitalized, once again a believer in hope and in the modest milestones (marriages, births...) of the modern man. Here, then, was a Marx Brothers researcher who tried and failed, on two successive nights, to find a simple momentary escape from his focus of study. That failure would seem to say a lot about the ongoing significance of the Marxes.

Allen's recognition of the importance of the Marxes is important because he has evolved into one of America's greatest creative artists. His accomplishments range from multiple Oscars to the O. Henry Award for best short story. And in 1986 the nominating theatre critics for the Pulitzer Prize in drama even recommended his screenplays should be eligible for the competition. This is especially relevant here, for besides calling Allen "America's Ingmar Bergman," the critics' action had been precipitated by the fact that the only narrative script they had agreed upon in their 1986 nominating capacity was *Hannah and Her Sisters,* with its pivotal reference to the Marxes.[2]

One might even say the spirit of the Marxes brings out the best in Allen. This Marx Brothers influence is most pervasively apparent in such early Allen films as *Take the Money and Run* (1969) and *Bananas* (1971). For example, in the latter film Allen's disguised return from San Marcos (where he, like *Duck Soup*'s Groucho, has become president!) is straight out of the *A Night at the Opera* (1935) scene where the similarly-costumed Marxes also attempt to re-enter the country. And though the most integrated Marx Brothers' influence on Allen (such as gag usage and overall comic framework) occurs early, his most pointed previous highlighting of the Marxes, or more specifically Groucho, had come at the opening of his most acclaimed film—the Academy Award-winning *Annie Hall* (1977). At that time he had quoted Groucho's famous real life putdown: "I would never want to belong to any club that would have someone like me for a member." But not before *Hannah and Her Sisters* had Allen so strongly showcased the importance of the Marxes' comedy art. Moreover, he offered no verbal or printed lead-in (such as even a "now showing" movie poster) as to whom or what the *Hannah* viewer was about to see in this movie-within-a-movie. The *Duck Soup* excerpt, from "The Country's Going to War" number (where the Marxes brilliantly satirize the unthinking jingoism that welcomes war), is simply presented without fanfare as the comic masterpiece it is. While it would be an overstatement to call the Marxes, or *Duck Soup*, the motivating spark behind *Hannah*, one must remember that Allen's narrative goal in the scene is to present a symbol of comedy at its greatest. High praise for these former low level vaudevillians.

With the world's ever increasing marketing, the importance of the Marx Brothers as cultural icons is neither to be denied nor to be avoided. Caricatures of them appear on nearly anything which can be purchased. Their much-hawked images rank with such diverse characters as Chaplin's Tramp figure, Monroe's sex goddess, and Bogart's tough guy—possibly the most universally recognized of American film icons. But the Marxes' significance as images goes beyond mere sales.

As with the others, caricatures of Groucho, Chico, and Harpo have become an enduringly popular logo for Americans, even for those who have not seen a complete Marx Brothers film. This is possible because it has become a common culture heritage to know what they represent.

Most specifically, the Marx Brothers as icons symbolize two things: pure comedy and anti-establishment spirit. Expanding briefly upon the former, the Marxes are not only funny, they look funny, whether you are watching them in a film or studying a caricature. As the great 1930s film critic Otis Ferguson observed in his *New Republic* review of *A Night at the Opera*, Groucho "would be funny in still photographs ...."[3] Most memorable, then, are Groucho's greasepaint mustache and eyebrows, the latter so comically powerful that the comedian refused to raise them when doing road tours of movie material, because they would win a laugh for any line. Ferguson might only have improved on his comment by stating the obvious: *all three* Marxes "would be funny in still photographs." Thus, as is true of the most traditional of clowns, one would be prone to laugh at them visually without prior knowledge of who, or what, they were.

Their significance as comedy symbols is doubly underlined by the frequency with which stage shows appear which include impersonations of one or more Marx Brothers. An excellent overview of this phenomenon can be found by examining recent back issues of another Marx Brothers fascination—The *Freedonia Gazette*, which bills itself as "*The* Magazine Devoted to the Marx Brothers" (New Hope, Pennsylvania).[4] Along these same lines one should note today's ongoing stage revival productions of two Marx Brothers celebrations which originally played on Broadway: *Minnie's Boys*, and *A Day in Hollywood / A Night in the Ukraine* (two independent one-act shows, with the first showcasing the Marxes). Appropriately, *Minnie's Boys* is a musical comedy biography of sorts, while *A Night in the Ukraine*, loosely drawn from Chekov's "The Bear," captures the spirit of the Marxes better. Moreover, *Animal Crackers* is also being revived for theatrical release in mainstream cinemas. That the team should still be generating so much interest in the 1980s is an ongoing tribute to their influence.

Besides being symbols of pure comedy, they also represent the ultimate in anti-establishment icons. As Martin A. Gardner has so thoroughly revealed in his 1970 doctoral dissertation, their talent for satirizing society can be grouped into three broad categories. They comically undercut history, politics, and the economy; manners and customs; and literature and popular entertainment.[5] While one most frequently associates them with the comic usurpation of high society (manners and customs, especially as personified by Margaret Dumont), their satire seems to touch nearly every aspect of American culture. Thus, *Duck Soup* is a satirical send-up of politics which makes comic inroads

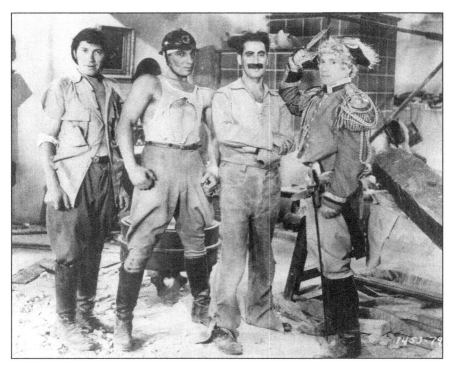

The Marx Brothers in their greatest film, *Duck Soup* (1933)—
left to right: Chico, Zeppo, Groucho, and Harpo.

into government policy on everything from the economy to diplomacy, managing effectively to scramble American history along the way, from Harpo's rendition of Paul Revere's ride, to the then current state of world depression. *Horse Feathers'* satire of university life manages to skew a range of literature and popular entertainment, from Theodore Dreiser's *An American Tragedy,* to college football.

The second broad influence of the Marxes, after their significance as comedy/anti-establishment icons, is in their impact upon schools of comedy. Most specifically, this means their involvement in the zany world of the comic antihero in American humor, best typified by *The New Yorker* writing of authors like Robert Benchley and James Thurber.[6] The Marxes did *not* invent this character type, but their memorable period successes with it (from vaudeville and Broadway to the movies) helped to widely disseminate the phenomenon. However, unlike so many of their contemporary screen comedians, such as Leo McCarey's Laurel & Hardy and W.C. Fields, they did not impersonate the frustration of the individual in the comic, antiheroic and absurd modern world. Instead, the Marxes donned the mantle of comic absurdity as a defense, and beat the world gone mad at its own game. In fact, they were cocky enough to "take what order there is in life and impose chaos on it."[7] The latter daydream victories of Thurber's Walter Mitty were business as usual for the Marxes.[8] Groucho is, however, often victimized by his Brothers, and in these encounters Groucho becomes the more traditional antiheroic male. Moreover, Groucho's solo writing for print more fully embraced the antihero's frustrations, be it essays like the 1929 *New Yorker* piece, "Press Agents I Have Known," or books like *Memoirs of a Mangy Lover* (1963).[9]

The Marxes acknowledge this tie to what they call "lunatic" comedy in a 1939 article in *Theatre Arts* magazine, correctly observing they were "followers" of such pioneering antiheroic writers as Stephen Leacock, Donald Odgen Stewart, and Robert Benchley.[10] The label "lunatic" is merely a characteristic of a comedy movement which generally focuses upon the comic frustrations of an antiheroic male, or what American humor historian Norris W. Yates frequently refers to as the "little man."[11] The authors noted by the Marxes all belong to this school of comedy, though today a more representative grouping would be: Benchley, Thurber, Clarence Day, and S.J. Perelman.[12] Not surprisingly, Benchley was a close friend of the Marxes, Perelman a Marx script-writer, and Thurber was a major Marx fan—see especially his comic mini-review of *A Day at the Races—Der Tag Aux Courses*—in the March 1947 *Stage* magazine.[13] And as early as 1931 John Grierson, in his very perceptive period criticism of the Marxes, was likening their work to Benchley's.[14]

Although the Marxes fittingly label themselves "followers," their intitial Broadway triumph in *I'll Say She Is!* (1924, which was essentially a zany anthropology of their "Greatest Hits" from years of vaudeville) was enough for Gerald Weales to justify placing the team in the vanguard of the movement. Their 1920s centerstage ascension as Broadway's resident crazies, on and off the stage (including participation in the Algonquin Round Table), does make them early participants in this comedy evolution. Thus, Weales has even suggested "it is more useful to think in terms of a shared intellectual and social climate [in 1920s New York, the center for the ultimate literary articulation of the movement] in which lunacy, verbal and physical, could flourish."[15] Although it is tempting to follow Weales' suggestion, especially since the Marxes' material is forever preserved on film, they are still best described as important early disciples of antiheroic comedy but not founding fathers.

Purists still distracted by the presence of Marx Brothers playwrights and screenwriters should keep in mind that while the Brothers did not control their film productions in the unquestioned total auteur manner of a Chaplin, they were, like W.C. Fields, largely undirectable. And yes, while one must acknowledge the team needed writers, it is frequently forgotten that Groucho was often involved, though uncredited, with the writing, and was a successful author himself. Harpo, though not as concerned with the overall scope of the play or film as Groucho, was generally the key "author" for his own visual material. In addition, much of the team's classic material for both stage and screen was first tinkered with daily as the Brothers either toured or tested it on the back roads of America. And finally, the Marxes exerted their influence even when they were involved with a pivotal antiheroic "lunatic" writer like S.J. Perelman in *Monkey Business* (1931), and *Horse Feathers*.[16] In fact, Perelman's own article, "Week End with Groucho Marx,"[17] has the satirist coming off as a Marx Brothers groupie, whose writing on *Monkey Business* would seem to borrow on Perelman's boyhood memories of the vaudeville Marxes. Still, one can hardly say that every Marx Brothers scriptwriter was under their spell. People like George Kaufman and Morrie Ryskind obviously had an impact on the team. But it is important to credit the Marxes with more of a collaboration status than they have been given.

Weales credits William Troy's negative review of *Duck Soup* as making an important connection between the Marxes and the lunatic comedy movement.[18] Troy had observed, "Like the whole 'crazy-fool' humor of the post-war epoch, it [Marxian humor] consists in a dissociation of the faculties rather than a concentrated direction of them towards any particular object in the body social or politic."[19] Troy might have exemplified his "dissociation of the faculties" analysis with the following *Duck Soup* conversation between the President of Freedonia (Groucho) and a peanut vendor (Chico):

> **Groucho:** Now listen here. I've got a swell job for you, but first I'll have to ask you a couple of… important questions. Now, what is it that has four pairs of pants, lives in Philadelphia, and it never rains but it pours?
> **Chico:** 'At'sa good one. I give you three guesses.
> **Groucho:** Now, lemme see. Has four pairs of pants, lives in Philadelphia. Is it male or female?
> **Chico:** No, I no think so.

Groucho: Is he dead?
Chico: Who?
Groucho: I don't know. I give up.
Chico: I give up, too .… [Chico insults Groucho]
Groucho: Just for that you don't get the job I was going
    to give you.
Chico: What job?
Groucho: Secretary of War.
Chico: All right, I'll take it.
Groucho: Sold!

The Groucho-Chico conversation nicely showcases their ability to personify the absurdity of the antiheroic modern world without also playing its comic victim, though Chico mildly gets the better of the argument. More often than most of their humor contemporaries, the Marxes comically vaccinated themselves against a zany world by assuming part of that zaniness themselves. Interestingly enough, this crazy comedy antidote is generally more apt to appear in the women who populate the comic antiheroic world, from the Looney Tunes Gracie Allen of (George) Burns & Allen, to the Thurber grandmother who thought electricity would leak from sockets without light bulbs.[20] But as eccentric as these women were, they made decisions (Thurber's grandmother was always screwing in bulbs), and then got on with living. Meanwhile, the comic antihero male generally attempts to make sense of it all (women and the world) and goes near crazy trying. In the film genre of screwball comedy this same type of antihero male/eccentric female dichotomy exists, but merely represents a more sophisticated feature-length variation which broadened the audience for the antiheroic misfit.[21]

Thurber later more fully articulates this antiheroic male-female difference in the story "Destructive Forces in Life," concluding:

> *The undisciplined mind [that of the woman] runs far less chance of having its purpose thwarted, its plans distorted, its whole scheme and system wrenched out of line. The* undisciplined *mind, in short, is far better adapted to the confused world in which we live today than the streamlined mind [the disciplined mind of the man]. There is, I am afraid, no place for the streamlined mind.*[22]

While the Marxes were much more likely to assume the "undisciplined" mind normally attributed to the female in this comedy movement, it should again be noted that interactions within the team often had Groucho playing the more traditional antihero male. This is best exemplified by the close of the long comedy dialogue between Groucho and Chico in the 1930 *Animal Crackers*. This is the conversation which includes Chico's classic irrational crime-solving suggestion to build a house next door in order to question the people who would then live there. Thus, the "undisciplined mind" of Chico has both so fractured reason and the language that Groucho's "disciplined mind" eventually is reduced to incoherency in trying to make sense of Chico. The mustached one stumbles out of the scene mumbling, "Ahh, ahh…." Although this victimization of Groucho to antihero status is not nearly so frequent as Groucho's own comic attacks on an absurd world, they do occur regularly. Examples would include the standing gag in *Duck Soup* that Harpo and his motorcycle sidecar will always leave Groucho behind, and the tootsie fruitsie ice cream scene in *A Day at the Races* (1937) in which Chico sells Groucho a library of unnecessary betting books. Moreover, what Marx author Allen Eyles calls "Harpo's *tour de force* in out-smarting Groucho," the *Duck Soup* "mirror scene" imitation of Groucho, is argumentatively the greatest of all Marx Brothers scenes.[23] Although variations of the mirror skit had occurred earlier, such as Chaplin's *The Floorwalker* (1916), the Marxes' version is so comically inspired that it is one to which film historians most often refer.

Added detail has been given to this examination of the Marxes' second broad influence, their involvement in the evolution of antiheroic comedy in American humor, for three reasons. First, unlike their high visibility as icons of comedy and the anti-establishment, their links to the world of the comic antihero are not always immediately apparent. Moreover, it is made more complex by Groucho's dual status—as comic aggressor outside the family (the stance which most readily comes to mind, especially when it involves Groucho's baiting of the Brothers' regular target Margaret Dumont), and as the sometimes antiheroic woman within the team. It is not that unlike the duality managed by his 1930s contemporary W.C. Fields, who fluctuated between his comic antiheroic male and that of carnival huckster—as well as sometimes joining them in the same role.[24] Second, understanding the Marxes' ties to antiheroic comedy makes Groucho's much more pronounced use of comic frustration in his solo writing considerably less jarring. Students of the Marxes frequently have expressed surprise over this apparent disparity, but the seeds of the antiheroic male were always in the Groucho persona, and comic frustration with his Brothers even made them surface, on occasion, in the team films. Third, joining the Marxes' often aggressive use of absurdity to the world of antiheroic comedy makes all the more understandable the ongoing pervasive influence of their comedy today. The same qualities which attracted surrealist Salvador Dali in the 1930s[25] moved Eugene Ionesco to declare that the three biggest influences on his work were actually Groucho, Chico and Harpo Marx.[26] Martin Esslin agrees upon the significance of the team to the theatre of the Absurd—a theatre which has also been called black comedy.

Like most things, black comedy is not in itself new, but its increased pervasiveness is. Thus, in a modern world which appears more and more unhinged, the Marxes seem even more contemporary. Moreover, their humor was often black to begin with. This is especially true in *Duck Soup*, where the foolishness of war is so effectively dramatized by Groucho's accidental machine-gunning of his own men. Indeed, Groucho's comic paranoia about the intentions of Ambassador Trentino, which satirizes the paranoia often connected with the decisions of American government,[27] has direct ties with the even darker comic paranoia of *Dr. Strangelove's* Sterling Hayden. Playing General Jack Ripper, he believes fluoridated water is a Soviet plot to assist in the takeover of America. Thus, one frequently thinks of the Marxes when dealing with the ironic absurdity of the modern world. This would include dark comedy film director Billy Wilder's early 1960s plan to use the Marxes in a *Dr. Strangelove*-type satire, the more recent view of playwright Dario Fo's darkly comic *Accidental Death of an Anarchist* as a "Left-Wing *Duck Soup*," and the Marxes' ties to *Brazil* mentioned earlier.[28] More visible popular culture footnotes to the Marxes' influence on today's dark comedy are countless. They range in diversity from the obvious debt Alan Alda owes Groucho for the anti-establishment, womanizing Hawkeye Pierce of TV's *M.A.S.H.*, to the frequent tendency among political cartoonists to comment on the escalating absurdity of today by including the Marxes in their drawings. For example, *The Freedonia Gazette*, which regularly includes these cartoons in its pages, has a devastatingly comic one in its November 1980 issue. A reprint of a *Washington Star* syndicated Marx Brothers caricature, it has the team as Pentagon heads preparing for a second mission after their involvement in the infamous failed hostage rescue under the Carter administration. Its black comedy detail might best be summed up by the fact that Chico is reading a booklet on "Helicopter Maintenance."[29]

The Marx's third broad influence on western culture has been their impact upon the complex, multifaceted phenomenon that is modern entertainment. The team might be called a cross-section of American humor, from the fast-talking Groucho and the dialect comedy of Chico to the mime of Harpo, which was forever supplemented by cartoon world sound effects. One might even count Zeppo as an example of the romantic light comedian for which sound comedy increased the need. Regardless of Zeppo, when the Marxes' comic diversity was married to their propensity for a scatter gun range of satire topics, the entertainment possibilities were almost overpowering. In fact, Irving Thalberg's M-G-M softening of the Marxes' screen characters, coupled with his addition of more traditional story elements was, in part, an attempt to make them more palatable to a general audience by making them less irrational. Numerous critics have commented on the danger of this homogenization. For example, Patricia Mellencamp says, "To be classically narrativized [as the Marx Brothers were] is to be sanitized [robbed of your humor]."[30] However, in fairness to Thalberg, his two productions, *A Night at the Opera* and *A Day at the Races* are still funny films; it is just that total anarchy no longer rules. (Though Thalberg died during the production of *A Day at the Races*, the extensive on-the-road testing of the script had been completed, and was finished according to a Thalberg blueprint.)

After the disappointing reception given *Duck Soup*, their last Paramount film and typical of their work for that studio, Thalberg thought the diversity of their comedy was too much for the 1930s audiences. Not surprisingly, today's more demanding viewer prefers the comically complex actions of the Marxes' Paramount films, especially *Duck Soup*, to their later work. This was the position Groucho himself later came to endorse.[31] Marx author Thomas H. Jordan quite logically observes:

> *They were without question the most prominent forerunners of the rapidly-paced saturation comedy reintroduced to modern audiences through such television programs as* Laugh-In, The Ernie Kovacs Show, That Was the Week That Was, *and in Britain*, The Goon Show and Monty Python's Flying Circus. *Few modern film comedies have been able to recreate the headlong rush of humor which characterizes the Marxes.*[32]

Related to this, Jordan goes on to note what has always been a popular refrain about the team and a key reason for their ongoing popularity:

"Their films can be seen many times without losing their appeal, for there are so many gags and jokes that no one can possibly remember more than a small number."[33] However, it should be underlined that the Marxes are still able to maintain their distinctive comedy character significance in this world of comedy chaos. Unlike other comedy team participants in similarly complex humor onslaughts, be it Olson & Johnson in *Hellzapoppin* (1941, which had also been an earlier success on Broadway), or Rowan & Martin in *Laugh-In*, the Marxes maintain center stage both by their talent and the simple fact that they monopolize the comedy roles. Unlike *Laugh-In*, which most people have forgotten was actually entitled *Rowan & Martin's Laugh-In*, there has never been a danger of forgetting the title characters in a Marx Brothers film.

Surprisingly, the influence of one Marx Brother has also been credited with setting just the opposite model (from saturation comedy) for television. Groucho Marx's casual conversations while sitting on a stool for the static camera *You Bet Your Life* was, according to television historian Max Wilk, instrumental in the similarly casual nature of many television programs which followed, especially the variety show.[34]

The Marxes' fourth broad influence was their early demonstration of the comic artistry potential of sound films, despite the often canned theatre nature of their first two movies. To the student of film comedy, their cross-section of American humor teams made the transition from silent to sound more palatable—especially with the mime of Harpo acting as a salve on the painful loss and/or decline of so many silent comedy stars. In fact, as early as 1937, Gilbert Seldes observed, "The arrival of the Marx Brothers and the reappearance of W.C. Fields saved screen comedy."[35] While Seldes goes on to credit Disney with being the ultimate sound replacement for the silent slapstick short, the live action team diversity of the Marxes (especially at a time when sound was decentralizing the formerly single comedy character focus of the silent films), demonstrated that film comedy's future could still be bright. More recently, theorists like Mellencamp have demonstrated the comic brilliance the Marxes brought to *sound* comedy. Their assault on the language produced a verbal slapstick every bit as iconoclastic as their attack on the establishment. Verbally as well as visually, their comic message remained the same: things are not what they seem! Moreover, the Brothers' early film success was so great they paved the movie way for a whole series of other zany period comedy teams, such as the Ritz Brothers and Olsen & Johnson. Indeed, M-G-M's failed early 1930s attempt to team Buster Keaton and Jimmy Durante does not seem so unlikely if seen as a variation upon a Harpo-Groucho duo. And even the earlier madcap team of Wheeler & Woolsey can be categorized as under the indirect assistance of the Marxes. While Wheeler & Woolsey entered film the same year as the Marxes (1929), the duo's initial Broadway teaming (1928) came at the height of the Marx Brothers' influential zany comedy reign on America's premier theatrical street.

Thus, one cannot disregard the influence of the Marxes as unique icons of both comedy and the anti-establishment, as major contributors to new developments in American humor, as pivotal early examples of what might best be called saturation comedy, and as a pioneering measuring stick for the great potential of sound film comedy. One must never, however, lose sight of their greatest and continuing impact: they make people laugh. There is no greater gift.

(Originally appeared in Canada's *THALIA: Studies in Literary Humor*, University of Ottawa, volume, xi, No. 1, 1989; Wes D. Gehring copyright.)

NOTES

1. Harpo Marx (with Rowland Barber), *Harpo Speaks!* (1961; rpt. New York: Freeway Press, Inc., 1974), p. 24. (The title of this essay "THE MARX OF TIME", was also the name of a shortlived Groucho and Chico 1930s radio program.)
2. Jeannie Williams, "Woody's film sparks Pulitzer tiff," *USA Today*, Weekend edition, April 18-20, 1A.
3. Otis Ferguson, "The Marxian Epileptic" (*A Night at the Opera* review), *New Republic*, December 11, 1935, 130.
4. Paul G. Wesolowski, "TFG Reviews *Groucho*," *The Freedonia Gazette*, Winter 1985, 7-8. This review lists Wesolowski's top five Marx Brothers impersonation stage shows.
5. Martin A. Gardner, "The Marx Brothers: An Investigation of their Films as Satirical Social Criticism," Ph.D. dissertation, New York University, 1970.
6. See especially: Wes D. Gehring, *Leo McCarey and the Comic Anti-Hero in American Film* (New York: Arno Press, 1980).
7. Joe Adamson, *Groucho, Harpo, Chico, and Sometimes Zeppo* (New York: Simon and Schuster, 1973), 156.

8. James Thurber, "The Secret Life of Walter Mitty," in *My World and Welcome To It* (New York: Harcourt, Brace and Company, 1942), 72-81.

9. Groucho Marx, "Press Agents I Have Known," *The New Yorker*, March 9, 1929, 52, 54-55; Groucho Marx, *Memoirs of a Mangy Lover* (New York: Bernard Geis Associates, 1963).

10. Marie Steton, "S. Dali + 3 Marxes ," *Theatre Arts*, October 1939, 734.

11. Norris W. Yates, *The American Humorist: Conscience of the Twentieth Century* (1964; rpt. Ames, Iowa: Iowa State University Press, 1967).

12. See: Walter Blair, *Native American Humor* (1937; rpt. San Francisco: Chandler Publishing Company, 1960), p. 169.

13. James Thurber, "Der Tag Aux Courses," *Stage*, March 1937.

14. John Grierson, "The Logic of Comedy," in *Grierson on Documentary*, ed. Forsyth Hardy (1947; rpt. Los Angeles: University of California Press, 1966), 55. (Marx Brothers segments originally appeared as an *Animal Crackers* review in *The Clarion* of December 1930 and a *Monkey Business* review in the *Everyman* of October 15, 1931.)

15. Gerald Weales, "Duck Soup," in *Canned Goods as Caviar: American Film Comedy of the 1930s* (Chicago: The University of Chicago Press, 1985), 58.

16. J.A. Ward, "The Hollywood Metaphor: The Marx Brothers, S.J. Perelman, and Nathanael West," *The Southern Review*, Summer 1976), 660.

17. S.J. Perelman, "Week End with Groucho Marx," *Holiday*, April 1952, 59, 126-33. Later anthologized as "I'll Always Call You Schnorrer, My African Explorer" in *The Most of S.J. Perelman* (New York: Simon and Schuster, 1958), 624-31.

18. Weales, "Duck Soup," 57.

19. William Troy, *Duck Soup* review, *The Nation*, December 13, 1933, 688.

20. James Thurber, "The Car We Had to Push," in *My Life and Hard Times* (1933; rpt. New York: Bantam Books, 1947), 41.

21. See Wes D. Gehring's *Screwball Comedy: A Genre of Madcap Romance* (Westport, Connecticut: Greenwood Press, 1986).

22. James Thurber, "Destructive Forces in Life," in *Let Your Mind Alone! and Other More or Less Inspirational Pieces* (1937; rpt. New York: The Universal Library, 1973), 18.

23. Allen Eyles, *The Marx Brothers: Their World of Comedy* (1966; rpt. New York: Paperback Library, 1971), 106.

24. See: Wes D. Gehring, *W.C. Fields: A Bio-Bibliography* (Westport, Connecticut: Greenwood Press, 1984).

25. Salvador Dali, "Surrealism in Hollywood," *Harper's Bazaar*, June 1937, 68-69, 132.

26. Eugene Ionesco's *The Shephard's Chameleon* review, *Time*, December 12, 1960, 63; Gardner, "The Marx Brothers," 2-3; Martin Esslin, *The Theatre of Absurd* (Garden City, New York: Doubleday & Company, Inc., 1961), 236-37.

27. For more on this, see Gardner's "The Marx Brothers," 94.

28. Lance Morrow, *Accidental Death of an Anarchist* review, *Time*, March 12, 1984, 70.

29. *The Freedonia Gazette*, November 1980, 17.

30. Patricia Mellencamp, "Jokes and Their Relationship to the Marx Brothers," in *Cinema and Language*, ed. by Stephen Heath and Patricia Mellencamp (Frederick, Maryland: University Publications of America, 1983), 76.

31. See: Hector Arce, *Groucho* (New York: G.P. Putnam's Sons, 1979). This "official" biography of the comedian by his close friend is also the most detailed look at the Marx Brothers.

32. Thomas H. Jordan, "The Marx Brothers," in *The Anatomy of Cinematic Humor* (New York: Revisionist Press, 1975), 90.

33. Jordan, 91-92.

34. Max Wilk, *The Golden Age of Television* (1976; rpt. New York: Delacorte Press, 1977), p. 92.

35. Gilbert Seldes, Chapter 5, in *The Movies Come from America* (New York: Charles Scribner's Sons, 1937), 41.

TELEVISION'S OTHER GROUCHO

Have you ever fallen out of a patient?
– Groucho Marx's questioning a *You Bet Your Life* tree surgeon contestant.

GROUCHO'S CAREER as a solo performer is best charted from 1947 and his association with a simple radio show—*You Bet Your Life*, which found equal success on 1950s television. But hosting a quiz show initially seemed a comedown for the former president of both Huxley College (*Horse Feathers*, 1932) and the land of Freedonia (*Duck Soup*, 1933), the only "Marxist" leaders America ever took to heart. Marx fans mourned that "it was like selling Citation to the glue factory."[1] *You Bet Your Life* creator and executive producer John Guedel said, "Having Groucho as emcee of a quiz show is like using a Cadillac to haul coal."[2] Even Groucho confessed, in an unpublished letter to long-time friend and correspondent Dr. Samuel Salinger, "It's not too distinguished a set-up [the show], but you know me; I have no shame."[3]

The career risk worked. The quiz show format proved a perfect entertainment setting for a solo Groucho to comically converse with and kid non-celebrity guests, the quiz itself being of secondary importance. In 1949 he received radio's greatest tribute—a Peabody Award as best entertainer. Groucho added television's highest honor in 1951—an Emmy for most outstanding personality. Even with this recognition, Groucho's position could generate affectionate attacks from friends; Goodman Ace described him as "presently occupied in the rather opprobrious business of operating a quiz show on radio and television."[4]

First broadcast on October 27, 1947, the program started slowly. Recorded long and then edited down for pace and to maximize the funniest material, the show caught on in popularity. Consistently highly rated, *You Bet Your Life* continued its acclaimed run on 1950s television with the last regular telecast in September 1961; during the final season it was entitled *The Groucho Show*.

As befitted a Marx Brother, *You Bet Your Life's* early commercial success even had a touch of the bizarre. Groucho lost his first sponsor, Elgin-American, because he was *too* popular. The company could not keep up with the product demand created by the program's hit status and decided not to continue advertising. With a "problem" like that, Groucho and company had no trouble attracting the sponsor Desoto-Plymouth.

THE QUESTION OF AD LIBS

The program maintained its top ten standing even after the 1954 public revelation that Groucho's *You Bet Your Life* wit was often less than spontaneous, a fact which long had been rumored. *TV Guide* said it most entertainingly, quoting an unnamed source: "'That show has all the spontaneity of a Swiss watch.'"[5]

Guests generally were not selected randomly from the audience, as had been previously suggested. Instead, they were screened and chosen for their colorful backgrounds and potentially comic personalities. Groucho did not meet them prior to the program, but the contestants were coached on how to tell their stories to the host, including key tagline openings designed for "ad libs" from the comedian host—ad libs he had time to prepare. Ironically, Groucho was good at legitimate ad libbing; it was the reason Guedel chose Groucho for the show (he had been impressed with the comedian's impromptu exchanges with Bob Hope on another radio program). Regardless, some of Groucho's *You Bet Your Life* ad libbing was real. But comedy chances were *not* taken.

Though not often utilized, the quick-witted Groucho had an already long-established gift for making the scripted seem spontaneous. For example, in the unpublished text for the Marx Brothers' Broadway stage production *Animal Crackers*, the character of Roscoe W. Chandler makes scripted "mistakes" to comically feed Groucho's Captain Spaulding.[6] This otherwise seemingly impromptu scene, where Chandler confuses character names, also surfaces (with slight variation) in the 1930 film adaptation.

It is disappointing to tarnish Groucho's legitimate ad lib reputation, but the program sailed through the revelation, even maintaining its number four Nielson ranking from the previous season (1953-1954). Continuing until 1961, *You Bet Your Life* became a 1970s phenomenon in syndication—successfully entertaining "nine of the top ten [United States] markets" as well as going into foreign distribution.[7] This was an ongoing tribute to Groucho's humor (regardless of ad libbing questions), because 1950s black and white quiz shows were not exactly hot properties in the 1970s rerun market. Watching the show in syndication also became a major personal event for Groucho in the years just prior to his 1977 death.

AN OLD COMPLAINT

Historically, however, one complaint has persisted since the show's inception: did Groucho comically misuse his "guests?" For instance, *Newsweek's* early panning review noted the vulnerability of the "mike-frightened contestants."[8] The magazine's later cover story praise of the program further added, "To grown people he [Groucho] was a little too bitter at times with his guests, but he was also very, very funny."[9]

Steve Allen addresses this subject in both his books on comedians, *The Funny Men* and *Funny People*.[10] The premise of this accusation begins that the movie Groucho (especially in the more comically aggressive Paramount films) unloaded his attack humor on pompously deserving subjects, from stuffy society matrons (frequently played by Margaret Dumont) to crooked big business financiers. Essentially, anyone who took himself too seriously was a valid target. In contrast, the argument continues, Groucho's quiz show unleashed such insults on the average person—who became undeserving victims, not legitimate comedy targets.

The show's ongoing popularity puts proponents of this position in the minority, or, as an early review phrased it, "none but the hyper-critical could take umbrage."[11] Yet its persistence as a detractor merits an answer: the *You Bet Your Life* Groucho is not quite the same as that fellow in the movies. The cynicism was still present, as well as the sexual innuendo and raised eyebrows which had won for him the title of film comedy's King "Leer." But compared to the iconoclast of the movies, Groucho the quiz master is much subdued. Even the aforementioned *Newsweek* cover piece (with its reference to "a little too bitter at times") admits the secret to Groucho's involvement was a softening of his television image. The magazine quotes Guedel as having convinced the comedian by way of a persona change: "I told Groucho you're as thin and brittle as a window

Here's a calmer radio/TV Groucho for *You Bet Your Life*.

pane. You should be given a chance to have depth and warmth, to say something nice once in a while."[12] The *New York Times* further emphasized the change: the quiz show "Groucho Marx is pretty much the [restrained] real man himself," as opposed to the outrageous screen persona and its "comic Frankenstein effects."[13] Groucho friend Goodman Ace described him as being "enchanted by people... for the dialogue he is able to draw from them by a special offbeat type of kindly questioning both on and off."[14] Ace then described several real-life Groucho-people encounters which could have occurred on the program. This realistic softening seemed more pronounced with the passing years (Groucho was nearly 71 when the last regular telecast aired). However, even the program's 1950 television pilot reveals a witty but less than aggressive host.

Incongruous as it may sound, since not everything was scripted, the host was also vulnerability realistic. He could "often [be comically] topped, as he was when he asked an elderly woman what people were wearing when she was a baby. Her answer: 'Diapers.' And he was almost speechless for once when a burlesque show employee identified a stripteaser as 'an anatomy award winner.'"[15]

Being more realistically human also included self-deprecating humor. To illustrate, Groucho once told newlywed guests: "I'll never forget my wedding day... they threw vitamin pills." (Both his second and third marriages were May-December affairs.) On another occasion he told a blood analyst guest: "Don't look at me unless you analyze Geritol." (The real-world Groucho was also best known for his self-deprecating humor, such as his celebrated comment, "I would never want to belong to a club that would have me as a member.")

The comedian's son Arthur later wrote about his father's television success as an extension of the real man in his critically and commercially acclaimed biography, *Life with Groucho: A Son's-Eye View*: "Father has become such a likable [television] personality... [because, in part] He can be funny on the air in the same way he's funny at home—commenting on life itself... [often as] the downtrodden father."[16] Fittingly, Groucho's then elementary-aged daughter Melinda (born 1946, of second wife Kay Gorcey) was a periodic guest on the program.

During the 1950s the realistically warmer *You Bet Your Life* image of Groucho was further enhanced by the phenomenal popularity of Arthur's biography itself. It was a funny and affectionate behind-the-scenes look at the comedian which also managed occasionally to juggle real pathos into its pages. For instance, Arthur quotes a letter from his father telling of his parents' separation:

> I was sorry to see her [first wife Ruth] go, for I am still fond of her, but obviously this uncomfortable set-up couldn't continue. I said good-bye to her before she drove

off… It was one of those awkward, half-serious, half-comic moments, and I didn't know quite what to say. I put my hand out and said, "Well, it was nice knowing you, and if you're ever in the neighborhood again, drop in." Your mother seemed to think that was a funny line—so for once in my life I got a laugh when I wasn't trying for one.[17]

Besides making a conscious effort to put the cinema Groucho behind him (to be expanded on shortly), the comedian recognized medium differences—"That small box [a television set] is no place for frenetic comedy. Casual shows like ours are the ones that last."[18] Groucho anticipates Marshall McLuhan's famous distinction between hot (film) and cool (television) media. While film does not demand much viewer participation because of its high definition information-laden picture, television's less data-filled image necessitates increased audience involvement. Consequently, the overly demonstrative performer, such as the movie Groucho, would not wear as well on television.

Ironically, one such seemingly frenetic show which did not last was Chico Marx's short-lived *College Bowl*, which premiered on television the same season as his brother's quiz program (1950). Not to be confused with the later TV quiz show of the same name, *College Bowl* featured a musical malt shop where Chico would showcase his comic piano skills.

Television historian Max Wilk has credited Groucho's relaxed conversations while sitting on a stool for the functionality visual *You Bet Your Life* as instrumental in establishing the casual nature of many television programs to follow, especially the variety show.[19] This distinct difference between the television and movie Grouchos is underlined all the more when one realizes that comedy theorist and Marx Brothers author Thomas H. Jordan credits the team's movies as a model for later more sophisticated TV audiences: without question the most prominent fore-runners of the rapidly-paced saturation comedy reintroduced to modern audiences through such television programs as *Laugh-In, The Ernie Kovacs Show, That Was the Week That Was,* and in Britain, *The Goon Show* and *Monty Python's Flying Circus*. Few modern film comedies have been able to recreate the headlong rush of humor which characterizes the Marxes.[20]

DIFFERENTIATING GROUCHO PERSONAE

While Groucho's main cinema persona was a comically outrageous looking and acting con man, his television counterpart often seemed more related to an atomic age crackerbarrel figure—comically wise and often self-deprecatingly funny. For instance, the *New York Times* described him as "a fellow with brilliant common sense," and *Cue* magazine said, "a rolling of the wise old owl eyes behind spectacles, can wrap his audience in stitches."[21] Marx Brothers author Allen Eyles states television's "Groucho decisively abandoned the old screen image to become a friendly avuncular figure, if with a roguish eye for the prettier guests."[22] These two Groucho comedy character types can be differentiated in seven ways.

First, on television, Groucho is without his con man costume of frock coat and grease paint mustache and eyebrows. As befits that old parental axiom of costume directs behavior, his mainstream street clothing and modest real mustache reflect an obviously older, more subdued individual in both appearance and actions. Now as he sits atop a long-legged stool, without the showstopping make-up or such equally diverting visual antics as the patented loping walk, Groucho's cynicism is also scaled down and no longer as flippantly aggressive. And while the self-deprecating humor had been encouraged by Guedel, it was a comic prose Groucho the author had long assumed in his comically antiheroic articles. This was especially true of his 1940s essays, in which he attempted to distance himself from his more aggressive con man screen image. See, for example, such largely forgotten *New York Herald Tribune* pieces as "Do you know enough to go home?" (1941), "Groucho turns himself in for scrap" (1942), and "How to crank a horse" (1943).[23] And the vulnerable real-life father Arthur Marx alludes to nearly surfaced professionally during the 1940s when Groucho helped develop and almost played Chester A. Riley of the original *Life of Riley*, a classic put-upon father that William Bendix would later make famous on radio and television. During the 1940s, Groucho was not without an occasional regression to the past persona, such as the brief return of the team in *A Night in Casablanca* (1946), but this was much less the case after the 1947 inception of *You Bet Your Life*.

Conversely, Harpo and Chico essentially maintained their Marx Brothers personae for the rest of their careers. In fact, probably the most famous non-team appearance made by either Harpo or Chico involved recycled movie material. A May 9, 1955, television appearance on *I Love Lucy* had Lucy and Harpo recreating the mirror scene from *Duck*

Soup, the key variation merely being that the common costume was now Harpo's, as opposed to the look-alike Grouchos of the film. Harpo also did a harp rendition of "Take Me Out to the Ball Game" (a song which figured prominently in the Marxes' *A Night at the Opera*). Fred and Ricky (William Frawley and Desi Arnaz) appeared in the television finale dressed as Chico and Groucho, respectively.

Groucho would be the only Marx brother to escape his movie image after the 1941 breakup of the team, but such an escape was not easy. For instance, in an unpublished letter to Dr. Salinger, he explained why he had rejected a Broadway show which had been expressly written for him: "The play wasn't bad but it didn't fill what I wanted. I wanted to play a legitimate character and they wrote a musical-comedy [movie] Groucho, so I asked them to let me out."[24] Both when *You Bet Your Life* debuted and when it then moved to television, Groucho had to fight the demands of others that he resurface in his frock coat and grease paint and presumably resume his mad movie antics. When the program's head writer Bernie Smith (credited as a director so as not to distract from what was to be an ad lib image) initially made such a demand in 1947 for the radio program, Groucho responded, "The hell I will. That character's dead. I'll never go into that again."[25] It was a position from which Groucho would not budge.

Besides the absence of his frock coat, grease paint, and cartoon-like antics, the second manner in which the television "common sense" Groucho differs from his movie counterpart focuses on words—lots of words. The film huckster Groucho buries his comedy target under an avalanche of words. In *Duck Soup* he tells perennial Marx Brothers victim Margaret Dumont, "You know you haven't stopped talking since I came here? You must have been vaccinated with a phonograph needle." But this is a description much more appropriate to the film Groucho himself. Indeed, his machine gun patter (peppered with puns and other verbal slapstick) was one of the attractions the team offered to an early sound film audience so newly mesmerized by words themselves. His fast talk had originated from a time when, unsure of his material, he hurried from bit to bit to minimize the comic failure of any one line.

In contrast, the television Groucho allows his comedy opponents to be their own worst comic enemies; they are the ones who run on. As Groucho noted, "I don't prod. When some contestant puts his foot in his mouth, I just push it in a little further."[26] And when television Groucho adds his little "push," it generally has neither the same aggressive comic edge so often associated with the movie Marx nor the accompanying absurdity. That is, in the movies Groucho and company often brought comic insanity to a relatively sane situation, whether it was hotel life in *The Cocoanuts* (1929) or travel by ship in *Monkey Business* (1931) and *A Night at the Opera* (1935). On television he is more apt to derail humorously the eccentric comments of his guests and to attempt to make sense of them. For instance, one recently married contestant credited her happiness to not having to feed the chickens. Groucho's response, after first making sure she had, indeed, said this, was, "That's certainly a good reason to get married. It's certainly much easier to feed one rooster than a flock of chickens." Thus, Groucho represents the voice of reason on television.

This is not to suggest, however, that his guests were often just so many clowns, à la the later *Gong Show*. To this misconception Groucho himself said:

> The big thing I've got going for me is that people are interesting… If at times I seem to have a sprinkling of characters on my show culled from the lunatic fringe, at least they're always interesting. It's obvious to my audiences that they're not professional entertainers and that for the most part what they're telling me is true.[27]

Third, while the movie con artist Groucho is most often self-serving (whether courting Dumont for her fortune in several films or demanding his share of the graft in *Duck Soup*), the television Groucho is literally giving away money! In this regard, his atomic age crackerbarrel figure is decidedly old-fashioned; the television Groucho seems to try genuinely to be helpful. Fittingly, as quiz shows go, *You Bet Your Life* questions are not that difficult. The guest couple may also discuss the question between them. And if they still failed to answer correctly, there was always a consolation prize dependent upon merely answering a gag question, such as "Who is buried in Grant's Tomb?" or "Who is President?" That this is, indeed, a softer Groucho is best echoed by what he invariably says on these occasions: "Nobody leaves here broke." The show even sports a benevolent stuffed duck that occasionally drops from nowhere with a one-hundred-dollar bill if a guest happens to say that night's sacred word ("It's a common word, something you see every day").

During the '50s, moreover, the always proper *Look* magazine described Groucho's treatment of tongue-tied guests bothered by stage fright as with "gentleness and consideration."[28] His patented comment on such occasions was, "You had no answer for that at all. Well, it wasn't much of a question."

Fourth, on those occasions when the television Groucho seems like his more aggressive movie huckster persona, the targets are often also similar. While the *You Bet Your Life* guest is generally closer to John Q. Public than anything Groucho encountered in the movies, there sometimes were celebrities. When this happened Groucho admitted, "I'll go after a… big-shot politician or something. The audience loves that… it's their alter ego at work [saying what they would like to say]. How often do you get a chance to insult a big-shot stuffed shirt—and before 30,000,000 people?"[29] On one occasion Groucho asked a visiting Congressman, "How long have you been incongruous, I mean, in Congress?" Receiving an answer of three terms, Groucho added, "Better look out. One more offense and you'll get life." This is refreshing stuff. Still, it does not approach the comic dressing down he so frequently gave the high and mighty in the movies.

Fifth, by the 1950s, the comedian had become so synonymous with the comic insult that people, regardless of position, were more apt to be upset if they were *not* insulted. This is not unlike the position more contemporary insult comedian Don Rickles finds himself in—his audiences *want* to be insulted. Consequently, while the movie victim of Groucho's wit often responded with a comic fit (such as frequent Marx Brothers nemesis Sig Ruman), the *You Bet Your Life* guest seemed to relish Groucho's cracks.

Sixth, unlike his brash huckster from the movies, who could never go too far with an insult, the *You Bet Your Life* "common sense" Groucho was more sensitive to decorum. For example, one program conversation with a retired admiral, whom he had been needling, revealed that the man had been a naval hero. Groucho promptly responded, mildly penitent, "Well that's about as big a thrill as anybody could have. I didn't know you were quite that much of a war hero. I wouldn't have cracked all those bum jokes about you." Groucho later explained, "I wasn't taking any chances in case any listener might have been offended."[30]

Seventh, Groucho's relationship with his television sidekick, announcer George Fenneman, is much less volatile that that with his film partners in fun—Brothers Harpo, Chico, and for a time, Zeppo. The family encounters were comic war, with the otherwise dominant Groucho often coming out on the short end, such as Harpo constantly leaving him behind in the ongoing motorcycle sidecar gag in *Duck Soup* or Chico unloading all the worthless betting code books on Groucho in the "tutsi-fruitsi ice-cream" scene from *A Day at the Races*. In fact, the scenes could become comically sadistic; witness Chico's continuous booting of Groucho off the train in *At the Circus* (1939). Groucho's feelings on these brotherly encounters are probably best summarized by the mustached one's direct-address comment to the viewer in *Monkey Business* (1931) after Chico, in his Italian immigrant persona, has unleashed another of his patently bad puns. Groucho observes, "There's my argument. Restrict immigration."

On television Fenneman represents more of what has become the medium's traditional second banana; there is none of the in-group comic aggression of the movie Marxes. For instance, Groucho once gave this reply to Fenneman's comment that railroad men were to be on the show: "Do you keep track of them yourself? That's the tie that binds." Indeed, one often sees kidding affection, not to mention real concern, when a gag backfires, such as in the episode where George "Peter Pan" Fenneman, airborne via wires, becomes momentarily out of control. Besides the affection, which softened the occasional Fenneman-as-guinea-pig bits, their marked difference in age made it only logical to let the much younger "George" do it (be the comic victim). Also, it seemed closer to a real father-son scenario than the sometimes suggested movie relationship of Groucho and Zeppo as father and son.

These, then, have been seven key differences between Groucho's television character and his more aggressive movie persona and do not negate the fact that some television viewers still found Groucho's humor occasionally too strong. But it should demonstrate that the earlier aggressive movie Groucho was *not* simply unleashed on 1950s television. While Groucho's film character was *satirically* anti-establishment, the television quiz master was part of a *comic* status quo. He was just the one with the money and the common sense, assisting the often eccentric guest (the category formerly occupied by the Marx Brothers).

McCarthyism

The "new" Groucho was largely a result of the comedian's desire to escape his old persona and his recognition of the difference in media demands between film and television. But an extension of the satire/comedy contrast bears further examination. The softer *You Bet Your Life* Groucho also reflects the nature of softer 1950s American comedy, just as the iconoclastic early 1930s Marx Brothers films mirrored that politically volatile period. In the age of Joseph McCarthy, the House Un-American Activities Committee (HUAC), Red witch-hunting, and blacklisting, it was not wise to be politically cutting in one's comedy. Groucho noted:

> There are no more Marx Brothers movies because we did satire, and satire is verboten today. The restrictions— political, religious, and every other kind—have killed satire. If Will Rogers were to come back today, he couldn't make a living. They'd throw him in the clink for being subversive.[31]

Groucho is quoted more fully and more politically in a *Los Angeles Mirror News* article of the same date: "McCarthy started it [the decline of '50s comedy, especially on television]. Everybody became afraid to say what they were thinking. This affected comedy and comedians. There used to be a lot of comedians telling political jokes. Bob Hope is the only one left."[32]

Groucho knew first hand about blacklisting. *You Bet Your Life* bandleader (and later accomplished film composer) Jerry Fielding was called before the HUAC in 1953. Having a history of involvement in left-wing causes, he took the Fifth Amendment. Labeled a Red, Fielding was dropped from the show, after the comedian initially tried to fight it. Groucho later observed, "That I bowed to sponsors' demands is one of the greatest regrets of my life."[33]

Fielding believed the HUAC wanted him to name Groucho: "What other service could I have been to them? Name a bunch of musicians? Had I gone in voluntarily to talk to them, I'm sure they would have brought his name up to me."[34]

It was not that Groucho had anything to hide, but then many HUAC victims could say the same thing. However, in 1947 Groucho had belonged to the "Independent Citizens Committee of the Arts, Sciences and Professions." Though the Hollywood chapter of the organization failed the same year, the United States Attorney General placed it on a list of subversive groups. In addition, a number of Groucho's friends and acquaintances from the now celebrated New York Algonquin Round Table days, persons like Donald Ogden Stewart and Dorothy Parker, were soon to be under a political dark cloud because of their far-left activities. And while writers like Stewart and Parker were then Hollywood-employed part of the time, this said nothing about Groucho's many liberal film friends, such as the always politically controversial Charlie Chaplin.

Groucho had also been a member of the Committee for the First Amendment, a group of film stars (including Humphrey Bogart, Lauren Bacall, and Frank Sinatra) who had flown to Washington D.C., when the HUAC surfaced in 1947 to support the now famous "Hollywood Ten" after they were subpoenaed to appear. But support from the Committee, and from liberal Hollywood in general, dissipated when the hearings turned ugly and Congress cited the Ten for contempt. With Hollywood executives quickly resorting to blacklisting (the "Waldorf Agreement," after the New York Waldorf-Astoria Hotel meeting place), Committee members reacted out of fear for their own careers.

Groucho was a concerned liberal. Indeed, the Marx Brothers had once been blacklisted (for non-political reasons) in vaudeville. But for Groucho to lend his name publicly to a left-wing cause (or to any cause) was unusual, 1947 notwithstanding. After this date he was exceptionally nervous about such involvement.

Given this background, and the increased witch-hunting of the early 1950s (in television and film), Groucho's lack of action on Fielding's behalf (especially after the bandleader suggested that the HUAC had a vendetta out for the comedian) suggests he might have had real reasons to avoid the controversial satirical television comment, thus further softening his television character.

THROUGH THE YEARS

The long-running *You Bet Your Life* was not a static entity. The more restrained television Groucho portrayed herein seems to have become more mellow on the air with the passing years. While there is not necessarily any one reason for this apparently ongoing transition, the comedian's age (as previously noted) probably was a factor—though period publications frequently credited him with being much younger.[35] Moreover, as *Look* magazine's perceptive article "The Secret of Groucho" suggests, Groucho's ongoing television success softened the "need for such automatic [sarcastic] defenses [with guests]."[36] In later years the show also relaxed its "just folks" guest policy and occasionally teamed a celebrity with the everyman contestant. These were generally stars for whom Groucho had open admiration. Such celebrities included his favorite brother Harpo and television comedy innovator Ernie Kovacs, who (with his off-beat humor, bushy eyebrows and mustache, and perennial big black cigar) had more than a little in common with the young Groucho. And Melinda Marx and her comparably-aged playmate Candice Bergen (daughter of Groucho friend and comedy contemporary Edgar Bergen) also appeared together. Fittingly, Groucho's humor was even more affable on such occasions. Regardless, as one studies the extensive period literature about *You Bet Your Life*, the general tone through the years describes an ever more congenial Groucho.

One program constant, however (which also supports the restrained *You Bet Your Life* Groucho argument) is that the show forever courted the family audience. For instance, it ran in an 8 P.M./7 Central family time slot from 1950-1958. Groucho's young fans are occasionally mentioned in period materials, and he lamented the potential loss of East Coast "kids" when the program moved to a 10 P.M./9 Central.[37] But even this slot change had a family connection. It was done to bolster the heartland audience in the Midwest, where 7 P.M. was seen as too early.

This "kid" factor contrasts sharply with such earlier non-film work as Groucho and Chico's short-lived (late 1932) radio program *Flywheel, Shyster, and Flywheel*. *Variety's* lengthy child-related review voiced concern over a skit in which crooked lawyer Groucho (drawing upon his amusingly amoral screen persona) comically turned out to be the mysterious other man in his client's divorce case:

> That's fine stuff for children! Chances are that if the Marxes proceed with their law office continuity along lines like this they will never be able to hold a kid listener…. Because parents don't want their children to hear about bad wives and divorces.[38]

The *You Bet Your Life* Groucho was just not the same fellow as the earlier one. He could still be sharp-tongued, but compared to his cinema comedy anarchist, he was much subdued. In addition, as a later critic observed, even if Groucho was being caustic, one felt like the comedian had just whispered into his contestant's ear: "Don't let it bother you. It's all in fun."[39] It is this human factor which lifts Groucho above the ranks of mere insult comedian—an element of compassion entirely alien from the comic opportunism of his film personae, such as the inspired Rufus T. Firefly of *Duck Soup*. To ignore that difference is to encourage repetition of a Groucho refrain popular with impressionists: "That's the most ridiculous thing I've ever heard."

(Originally appeared in *HUMOR: International Journal of Humor Research*, 5-3, 1992; Wes D. Gehring copyright.)

Notes

1. "Master Marx," *Newsweek*, May 2, 1949, 53.
2. "What Comes Naturally," *Time*, November 7, 1949, 69.
3. Groucho Marx, Unpublished letter, October 3, 1947, in *The Groucho Marx Papers*, Box 1, Folder 3, State Historical Society of Wisconsin (Madison).
4. Goodman Ace, "Groucho vs. the People," *Saturday Review*, September 28, 1952, 27.
5. "For the First Time: The Truth About Groucho's Ad Libs," *TV Guide*, March 19-25, 1954, 5-7.
6. George Kaufman, and Morrie Ryskind, *Animal Crackers. The Groucho Marx Papers* (unpublished, 1928), in Box 1, script section, State Historical Society of Wisconsin (Madison).
7. Steve Allen, Groucho Marx, *Funny People* (New York: Stein and Day, 1981), 193-215.
8. "You Bet Your Life," *Newsweek*, November 24, 1947, 57.
9. "Groucho Rides Again," *Newsweek*, May 15, 1950, 56-59.
10. Steve Allen, *Funny Men* (New York: Simon and Schuster, 1956) 237-251; and Allen's *Funny People*, 193-215.
11. "Groucho Marx Show," *Variety*, October 12, 1949, 28.
12. "Groucho Rides Again," 56-59.
13. Val Adams, "Goucho in Mufti," *New York Times*, April 4, 1950, Section 2:9.
14. Goodman Ace, 28.
15. "Hot Out of Vassar," *Time*, May 1, 1950, 36, 38.
16. Arthur Marx, *Life with Groucho: A Son's-Eye View* (New York: Simon and Schuster, 1954), 279.
17. Ibid., 245-246.
18. "The Stupider the Better," *Newsweek*, September 2, 1957, 52.
19. Max Wilk, *The Golden Age of Television* (New York: Delacorte Press, 1976), 92.
20. Thomas J. Jordan, *An Anatomy of Cinematic Humor* (New York: Revisionist Press, 1975), 89-157.
21. Val Adams and Joe Hyams; "The Givin' Is Easy," *Cue*, April 3, 1954, 17, 36.

22. Allen Eyles, *The Marx Brothers: Their World of Comedy* (New York: Paperback Library, 1971), 189.

23. Groucho Marx, "Do You Know Enough to Go Home?" *New York Herald Tribune*, March 23, 1941; "Groucho Turns Himself In For Scrap," *New York Herald Tribune*, November 8, 1942; "How To Crank a Horse," *New York Herald Tribune*, April 4, 1943.

24. Groucho Marx, Unpublished letter, August 11, 1942, in *The Groucho Marx Papers*, Box 1, Folder 2, State Historical of Wisconsin (Madison).

25. Groucho Marx (with Hector Arce), *The Secret Word Is Groucho* (New York: Berkeley, 1976), 17.

26. "The Stupider the Better."

27. Pete Martin, "I Call on Groucho," *Saturday Evening Post*, May 25, 1957, 85-86, 89.

28. George Eells, "The Secret of Groucho," *Look*, July 9, 1957, 30-34.

29. Bob Salmaggi, "[Groucho and *You Bet Your Life*]," *Look*, July 27, 1958, 33.

30. Adams.

31. "The Marx Brothers Now," *Newsweek*, March 17, 1958, 104, 106.

32. Hal Humphrey, "Groucho Diagnoses Our Ailing Comedy," *Los Angeles Mirror News*, March 17, 1958, in Marx Bros. Files, Special Collections, Academy of Motion Picture Arts and Sciences (Beverly Hills, CA.).

33. Marx (with Hector Arce), 85.

34. Ibid., 355

35. Cecil Smith, "Why Groucho Sends Viewers," *Los Angeles Times*, January 1, 1957, 1, 5.

36. Eells, 31.

37. Smith.

38. "Refineries' *Five-Star Theatre* For Every Type of Radio Listener," *Variety*, December 6, 1932, 34.

39. Richard Whelan, "Cruelty vs. Compassion Among the Comics," *New York Times*, October 2, 1977, D-29.

CHARLIE CHAPLIN & STEVE MARTIN:

Two Late Career Parallel Films

KNOWING THAT MY FAVORITE "golden age" comedian is Charlie Chaplin, while Steve Martin holds that distinction for modern-day funnymen, one of my students asked what was each's most underrated movie, and could I make a connection between the two, beyond the comic link. I pinpointed Chaplin's *Limelight* (1952) and Martin's *Shopgirl* (2005). While the films have many complexly conflicting nuances, each poignantly has examined the loneliness of an older man briefly placated by the love of a younger woman. Both are based upon autobiographical novels—Chaplin's unpublished *Footlights* and the Martin bestseller *Shopgirl*.

Chaplin's *Limelight* came out at a time when he was being hounded by America's reactionary right for his liberal political views. It was the height of the McCarthy Era, and the House Un-American Activities Committee was making life difficult for leftist artists in every entertainment field. Indeed, upon leaving the U.S. for the London opening of *Limelight*, Chaplin's reentry visa was revoked and he became a permanent exile from his adopted country. Harassment, however, had been dogging Chaplin for years, since the 1947 release of *Monsieur Verdoux*, a controversial dark comedy that further soured the comedian's relationship with the general public—though the picture is now considered a pioneering example of the genre.

Given the comedian's fall from grace, *Limelight* tells the story of the once famous London music hall clown Calvero (Chaplin), drawing from a stage tradition that launched the real Chaplin's career. The comedian then added a further autobiographical twist by setting the movie in 1914, the same year he had found international film fame, just removed from those music halls.

The *Limelight* plot turns upon Calvero saving a young ballet dancer (Claire Bloom) from a suicide attempt. Chaplin's character takes it upon himself to nurse his fellow boarding house lodger back to health and revitalize her passion for life and the theatre. Bloom's character (Terry) was inspired, in part, by the love of Chaplin's life—his fourth wife, Oona O'Neill, 35 years his junior and the daughter of playwright Eugene O'Neill. Yet, art does not completely imitate life here because, while Terry and Calvero do fall in love, he rejects the relationship and orchestrates a romance for her with someone closer to her age (Neville, a character played by the comedian's son, Sydney Chaplin). The movie's bittersweet conclusion, a joyful theatrical showcase and tribute that allows Calvero one last opportunity to perform before an appreciatively large audience, is tempered by his dying tragically in the wings as Terry performs. However, this underlines Calvero's ongoing lesson to the girl after her suicide attempt—life and art (the show) must go on.

Though an artist imagining his own death could be termed the supreme act of ego, Chaplin's fatherly Calvero is the most nurturing of figures, consistent with such early watershed Tramp pictures as *The Vagabond* (1916), in which Chaplin cares for another young girl (Edna Purviance) but whereas this picture had the Tramp suffer through the fate of unreturned love, Calvero sacrifices romance. Both protagonists rescued lives and played muse to fellow artists.

Martin was 60 years old when he adapted his *Shopgirl* novella to the screen, versus Chaplin's 63 at the time of *Limelight*. Claire Danes, and Bloom, were twentysomething actresses. Martin's scenario was a rescue, of sorts, too. Dane's character (Mirabelle) is not suicidal, but she is a photography artist "dying" in an exclusive Beverly Hills "shopgirl" position. Unlike *Limelight*, however, Martin's sophisticated older businessman Ray only has romance in mind. Still, Ray and Calvero are similar in that their feelings border more on compassion than passion, and each is parental in his attention to the respective young woman.

Though not an artist, Martin's figure has an artistic temperament, which is underlined by his appreciation of her photography and his character's elegantly minimalist residence. The dwelling is reminiscent of the comedian's own starkly modern home, which uses its minimalism to better showcase Martin's collection of 20th-century art. In fact, *Shopgirl* often has the freeze frame under glass look of a painting by an artist

Martin greatly admires—Edward Hopper, whose signature 1942 work, *Nighthawks*, is a study of late loners in New York. *Shopgirl* also showcases a tastefully done nude shot of Danes that comes across as erotic and abstractly

Charlie Chaplin as Calvero in *Limelight* (1952).

artistic—a modern "canvas" that would not be out of place among the sometimes sexy surrealism of Georgia O'Keeffe's desert paintings.

As with Bloom's Terry, Danes' Mirabelle ends up with a younger lover (Jason Schwartzman). Yet, while the *Limelight* arrangement seems appropriate, the *Shopgirl* viewer genuinely is disappointed that Martin's sophisticated Ray does not commit to the relationship, especially with the lovely Danes being so in love. Granted, Ray professes from the beginning he does not want a permanent coupling, but the much-needed attention he showers on Mirabelle, and his delight in giving her gifts, seems to have the promise of another May-December romance, á la Billy Wilder's 1957 *Love in the Afternoon*, starring Gary Cooper and Audrey Hepburn—with its wonderfully metaphorical title.

Ultimately, Ray's rejection is more a reflection of the complexity inherent in any modern relationship, though one wishes his generosity had focused less on the financial and more on the emotional, although even Martin's melancholy close would have been more palatable had there been something like the undisclosed whisper between Bill Murray and Scarlett Johansson in *Lost in Translation* (2003). That is, a disconnect that was ambiguous enough to allow the romantic viewer the hope for some future get-together.

Regardless, the greatness of *Limelight* and *Shopgirl* is that two mature artists continue to do what they always have done—celebrate the human comedy by way of that most ephemeral phenomenon called love.

AMERICA'S MISUNDERSTOOD PATRIOT:

Young Charlie Chaplin

THE LIBERAL POLITICS OF CHARLIE CHAPLIN, creator of arguably cinema's most iconic figure ("the little fellow" Tramp), ultimately found himself being labeled un-American during the reactionary period now known as the witch-hunting Joseph McCarthy era. This travesty resulted in him being hounded from the country in 1952. Twenty years later, the U.S. would make amends with a series of awards culminating in an honorary Academy Award (April 10, 1972) for "the incalculable effect he has had in making motion pictures the art form of the century."

What had fallen through the cracks of time, however, is a more fleshed-out portrait of Chaplin as a World War I American patriot. During this conflict, the comedian and fellow pioneering filmmakers Douglas Fairbanks Sr. and Mary Pickford raised millions of dollars [which would translate to over a billion dollars today] through a series of war bond rallies. This trio, dubbed the "Three Star Special," launched the Third Liberty Bond tour in Washington, D.C., moved the tour to New York City, and then split up to cover a series of Eastern and Southern states.

While these events often are noted briefly in Chaplin texts, they invariably get short shrift, but a closer examination of period publications provides a vivid account of these rallies and how passionately Chaplin, a native of England, embraced his adopted country, and how American citizens reciprocated these affectionately patriotic feelings. When coupled with Chaplin's later single-handed cinematic capture of the Kaiser in the groundbreaking dark comedy, *Shoulder Arms* (1918), one has quite the patriotic portfolio for World War I. If these events then are refracted through the overt un-American McCarthy era slandering of the comedian, one experiences a poignant lesson in the inherent history-impaired nature of humanity.

The war bond tour's greatest splash occurred when Chaplin, Fairbanks, and Pickford appeared on April 8, 1918, before a Gotham crowd in which the *New York Sun* stated, "The police estimated … 50,000 were present."

Charlie Chaplin selling war bonds in 1918 New York.

People had begun to gather early on Wall Street (from Broadway to William Street) and on Broad Street (from Wall Street to Exchange Place).

The *New York Telegram* reported, "There was a roar as Charlie Chaplin … mounted the platform to announce that he had just come from addressing a Liberty Loan meeting in Washington, and that his 'British heart was 100 percent American today.' He said that if he would be not physically unfitted [sic] he would be in the trenches himself. He wore his trick derby and with the aid of a cane did the celebrated Chaplin walk."

However, the full extent of Chaplin's New York rally speech, and all-around shtick, only can be pieced together by a sampling of the broad print coverage of the event. (For instance, the comedian's signature derby and cane sometimes are reported as being present, as in the *Telegram* account and sometimes the props are noted as missing.)

The *New York Herald Tribune* keyed upon the entrances of the stars, with Chaplin appearing first: "There was a mighty howl of delight when Chaplin, with his mincing dance steps, bounded into view from the interior of the [Federal Reserve Bank] and pranced to the front of the Washington statue. 'Charlie' was not in costume. Grabbing a megaphone the little comedian, looking smaller than ever beside the heroic statue of [George] Washington … led his admirers in three cheers for the Army and Navy and three more for the Liberty Loan."

The *New York American* focused upon an artist initially stunned by the crowd's size: "Charlie, sans cane and mustache, was obviously suffering from stage fright. He was vociferously cheered." The *Wall Street Journal*, meanwhile, provided a lengthy sound byte from the comic patriot's speech, sharing, in part, "Don't think of the percentage of the loan; think of the lives that are being sacrificed. America's richest blood is now being given up for democracy. The Germans are now in an advantageous position and we must get them out of it."

Still, the most entertainingly detailed of all the print coverage came from the *New York Sun*, especially in its winning description of Fairbanks' acrobatic treatment of his close friend. Just after Chaplin said he was "144 percent American … Doug reached for the slim waisted little Charley [sic] and gripped him below the belt on the East River side while Charley was facing the Hudson. Then the muscular Doug held Charley high in the air with one hand and jiggled him above the roaring crowd."

Chaplin's greatest friend during a long life was Fairbanks. The comedian profoundly admired the charm and the off-the-cuff humor of his swashbuckling colleague. Nowhere was this more apparent than in the coverage of the bond tour. For example, during Fairbanks' comments, he asked the crowd, "How did you like Chaplin's speech?" [Cries of "Great!"] "I wrote it!" This produced a wave of laughter, according to the *New York Telegram*.

More humor followed the rally when Chaplin and Fairbanks were invited to a tour of the sub-Treasury Building vault. Shortly after being privy to millions, "Doug called Charley's [sic] attention to the fact that he was hatless. 'Sure enough!' cried Charley, with every semblance of surprise. 'Yes, I must have left the little old trick hat back there in the vault room. Doug, you ... and all you guards go on right up to the main floor and I'll join you as soon as I've stepped back in the vault and found my hat. Go on—all the guards and everybody; don't wait for me—I couldn't think of detaining you gentleman.' But they wouldn't let Chaplin go back. [Later a tongue-in-cheek Fairbanks told the press] he had seen Charley deliberately place the trick hat on top of $85,000,000 in a dark corner of the vault room when no one was looking" (*New York Sun*).

Three days earlier, Fairbanks' humorous savoir faire took center stage when the members of the Three Star Special were honored guests at the White House, but the trio initially struggled in their response to Pres. Woodrow Wilson's question, "What are you going to say in your speeches about the Third Liberty Loan?" At last Fairbanks spoke up, "Mr. President, the only general scheme I've got for a speech is to mention your name wherever I get stuck. That'll get a cheer every time, and while the crowd is making a lot of noise I'll keep waving my arms and working my lips as if I was saying something. And when the noise dies down again I'll shout, 'And fellow citizens, this great, great President, Woodrow Wilson....' Bingo, they'll begin to cheer again." The *New York Sun* concluded this coverage by adding, "All of which the Hon. Woodrow Wilson enjoyed immensely."

After this sit-down with the President, the watershed fundraiser in New York, and solo bond rallies by Chaplin throughout the South, the comedian eventually released his patriotic piéce de résistance, *Shoulder Arms*. As the *New York Sun* observed, "The best of the picture is that it is not simply old slapstick tricks transferred to a trench [war] background but is a Chaplin satire on the life of a soldier." *Variety* added, *Shoulder Arms*, with Charlie Chaplin in uniform, without his derby hat and cane, says Charlie Chaplin is a great film comedian—the greatest."

Flash forward to the 1950s, and somehow this patriot had become un-American. Yet, Chaplin never had ceased his positive actions for the causes of peace and freedom. For instance, even before the U.S. entered

World War II, Chaplin produced a second watershed dark comedy about another German (moving from Kaiser Wilhelm to Adolf Hitler) with *The Great Dictator* (1940). Besides a portion of the film's sizable premiere profits going to the families of U.S. servicemen, Chaplin gave several war-related humanistic speeches (on radio and at rallies) during the war. These passionate talks were almost always variations of the comedian's close to *The Great Dictator*. With Chaplin playing two lookalike parts (Hynkel the dictator and the Tramp as a Jewish barber), the picture concluded with the Tramp being mistaken for Hynkel, but as the Jewish barber begins his poignant speech for peace, it is clear that Chaplin has taken an artistic risk—deciding to step out of character and personally address the audience as the most articulate of concerned citizens.

Though some period critics saw the finale as a flaw in an otherwise groundbreaking picture, the passage of time now finds historians celebrating this artistic choice. The speech invariably was a crowd-pleaser when Chaplin performed it for wartime audiences. Plus, given the general isolationist sentiment of the U.S. in 1940—as well as the country's own lingering anti-Semitism—*The Great Dictator* now is credited with being the most prophetic of pictures. (Keep in mind, conservatives, both inside and outside of the film community, initially had put pressure upon Chaplin not to release the movie, but Pres. Franklin Roosevelt told Chaplin that this cinematic effort was important, and that made all the difference.) Moreover, the film has a seamless connection with *Shoulder Arms*, as both pictures start with the Everyman Tramp as a hapless WWI soldier. (This universality is underlined by Chaplin being an antiheroic American doughboy in one film, and as a misfit Jewish German private in the other.)

So, how did this disconnect occur, in which Chaplin the patriot came to be perceived as un-American? There is no simple answer. After WWII, his ultraliberal views had him labeled a Communist. Then again, his post-World War I outspokenness had him being labeled a Bolshevik. (Chaplin best chronicles these events in a 1922 memoir-travel book, *My Trip Abroad*.) Indeed, conservatives trumped up a "Red Scare" after World War I as well.

More significant for the political derailment of Chaplin was the unofficial retirement of the Tramp with *The Great Dictator*. In the past, whenever his frequently controversial private life made the scandal sheets (from accepting an award from a left-wing organization to having a very young lover), the next installment in the beloved misadventures of "the little fellow" always smoothed things over. Instead, his first movie after *Dictator* was *Monsieur Verdoux* (1947), in which Chaplin's title character marries and murders little old ladies for a profit. His dapper Parisian was inspired by the "career" of Frenchmen Henri Landru, better known as the "modern Bluebeard," who was guillotined in 1922 for liquidating 10 of his girlfriends.

Immediately acclaimed in Europe as another pioneering example of black humor (a "reading" which now is the norm), the initial verdict in the U.S. was different entirely. Upon the 1964 reissue of *Verdoux*, to universal acclaim in the U.S., *The New York Times* best summarized the original domestic debacle of 1947: *Verdoux* received "the most antagonistic critical and public reception ever accorded a Chaplin film."

Another "red flag" for conservatives was that Chaplin never had become an American citizen, despite living in the U.S. for decades, although this hardly was unusual in Hollywood's international film community. For every foreign national who eventually became a U.S. citizen, two others maintained their old passport. Indeed, no less an iconic *American* than Frank Capra pitched one nation of the world in his *State of the Union* (1948), via another pivotal USA Everyman, Spencer Tracy, the picture's star.

The real reason for the smearing of Chaplin—and this is just a personal hypothesis—may be found in a simple irony: silent cinema's greatest artist never stopped being a vocal dissenter to what he saw as injustice. Fittingly, when CBS journalist Edward R. Murrow helped bring down McCarthy, he ever so eloquently tutored the demigod on the true nature of patriotism: "Never confuse dissent with disloyalty." The U.S. was forged through dissent, and a true patriot is ever watchful against lock-step complacency. Whether Chaplin was volunteering generously of his time and energy for war bond rallies, or later assuming a questioning demeanor for democracy, he forever remained the quintessential poster child for that ephemeral phenomenon known as patriotism.

Thus, when Chaplin was later denigrated by narrow-minded, history-impaired "love it or leave it" type Americans, his victimization showed, as in so much of life, that the "enemy" quite often is on this side of the fence—or, since Chaplin is so synonymous with comedy, one might best close with another rendition of this disturbing axiom, from the cartoon strip character "Pogo": "We have met the enemy and he is us."

MR. KEATON

Goes To Yankee Stadium

ACCORDING TO JAMES AGEE'S 1949 essay in *LIFE* magazine, "Comedy's Greatest Era," the four pantheon figures of the 1920s were Charlie Chaplin, Harold Lloyd, Harry Langdon, and Buster Keaton. During that silent-film decade, there is no question that Chaplin was the greatest personality comedian and overall auteur (writing, director, producing, and starring in his Tramp films). However, since Chaplin allowed years to pass between his movies, the prolific Lloyd and his inventive gag team, mixed with the comedian's timely 1920s go-getter persona, made him the decade's comedy box office king.

Langdon's inclusion among Agee's iconic group is somewhat tangential, given it is largely based upon just three 1926-27 features: *Tramp, Tramp, Tramp, The Strong Man* (both 1926), and *Long Pants* (1927). There is no denying the whimsical appeal of his wide-eyed man child, whose only ally seems to be a deus ex machina ending. Yet, this popular trio of features were influenced heavily by Frank Capra, who assisted in their writing and direction. Once Langdon severed his ties with Capra, he lost favor with 1920s audiences. Indeed, his feature film career essentially was over even before the coming of sound.

Keaton, however, is the wild card in this quartet. Like Lloyd, Keaton made 12 features during the 1920s, but the pictures did not find the universal critical and commercial success of Lloyd's work. The latter's still-entertaining all-American hero remains tied to that period, while Keaton's otherworldly persona and minimalist "Great Stone Face" belong to the past, present, and future, such as his Sisyphus-like fate of endless walking on a riverboat paddlewheel in the short subject *Day Dreams* (1922).

Baseball loving Buster Keaton in real diamond garb (circa mid-1920s).

Keaton's world of surrealism meets existentialism is full of these Kafkaesque images, such as the ability to enter a projected film within his film (*Sherlock Jr.*, 1924); miss a major Civil War battle backdrop as he chops wood on his otherwise empty train (*The General*, 1926); win the girl, only to close with a series of dissolves showing the unhappy marriage to follow (*College*, 1927); and find himself walking into a nightmarish cyclone at a 60-degree angle (*Steamboat Bill Jr.*, 1928). It is, as critic David Thomson once observed, "Keaton instructing Franz Kafka on the pitiless futility of taking sides in life."

While Lloyd and Langdon are exceptional comedians, they do not transcend their era in the unique manner of Keaton and Chaplin. Indeed, Keaton's dark side, "like a mute in a monologue," to borrow a phrase from British playwright Tom Stoppard, is more germane to the modern world than the romantic silent film Tramp. However, Chaplin's "Little Fellow" remains current by the sheer ingeniousness of both his comic gift, such as the Thanksgiving boot-eating scene (*The Gold Rush*, 1925), or the aching poignancy of his film-closing rejection by the former blind girl he enabled to see (*City Lights*, 1931).

Ironically, a favorite Keaton moment of other worldliness actually involves America's national pastime. The comedian's title character in *The Cameraman* (1928) has gone to Yankee Stadium for some freelance footage. Naturally, the team is out of town. Just as an empty ocean liner seems to swallow him up in *The Navigator* (1924), he finds himself alone in the cavernous "House That Ruth Built." What occurs next by this refugee from an Edward Hopper painting is yet another example of Keaton's peculiar under glass world—he decides to play an imaginary game of "shadow ball."

Keaton goes to the mound, shakes off the catcher's sign, and then nods "yes" to the next pitch call. However, he initially holds the runners on first and third, and even throws to third. Once the comedian gets the ball back, he looks at another phantom runner on second while motioning his right fielder over. Finally, he delivers the ball and it is a hot grounder to him. He fields it and starts a second-to-first double play. The opponent on third is caught in a rundown attempting to score. Keaton takes a high throw from the third baseman and manages to tag the runner at the plate. Keaton is out of the inning and acknowledges imaginary applause.

The "game" continues as Keaton comes to bat. He dirties his hands for a better grip, and steps into the box. Keaton takes some practice swings, digs in, and suddenly hits the ground—the pitcher has tried to "stick it in his ear." Angry over the knockdown, he takes a few steps towards the mound and words are exchanged. Keaton shakes it off, nods to the umpire that he is ready, and digs in again. This time he hammers the horsehide. Tearing around first base, he momentarily slows at second, but the ball gets by the left fielder. He sprints to third and is given the green light to go home. Keaton scores with an unyielding headfirst slide. Casually brushing himself off, he again accedes to the appreciative fans—until a groundkeeper appears and Keaton's mind game is over.

Unable to interact in social situations, Keaton's robotic figure survives best in the most lonely of settings—venues meant for people, such as an empty ship, train, or stadium. As novelist and playwright Samuel Beckett's Vladimir observes in the absurdist play, *Waiting for Godot* (1953), "This is becoming really insignificant [but] it'd pass the time." Fittingly, Keaton later plays the puzzling central role of O in Beckett's only movie, a short subject entitled *Film* (1965). The picture could be a description of Keaton's solo sojourn to Yankee Stadium—a camera following a peculiar outsider. Regardless, since existentialism essentially is about killing time until life's ninth inning, watching the exploits of the diamond works for me. Moreover, maybe Keaton anticipated linking Beckett to baseball. After all, as Yogi Berra warned, "The future ain't what it used to be."

FILM/
LITERATURE
HUMOR

KIN HUBBARD'S
ABE MARTIN:

A Figure of Transition In
American Humor

DURING THE FIRST THREE DECADES of the twentieth century one of America's most important humorists was Indiana's Frank McKinney "Kin" Hubbard, creator of "Abe Martin." For twenty-five years, from 1904 to 1930, the comic sayings of Martin and his neighbors in Brown County in southern Indiana were highlights of the newspaper to millions of Americans. By 1910 the Abe Martin mania had so enthralled the country that there were "Abe Martin cigars, overalls, cookies, whiskey, porch-furniture, lead pencils and moving picture theatres...."[1] At the time of Hubbard's death in 1930 his humorous comments were nationally syndicated in more than three hundred newspapers and magazines.[2]

Hubbard's Abe Martin appeared during the waning years of the crackerbarrel ascendancy in American humor. The nineteenth-century crackerbarrel figure traditionally focused on political involvement, rural residency, the fatherly image, employment, and success. Above all else he was a capable figure in a world still based in eighteenth-century rationalism. If problems arose, common sense and past experience would be enough to make any life well-ordered again. The inability to cope with a dilemma was an individual rather than a societal problem. The crackerbarrel figure was thus a symbol of American individualism.[3]

By the early twentieth century a transition was taking place in American humor. This change would first find its full articulation in the *New Yorker* magazine of the 1920s, especially in the writings of Robert Benchley, James Thurber, Clarence Day, and S.J. Perelman. Unlike the crackerbarrel, the antihero was nonpolitical, urban, childlike, leisure-

77

oriented, and frustrated—often at the hands of his domineering wife. In his earlier appearances in the comedy world the comic antihero had invariably represented the whipping boy for the capable hero, and his frustration usually resulted from a failure to follow the common sense model of his crackerbarrel counterpart. By the second decade of the twentieth century, however, the antihero was appearing on center stage. Abe Martin was a product of this transitional period. He was in most respects a typical nineteenth-century crackerbarrel figure; yet, he was increasingly at home in the twentieth century world of the antihero. An examination of this dichotomy will perhaps help to restore both Hubbard and Martin to their proper places in American humor.

The most dominant characteristic of the crackerbarrel figure, his fascination for politics, is a trait for which Martin became famous. In fact, the birth of the character was the result of the 1904 presidential election. Hubbard had followed the Theodore Roosevelt-Alton B. Parker campaign for the *Indianapolis News*—he traveled with the candidates in Indiana— and had accumulated a notebook full of drawings, including the figure of the eventual Abe Martin.[4] Never one to waste things, Hubbard introduced this character to the newspaper shortly after the election. In the years that followed "Abe" became famous for such classical political observations as "It's purty hard t' underpay a city official" and "We'd all like t' vote fer th' best man, but he's never a candidate."[5]

Although Abe Martin was born in the political arena, political perspective did not play the dominant part in the Hoosier character's comedy world as it did in the humor of other crackerbarrel figures such as Will Rogers and Finley Peter Dunne's Mr. Dooley. Political observations occur in Hubbard's work as *one* of the fixtures of life, not *the* fixture. Even in the humorist's first collection of sayings, *Abe Martin of Brown County, Indiana*, in which one would expect a political focus due to the origins of the character, politics is not an overriding theme. In fact, the book opens with a nonpolitical question: Have you ever had a "bald-headed barber talk for an' hour t' git you t' try some hair restorer?"[6] In the World War I collection, *Abe Martin on the War and Other Things*, politics retains its secondary status. Instead of being "on the war," a topic which would logically lend itself to political observation, the book is primarily about "other things."[7]

Despite the balance of subject matter in Hubbard's humor when Abe Martin emerges from his relative obscurity in the late twentieth century, he is usually quoted in a political context. Two possible reasons occur.

First, audiences have come to expect a political emphasis from the crackerbarrel humorists; hence, readers focus on politics even though Hubbard did not. Second, the political observations that Hubbard did make have weathered the passage of time somewhat more gracefully than those of other, more political, crackerbarrel figures such as Will Rogers, Seba Smith's Jack Downing, and Dunne's Mr. Dooley. The political sayings of Rogers and Dunne are more readily available and more frequently quoted than Hubbard's; but politics was their main theme, and they dealt with more topical—although quickly dated-subjects. Hubbard, on the other hand, generally wrote in political generalities; such as, "How'd you like t' be marooned in Napolean,

The below 1908 Abe Martin observation juggles characteristics of both crackerbarrel and antihero humor. "'Th' worst feature of a new baby is its mother's singin.'"

Indianny, an' dependin' on th' Congress t' git you out?"[8] When he did deal with politics, he was thus seldom off the mark; for example, "You can lead a feller to the polls, but you can't make him think."[9]

That Abe Martin and his friends resided in rural, isolated Brown County, Indiana, was in keeping with another basic trait of the crackerbarrel figure—residency in small-town, rural America, of which Hubbard himself was a product. Idealization of country life was a characteristic of eighteenth-century rationalism, which saw the city as an unhealthy, unnatural place to live. The key to freedom was an agriculturally-oriented America in need of little government. Throughout his life Hubbard strongly believed in the superiority of this self-reliant, small-town

America. Abe Martin comments in 1908, "Th' biggest 'rubes' at a State Fair er city people";[10] in 1929, near the end of his career, he cracks: "I'm continually readin' o' fellers who've made good in the city, but makin' good in a little town is the real test."[11] Hubbard populated Martin's small-town America with a large collection of other eccentric, crackerbarrel neighbors reminiscent of the family Seba Smith gave Yankee Jack Downing in his tales. It is from one of Abe's friends, the Reverend Wiley Tanger, that the most thorough praise of the rural way of life is presented:

> Some folks jist seem t' be cut out fer th' artificiality o' th' city, an' that's where they ought t' live. But if you want t' live an honest, quiet, peaceful life an' enjoy th' love an' confidence o' your friends an' neighbors, ther's no place like th' little town where one-half th' people knows how th' other half lives, where respectability is a real asset, where a K. of P. [Knights of Pythias] watch charm won't save you if you can't toe th' mark an' where you're remembered long after th' hearse gits back t' th' livery stable.[12]

Hubbard consistently practiced what he preached. The national popularity of his writing created lucrative opportunities in New York City on more than one occasion, but his answer to the possibility of moving to the city was always the same: "I'd rather stay here where I'm known [small-town Indiana] and can play in the band."[13]

In true crackerbarrel tradition Abe Martin is an older, fatherly figure. His crackerbarrel wisdom is a product of tried and tested experience, a valid premise in a world considered to be rational. Situations and experiences repeated themselves, rationalists thought; thus, cause and effect became predictable. In the crackerbarrel world, therefore, age is equated with wisdom and is venerated because it represents an accumulation of experiences. Abe Martin neighbor Tell Binkley perhaps best expresses this philosophy in a short essay entitled "Sixty." (Hubbard "just happened" to be sixty at the time.) Binkley noted, one "has only reached the shank o' young manhood at sixty," a condition with "judgment an experience...piled up ...."[14] Hubbard had earlier claimed that people only improve with age: "Cato took up Greek an' learned it at eighty; Goethe wuz eighty when he put the finishin' touches on Faust; Sophocles wrote Oedipus at four-score an Theophrastus wuz ninety before he became popular as a writer."[15]

A major axiom for Abe Martin was that life is the only real teacher: "Ther hain't no favorites in th' school o' experience"[16] and "Experience is a dear teacher but delivers th' goods."[17] Thus, like the vast majority of crackerbarrel figures, from Sam Slick to Will Rogers, Martin questions formal education: "Lester Mopps has been out o' school fer nigh on two years an' he can't even play the saxophone," Hubbard wrote in 1924.[18] In fact, in typical crackerbarrel style, Abe often suggests that formal schooling is a liability: "Miss Tawney Apple's cousin says he's never been able t' find as good a job as he had before he went thro' college."[19] Hubbard himself had profited little from formal education: he had dropped out of school during the grades, and his one attempt at an advanced academic setting (the Jefferson School of Art in Detroit) did not last a week.[20] He had, nevertheless, achieved great critical and commercial success through the time-honored crackerbarrel "school o' experience." Hubbard and Abe Martin obviously understand each other.

Martin's crackerbarrel credentials have thus far been impeccable. He has personified the wise, elder statesman of rural, small-town America. Two final characteristics associated with the traditional crackerbarrel figure, career and success, are not, however, consistently apparent in Abe Martin. Though Hubbard's drawings of Abe suggest that he is a farmer, they also depict a perennial loafer; and Martin's sayings often underline this inactivity: "more people die from overwork than all th' loafin' put t'gether."[21] That the posture of a loafer was a conscious move is implied by Hubbard biographer Fred C. Kelly, who notes that early in the humorist's career he experimented with, but discarded, being a more "industrious farmer."[22] Comedy historian Norris Yates thus seems justified in calling Martin a "pensive loafer."[23] Yates might also have added that Abe was often a most "frustrated pensive loafer."

Martin's deviation from the crackerbarrel mold in terms of leisure and frustration reflects events in and characteristics of Hubbard's own personal life. Leisure-time activities had always been a central focus in the humorist's life; certainly his love affair with this antiheroic trait predates the Abe Martin period. From childhood Hubbard had had a special weakness for circuses and traveling theater productions, and his lifestyle had always been structured to meet that fascination. As a young man he had become something of a carnival vagabond, moving from job to job and place to place—always in or on the fringes of the entertainment world. During this period he was employed as gatekeeper at an amusement park, ticket seller for a traveling show that featured a mummified Aztec mother and child, and manager and performer in his own minstrel show. Not surprisingly, people close to the young humorist often saw him as something of a pensive loafer. When Hubbard eventually moved into newspaper work, several of his early positions often seemed contingent on his ability to get free passes to local vaudeville performances; moreover, he had a tendency to spend much of his early, modest newspaper salary on flashy clothing that he felt replicated that of the touring vaudevillians.[24] By the time of Abe Martin's success at the *Indianapolis News*, leisure had actually became a problem for Hubbard. His comedy work came so easily that he had trouble keeping busy. Much of his time at the *News* was spent in practical jokes and popular entertainment for the rest of the staff, especially in relating the latest vaudeville stories and routines.[25]

Abe Martin's great success allowed Hubbard to feed his vagabond nature in a grander style. In 1924 he took a trip around the world. Unlike most crackerbarrel figures, who used travel to report on national politics (such as Rogers's fame for covering each party's presidential convention), Abe focused his travel reports on such leisure activities as girl-watching in Florida: "One don't have t' loaf around Miammy Beach very long t' appreciate what an awful time Flo Ziegfield must have in findin' material t' glorify."[26]

The second antiheroic characteristic in Hubbard's work—frustration—is more a product of changes that the humorist experienced while writing the Martin material than an innate characteristic of the man. Comedy references about wives and/or marriages—generally a key focus of frustration for the antihero although virtually nonexistent in crackerbarrel humor best exemplify this developing frustration. Marriage was a rare institution among the always independent Hubbard clan. None of the humorist's five older brothers and sisters ever married, and Kin did not find his way to the altar until 1905 when he was in his late thirties. Even then he felt so embarrassed about being a bridegroom that wedding guests were not allowed to watch the ceremony.[27] His union with Josephine Jackson, though generally considered quite happy, seemed to have a fair share of conflicts; for example, the couple bought two complete sets of furniture for their first home because neither one would give up his or her preference. At the same time, as Kelly notes in his Hubbard biography, "Married life gave Kin a new source of material for Abe Martin."[28] It was, of course, material based in comedy frustration. Marriage was also a key source of frustration in the world of Abe Martin in his role as a comic antihero. Martin jabbed at the wedded state throughout his career. In

1906 he quipped: "O' all the woman's clubs th' rollin' pin is th' wust";[29] in 1926: "Marriages are made in Heaven, an' very few o' them ever git back t' th' factory."[30] As crackerbarrel-type political comments grew fewer as Abe's career progressed so the antiheroic cracks about marriage represent an increasing percentage of his material.

A host of marriage-related "domestic" problems also plagued both Hubbard and Martin the antihero. The rather tightfisted Hubbard found it difficult, for example, to accept the increased expense involved in marriage. Thus Abe Martin noted: "Two can live cheaper than one—but not as long."[31] When the Hubbards built their first home, it was quite an ordeal for Kin; and his alter ego said, "After a feller gets through havin' a house built he reads ever'thing he signs."[32] Houses need furniture and decorations, and as already noted, the Hubbards did not always agree. Not surprisingly, Martin joked: "I guess pickin' out wall paper hez caused 'bout ez many tragedies ez liquor."[33] Children, too, created special frustrations; the Hubbards had three such "blessings." Again, Abe capsulizes things nicely, "Th' worst thing about bein' a parent is havin' a little child come home from school ever' evenin' loaded down with algebras, histories, French text books, an' writin' pads, an' believin' we know enough t' help it."[34]

As the years passed, the frustrations visited upon Hubbard and Abe Martin were not limited to the domestic scene. The most dramatic example stemmed from another real event in Hubbard's life: during the 1920s he was robbed at gunpoint in his own home. The humorist drew several comic sayings based in frustration from this incident as well as from the apparent increase in crime during the 1920s. Martin noted, "The first thing a feller does when he's held up is change his mind about what he used to think he'd do."[35] Automobiles also gave Hubbard problems. His alter ego moaned, "Why does a tire allus go flat on the side where we're liable to git bumped off changin' it?"[36] The ever-increasing sense of absurdity in the world—the whole Hubbard clan was considered to be eccentric—was a constant source of comment: "Th' Father o' Oscar Kite wuz found dead in two feet o' water, t'day, weighed down by a sack o' doughnuts."[37]

Although Abe Martin's frustrations and his focus on leisure are not enough to make this crackerbarrel-based figure a true comic antihero, Hubbard's comedy tended more in that direction with each successive year of the twentieth century. By incorporating the relatively new, antiheroic motifs into the more established milieu of the crackerbarrel figure, the Hoosier humorist emerges as something of an innovator. His significance as a major figure of transition between two worlds of comedy should be recognized.

> (Originally appeared in the *Indiana Magazine of History*, March 1, 1982; Wes D. Gehring copyright.)

NOTES

1. Margaret Rohe Howard, "The Hoosier Humorist," *Human Life*, XXXII (September, 1910), 14.
2. J.Harley Nicholas, "Kin Hubbard," *Indiana Magazine of History*, XXVII (March, 1931), 5. During his lifetime Hubbard received high praise from contemporary comedy writers such as fellow Hoosier George Ade and the renowned Will Rogers. Rogers wrote: "No man in our generation was within a mile of him… I have said it from the stage and in print for twenty years." Quoted in *Dictionary of American Biography*, V (New York, 1961), 324.
3. Walter Blair, *Native American Humor* (New York, 1937; reprint, San Francisco, 1960), 168-69.
4. Fred C. Kelly, *The Life and Times of Kin Hubbard: Creator of Abe Martin* (New York, 1952), 81-82.
5. Kin Hubbard, *Abe Martin's Almanack for 1908* (Indianapolis, 1907), [8]; Hubbard, *Abe Martin's Primer* (Indianapolis, 1914), [62, some Hubbard texts were not numbered].
6. Kin Hubbard, *Abe Martin of Brown County, Indiana* (Indianapolis, 1906), [1].
7. Kin Hubbard, *Abe Martin on the War and Other Things* (Indianapolis, 1918), [16].
8. Kin Hubbard, *Abe Martin: Hoss Sense and Nonsense* (Indianapolis, 1926), 126.
9. Kin Hubbard, *Abe Martin's Town Pump* (Indianapolis, 1929), 44.
10. Hubbard, *Abe Martin's Almanack for 1908*, [62].
11. Hubbard, *Abe Martin's Town Pump*, 138.
12. Hubbard, *Abe Martin's Primer*, [160].
13. Kelly, *Life and Times of Kin Hubbard*, 107. Hubbard's comment could possibly have influenced the musical reluctance of a celebrated fictional crackerbarrel figure to go to New York. Film director Frank Capra's Longfellow Deeds, of *Mr. Deeds Goes to Town* (1936), is not

impressed by the monetary windfall beckoning from the city. In this film Deeds (played by Gary Cooper) consents to visit New York, but his chief concern about leaving home is his place in the small-town band.

14. Hubbard, *Abe Martin's Town Pump*, 41.

15. Hubbard, *Abe Martin on the War and Other Things*, [16].

16. Kin Hubbard, *Short Furrows* (Indianapolis, 1912), [9]. There is also a volume published in 1911 that is entitled *Short Furrows*. It is somewhat different from the 1912 edition.

17. Kin Hubbard, *Abe Martin's Brown Country Almanack* (Indianapolis, 1909), [111].

18. Kin Hubbard, *Fifty-Two Weeks of Abe Martin* (Indianapolis, 1924), 25.

19. *Ibid.*, 86.

20. Kelly, *Life and Times of Kin Hubbard*, 50, 59-60.

21. Hubbard, *Abe Martin: Hoss Sense and Nonsense*, 127.

22. Kelly, *Life and Times of Kin Hubbard*, 82.

23. Norris W. Yates, *The American Humorist* (Ames: Iowa State University Press, 1964), 100.

24. "'Kin' Hubbard, Hoosier Humorist and Creator of 'Abe Martin,' Dies," *Editor & Publisher: The Fourth Estate*, LXIII (January 3, 1931), 10; Richard E. Banta, comp., *Indiana Authors and Their Books, 1816-1916* (Crawfordsville, Ind., 1949), 162.

25. "'Kin' Hubbard, Hoosier Humorist," 10; Kelly, *Life and Times of Kin Hubbard*, 107-11.

26. Hubbard, *Abe Martin: Hoss Sense and Nonsense*, 56.

27. Kelly, *Life and Times of Kin Hubbard*, 18.

28. Ibid., 91, 99.

29. Hubbard, *Abe Martin of Brown County, Indiana*, [89].

30. Hubbard, *Abe Martin: Hoss Sense and Nonsense*, 31.

31. Hubbard, *Abe Martin's Brown County Almanack*, [104].

32. *Ibid.*, [40]; Kelly, *Life and Times of Kin Hubbard*, 99.

33. Hubbard, *Abe Martin of Brown County, Indiana*, [71].

34. Kelly, *Life and Times of Kin Hubbard*, 97-98, 139; Hubbard, *Fifty-Two Weeks of Abe Martin*, 142.

35. Kelly, *Life and Times of Kin Hubbard*, 145-46; Hubbard, *Abe Martin's Town Pump*, 183. The fear of robbery at home characterized the frustration of other comic antiheroes, especially those in the work of James Thurber. See, for example, James Thurber, "Mr. Monroe

Holds the Fort," *Owl in the Attic and Other Perplexities* (New York, 1931), 55-63; Thurber, "The Night the Bed Fell," *My Life and Hard Times* (New York, 1933), 19-31. In fact, Hubbard's recognition that a victim of crime rarely does what he thought he would do anticipates Thurber's most famous antihero, Walter Mitty, the milquetoast husband whose only bravery came in daydreams.

36. Kelly, *Life and Times of Kin Hubbard*, 129-36; Kin Hubbard, *Abe Martin's Broadcast: Kin Hubbard Announcing* (Indianapolis, 1930), 54.

37. Hubbard, *Fifty-Two Weeks of Abe Martin*, 28; Kelly, *Life and Times of Kin Hubbard*, 25-36.

FIELDS AND FALSTAFF

IN WRITING A BOOK on America's greatest native-born comedian (see *W. C. Fields: A Bio-Bibliography,* Greenwood Press, 1984), the author happened upon occasional fleeting comparisons to Shakespeare's Falstaff. For example, *New Republic* film critic Otis Ferguson, the most poetically articulate of Fields' critical champions, described the comedian as a "natural resource. . . a minor Jack Falstaff on the sawdust of the twentieth century."[1] Fields, a self-taught student of literature, was not beyond comparing himself humorously with Falstaff. Author Gene Fowler, Fields' friend, drinking companion and later biographer, remembers the comedian observing "If Falstaff had stuck to martinis [Fields' favorite drink], he'd still be with us. Poor soul!"[2]

Unfortunately, no one ever pursued this comparison. Yet today, one argument for the ongoing popularity of W. C. Fields is that he has become a universal symbol as important in today's age of mass communication as the celebrated literary characters of the past.

The most analogous argument is probably film theorist André Bazin's interrelating of Chaplin's Charlie with epic characters of literature: "For hundreds of millions of people on this planet he [Charlie] is a hero like Ulysses or Roland in other civilizations."[3] A character of this type transcends any one story or collection of stories, whether they are printed or cinematic. Such a character has withstood the test of time, and the works in which he is showcased are "read" and "reread" through the years. All of this applies to the art of W. C. Fields.

Fields has been equated with many important literary characters, from Charles Dickens' Micawber (*David Copperfield*) to Mark Twain's Jim Smiley ("The Notorious Jumping Frog of Calaveras Country"). This article, however, will focus upon the parallels between Fields and Falstaff because of the latter's significance as the most important literary comedian in the English language. In fact, according to honored literary critic and historian J. B. Priestley, "With the exception of Hamlet, no character in literature has been more discussed than this Falstaff, who is, like Hamlet, a genius, fastening immediately upon the reader's imagination, living richly in his memory."[4] It seems only fitting that America's foremost film comedian should be compared to English literature's greatest fictional comedian, especially since ties have long been suggested. Therefore, the two will be examined according to the following criteria: (1) celebration of alcohol, (2) bragging and telling of tall tales, (3) quickness of wit and gift for language, (4) physical incongruity of their being men of action, (5) performance of the cowardly act, (6) pathos, and (7) characteristics and general ties between Falstaff's circle of supporting players and Fields.

Falstaff's and Fields' personae frequently are tall tale-telling revelers who like nothing better than the comradery of male drinking companions, just as Gene Fowler chronicled the real Fields inner circle in *Minutes of the Last Meeting*. Fascination with drink would seem the best starting point for comparison. After all, a beer was even named for Falstaff. And not surprisingly, in the fourth act of Shakespeare's *Henry the IV, Part II*, Falstaff expands at length on the merits of alcohol:

> A good sherries sack [wine] hath a twofold operation in it. It ascends me into the brain; dries me there all the foolish and dull and crudy vapors which environ it; makes it ... delectable shapes, which delivered o'er to the voice, the tongue, which is the birth, becomes excellent wit. The second property of your excellent sherries is the warming of the blood. [5]

Fields' films represent a nonstop celebration of drinking, but he best articulates the importance of imbibing (in preference to man's best friend, the dog) in the essay "Alcohol & Me." Fields cites a number of uncontested facts on why alcohol (in this case, whiskey) is preferable to the pooch: "Whiskey does not need to be periodically wormed, it does not need to be fed, it never requires a special kennel, it has no toenails to be clipped. ... Whiskey sits quietly in its special nook."[6] Moreover, he appeals to the reader's common sense: "When two kindred souls get together for a friendly session, do they sit there and pet dogs?"[7]

As one might assume of a comedy character so closely associated with drinking, the Fields persona forever approaches his defense of alcohol in mock religious terms, not unlike Falstaff:

> The responsibility for this crusade has weighed heavily
> upon my shoulders. Many times I have felt I was a lone
> voice crying in the wilderness. … Then I would let my
> voice really cry out in all its power and glory. I would cry,
> "Set 'em up again!"[8]

Fields' most comic exultation of alcohol, however, is "The Temperance
Lecture," the title notwithstanding. Easily the most anthologized of all his
radio recordings, it provides a Fieldsian version of the past which makes
him a much closer historical neighbor to Falstaff:

> Throughout the Middle Ages the use of liquor was
> universal. Drunkenness was so common it was unnoticed.
> They called it the middle ages because no one was able to
> walk home unless they were between two other fellows. I
> was the middle guy.[9]

Alcohol was just as important in Fields' private life as in his professional
one, though he always claimed his red nose was a product of numerous
childhood beatings, because his runaway freedom was a source of envy
to some boys. Serious drinking came later as a way of coping with the
stress of nearly nonstop juggling practice and performing. And while there
were few drinks he had not tried, eventually the martini became his staple.
His martini intake was massive; during the California years most sources
suggest nearly two quarts daily.[10] Fields claimed martinis were best for
him because "they work fast, and the sensations are lasting. They prick my
mind like the cut of a razor blade. I work better with them inside me."[11]
And they seemed to have this positive effect, for he drank continuously,
even during film productions, and did not become drunk. (In fact, he
strongly disliked drunks.) During film production Fields' only cover-up
for his martini cocktail shaker was to claim that it was full of pineapple
juice—a hoax generously accepted by all, though pranksters once filled
it with real pineapple juice, causing him to boom, "Somebody's been
putting pineapple juice in my pineapple juice."[12] And while Falstaff takes a
portable bar onto the battlefield in Act V of *Henry the IV, Part I* (Prince Hal
discovered Falstaff is carrying a bottle of wine in his pistol case),[13] Fields
is equally inventive in his films. Moreover, Fields's real life excursions on
his estate, or in his Cadillac, were never complete without his portable bar.
(His in-house stock could have doubled for a commercial outlet store.)

Both Falstaff and Fields are also excellent at bragging and telling tall tales. Possibly the most comic example involving Falstaff occurs in the second act of *Henry the IV, Part I,* just after Prince Hal and Poins have robbed Falstaff and several companions—only moments after the latter gang has done some robbing of its own. Falstaff's initial response is to claim the gang was beset by a hundred robbers, though the prankster Prince keeps Falstaff on a braggart's defensive: "if I fought not with fifty of them, I am a bunch of radish! If there were not two or three and fifty upon poor old Jack, then am I no two-legged creature."[14]

Fields, of course, is never far from the tall tale. The antiheroic Ambrose Wolfinger of *The Man on the Flying Trapeze* (1935) claims to have a wrestling hold so unique "there isn't a man or boy born in the United States or Canada that could get out of ... [it]"; the con-man Commodore of *Mississippi* (1935), relating his Indian-fighting career, is forever describing how he "cut a path through this wall of human flesh."

In real life Fields was also forever spinning tales, which, as he admitted in a 1934 article, were starting to catch up with him.[15] That is, he had been creative with so many facts that when friends and associates requested rehashes of specific stories, he frequently was at a loss. However, there is no denying ties between Fields' public and private yarns. For example, his last mistress Carlotta Monti observed:

> At dinners Woody [Fields] sometimes grew verbose knowing he had a captive audience, and would grossly exaggerate happenings that supposedly occurred to him in far-off and generally unheard-of spots in the world. The "Rattlesnake" story [about the close friendship of a particular man and his snake] from [his 1939 film] *You Can't Cheat an Honest Man* [the mere word "snake" always made the film's stuffy Mrs. Bel-Goodie wail and faint] is a good example.[16]

While the tales of Falstaff and Fields sometimes got them both in trouble, their quick wit and continued gift for language often came to the rescue. For instance, Prince Hal eventually calls out Fallstaff's yarn about bravely fighting a veritable army of robbers on the highway—an army only of the disguised Prince and Poins—by stating, in part, "Falstaff, you carried your guts away as nimbly, with as quick dexterity, and roared for mercy, and still run and roared, as ever I heard bullcalf ... . What trick ... canst thou now find out to hide thee from this open and apparent shame?"[17] Falstaff smoothly replies, "By the Lord, I knew ye as well as he that made ye. ... Was it for me to kill the heir apparent? ... Why, thou knowest I am as valiant as Hercules, but ... I was now a coward on instinct."[18]

In a similar manner, the bravery of Fields' former Indian-fighting Commodore is called into question on the point of his character having pulled a revolver during a battle royal years before. Revolvers had not been invented at this time, interjected some skeptic, to which Fields' Commodore coolly replied, "I know that but the Indians didn't know it." (Regarding the verbal magic of Fields' personae, one should not, of course, fail to mention his ability to sell someone a talking dog in *Poppy,* 1936). The private Fields was, if anything, even more determined not to lose a point of debate on any issues. A typical example can be drawn from the comedian's earlier tendency during touring years to open banking accounts all over the world as a safety-valve reflection of both his poor beginnings and the hazards of being stranded on the road. Thus, during a World War II gathering of friends, Fields revealed he had approximately ten thousand dollars in a Berlin bank. David Chasen thought he must be kidding, while Gene Fowler volunteered, "Or else you're nuts. With the war on, and the inflation in Germany, how do you expect to get your dough from Hitler?" Fields, never one to underestimate a villain, "put on a superior expression, and the toothpick [in his mouth] stopped moving." (A motionless toothpick meant he was disgruntled. Fowler compared it to a "readied stinger.") The comedian then replied, "Suppose the little bastard wins?"[19]

It should also be noted that the real world frequently echoed (and continues to echo) the words of this performer—words which frequently also represented clever bypasses of difficult situations, such as Fields' use of "Godfrey Daniel" as a substitute for "god damn" in the censorship era, or his often blanket endorsement of both the pretty and the not so pretty with terms of endearment such as "my little chickadee," "my glowworm," and "my dove." Of course, many of Fields' nationally acclaimed statements or catchwords merely turn a traditional observation on its ear, such as his widely quoted *Bank Dick* (1940) comment on bathing. Fields, as Egbert Sousé, requests of the bartender, "Make it another one, and another chaser. I don't like to bathe in the same water twice."

While Falstaff and Fields look and feel most natural in taverns and other locations of leisurely debauchery, they often are called upon to be men of action—obviously a visual source of much of their humor.

W. C. Fields as title character "warrior" in *The Bank Dick* (1940).

To see the big-bellied, uncourageous Falstaff on a battlefield—despite his position as a soldier—is the most delightful of comic incongruities, probably best captured by Orson Welles (in the title role) in his own outstanding film production *Falstaff* (1967, sometimes titled *Chimes at Midnight.*)

Comedian Fields is not unknown to military settings. In *Janice Meredith* (1924) he plays a drunken British sergeant during the American Revolution; in the 1928 remake of *Tillie's Punctured Romance* Fields' circus assists the World War I Allies' cause by a slapstick involvement with the German Army. One might say the comedian even improves upon Falstaff's military incongruity, because in both noted cases Fields' greatest involvement is with the losing side. (Fields also co-wrote and copyrighted, with co-author Mortimer M. Newfield, a three-act army farce set on an American base at the time of the United States entry into World War I. The farce was entitled "Just Before the Dawn."[20])

Despite these comedic army involvements of Fields, he is much better known for his civilian skirmishes, all showcasing admirably the comic incongruity of Fields in battle. In *The Man on the Flying Trapeze* (1935), the gun-toting, pajama-clad Ambrose Wolfinger falls down the cellar steps (in the best tradition of the antihero) as he hunts for burglars. Professor McGargle takes it on the lam in *Poppy* when a posse materializes. In *My Little Chickadee,* Cuthbert J. Twillie attempts to fight Indians with a slingshot. And in *The Bank Dick,* Egbert Sousé, is at his uniformed-guard best when he attempts to strangle a cowboy-clad child toting a toy pistol.

The real Fields maintained his own private war with the world, a war that sounds as if he were direct from the anti-hero pages of James Thurber. For instance, like Thurber's eccentric collection of relatives in "The Night the Bed Fell," Fields had his own established routine when he was especially aroused by fears of burglars.[21] He would prowl the grounds of his estate, gun in hand, frequently adding a monologue suggesting someone was with him—no doubt intended to further intimidate any crooks in the area, yet also lessening the chances of a direct confrontation.[22] During another period his fears of being kidnapped caused him to multiply his fictitious companion to several equally fictitious bodyguards. And in the middle of the night he would give his crew, who answered to names like "Joe, Bull and Muggsy," directions such as: "I know you boys are former prize fighters and gunmen but I'd rather you didn't shoot to kill. Try to get them in the spinal cord or the pelvis. Ha ha ha ha …."[23] (The 1932 kidnapping of the Charles Lindbergh baby only seemed to fuel a rash of abductions and/or attempts during the 1930s.) There was also a comic military air in the daylight manner in which Fields frequently surveyed his estate from the house with a large pair of binoculars. Gene Fowler even went so far as to liken Fields to "an admiral on the bridge of a flagship."[24] In addition, the comedian had a loudspeaker over the main door, and thanks to his binoculars, he was more than prepared for unwanted visitors. For Fields, just about the whole world was the enemy. Thus, he once scared away two nuns collecting for a charity by impersonating:

> the violent quarrel of lovers—snarled in his own voice, then answered in falsetto. There were threats by the male voice, piteous entreaties by the artificial voice, such as, "I'll murder you with this baseball bat, you double-crossing tart!" "Don't! Please don't beat me again, Murgatroyd! Think of poor little Chauncey, our idiot child!"[25]

(Fields also plays spy, having all his rooms wired so that he could monitor any potentially dangerous conversations from his servants, who were people he rarely trusted.)

Real war did, however, touch Fields' private life. During World War II (at sixty-plus years of age, he and several drinking companions, all of whom were suffering from various physical ailments, appeared at an army center prepared to register for home defense. While they were given forms to fill in (Fields is said to have requested a commando assignment), the woman on duty caught the comic absurdity of the event quite nicely when she inquired, "Gentlemen, who sent you? The enemy?"[26]

Not only are Falstaff's and Fields' personae comically incongruous to "battle," they are very capable of performing the cowardly deed, if it serves their purposes. Thus, in Act IV of *Henry the IV, Part I,* Falstaff first plays dead during battle and later stabs an already-deceased Hotspur, claiming credit for his death.[27] Fields' entertainment alter egos are just as apt to do such deeds, from booting Baby LeRoy in *The Old-Fashioned Way* (1934) to pushing his rival (Leon Errol) for Margaret Dumont off a mountain in *Never Give a Sucker an Even Break* (1941). But probably the best example of this, and certainly the one in which the on-screen Fields projects the most pride, occurs in *My Little Chickadee* (1940). Twillie, tending bar, tells a customer how he knocked down Chicago Molly. But when someone else claims credit, Fields replies yes—but he was the one who started kicking her. Then he tops the black-comedy effect of this proud admission by going into depth on the kicking experience, "So I starts to kick her in the midriff. Did you ever kick a woman in the midriff that had a pair of corsets on?" The customer replies, "No, I just can't recall any such incident right now." Twillie continues, "Why, I almost broke my great toe. I never had such a painful experience." (Later, however, it is revealed that

Twillie and another man were eventually beaten up by the victim and an elderly gray-haired woman with her.

One would not say the real Fields performed cowardly acts, but his methods could be dangerously eccentric. Probably the most famous case in point is the night he was doing his pool routine in the Ziegfield Follies and found the laughs were not coming at the right times. Eventually he discovered a mugging Ed Wynn under the table. Fields was not amused, and he promised fatal consequences if it happened again. It happened again. This time Fields brained Wynn under the table. Fields continued his popular pool routine, which still received additional laughs when Wynn uttered unconscious moans. Fields later offered to incorporate the whole thing into his act, but Wynn declined.[28]

In later Hollywood years, Fields had a muscle-bound butler who worked out on still rings in the garage. The comedian was intimidated by him and eventually sensed disrespect. Thus Fields acted … maybe. That is, the next time this live-in Charles Atlas took a swing on his rings, they gave way at the most inopportune of times. "As he lost consciousness, he said later, he heard a kind of hoarse, maniacal laughter from a darkened corner of the building."[29] The two parted company.

Both Fields and Falstaff are comic figures touched by pathos. For Falstaff, this is most poignant when he is banished by a king who was once a fellow reveler—Prince Hal. For Fields, the moments of pathos are smaller but no less moving, such as his character's attempt at suicide in *So's Your Old Man* (1926), which he repeated in his sound era remake, *You're Telling Me* (1934). In either case, additional pathos occurs when Fields thinks he is rescuing a beautiful young woman from suicide. Appropriately, as if to parallel Falstaff's hobnobbing with royalty, the young beauty is a princess— although Fields does not learn this until later. (Both films are based upon Julian Street's "Mr. Bisbee's Princess," which had won the O. Henry Memorial Award as the best short story of 1925.) While pathos is not something as readily associated with Fields as it is with a Charlie Chaplin, 1930s film critics not infrequently made reference to Chaplin when describing pivotal moments in Fields.

As has been so often the case in this comparison, the characteristic is also true of Fields himself. The comic foibles of Fields' screen personae did not stop when the cameras did. There is a very real pathos to a master comedian whose on-screen source of humor (the ongoing battle of day-to-day existence) frequently turned to a series of "persecution complexes" in private life, such as the aforementioned example concerning Fields's musclebound butler.[30]

These, then, have been the obvious parallels between Falstaff and Fields. But the comparison does not stop there. Several of Falstaff's supporting players also seem to have similarities or ties with Fields. Most obvious is the case of Bardolph, attendant to Falstaff and possessor of an impressive red nose which invites witty comment. For example, when Bardolph suggests Falstaff is too heavy, the latter directs an attack against the attendant's nose: "Do thou amend thy face, and I'll amend my life. Thou art our admiral [flagship], thou bearest the lantern in the poop— but 'tis in the nose of thee: thou art the knight of the Burning Lamp."[31] Fields, of course, owned quite a "Burning Lamp," too, and references to it are frequent in his comedy, including print, radio, and the movies. For example, in his celebrated radio rivalry with Edgar Bergen's Charlie McCarthy, McCarthy once asked: "Is it true, Mr. Fields that when you stood on the corner of Hollywood and Vine forty-three cars waited for your nose to change to green?"[32] (See also Jack Grant's interview/essay with Fields, "THAT NOSE of W. C. Fields."[33]) With the possible exception of Jimmy "Schnozzola" Durante, no major American comedian probably ever better utilized his proboscis (the term Fields preferred over nose). Strangely enough, however, he was unusually sensitive about his nose in private life and could become easily offended, even when the cracks were from close friends. One such offending comment was actually reminiscent of Falstaff's aforementioned jab at Bardolph's nose. After John Barrymore's death, his friends had difficulty convincing Fields to serve as a pallbearer, because he felt the time to help pals was when they were alive. But when Fields continued with his "why me" manner the reply was, Well, in case it gets dark, your nose would make an excellent light."[34]

Prince Hal's companion Poins, who devises the comic robbing of the robbers (Falstaff and company), suggests Fields' con-man persona. Pistol, the tavern warrior whose overblown speeches cover a coward, can be like a boastful Fields. Silence, the truly "silent" partner-stooge to country justice Shallow, is like any number of stooges Fields had on stage and in films, as well as in real life. And Dame Quickly, hostess of Boar's-Head Tavern and lender of money to Falstaff, rather anticipates those gullible women whom a conning Fields could manipulate in so many films.

This comparison does not imply that the character of Falstaff directly affected Fields (though it well could have), as seems to have been the case with Dickens' well-represented Micawber. (When Fields had traveled in vaudeville, one of his trunks was entirely given over to books.) Regardless, this Shakespeare tie puts into perspective the significance of Fields as a modern-day Falstaff, à la Bazin's analogy between Charlie Chaplin and Roland. Moreover, without trying to be sacrilegious in the halls of literature, Fields is now undoubtedly more universally recognizable by the general public than Falstaff, and he has been for some time.

> (Originally appeared in Canada's *THALIA: Studies in Literary Humor*, Fall & Winter 1985; Wes D. Gehring copyright.)

Notes

1. Otis Ferguson, "The Great McGonigle," *New Republic,* August 21, 1935, 48.
2. Gene Fowler, *Minutes of the Last Meeting* (New York: Viking Press, 1954), 224.
3. André Bazin, "Charlie Chaplin," in *What is Cinema?*, vol. 1 selected and trans. by Hugh Gray (1958; rpt. Los Angeles: University of California Press, 1967), 144.
4. J. B. Priestley, *The English Comic Characters* (New York: Dodd, Mead, 1931), 69.
5. *Henry the IV, Part II*, act 4, sc. 3, lines 97-105.
6. W. C. Fields, "Alcohol & Me," PIC, October 13, 1942, 32.
7. "Alcohol & Me." 34.
8. "Alcohol & Me." 32.
9. *The Best of W. C. Fields*, previously released recordings (Columbia, BL 34145), 1976.
10. Carlotta Monti (with Cy Rice), *W. C. Fields & Me* (1971; rpt. New York: Warner Books, 1973), 205.
11. Monti, 206.
12. Robert Lewis Taylor, *W. C. Fields: His Follies and Fortunes* (Garden City, New York: Doubleday & Company, 1949), 242.
13. *Henry the IV, Part I*, act 5, sc. 4, lines 52-55.
14. *Henry the IV, Part I*, act 2, sc. 4, lines 185-88.
15. Sara Hamilton, "A Red-Nosed Romeo," *Photoplay* (December 1934), 33.
16. Monti, W. C. *Fields & Me*, 78.
17. *Henry the IV, Part I*, act 2, sc. 4. lines 158-61, 263-65.
18. *Henry the IV, Part I*, lines 268-74.

19. Fowler, *Minutes of the Last Meeting*. 101.
20. "W. C. Fields Papers," Library of Congress. Manuscript Division (Madison Building), Washington, D. C.
21. James Thurber, "The Night the Bed Fell," in *My Life and Hard Times* (1933; rpt. New York: Bantam Books, 1947), 19-31.
22. The domestic private battles of Fields often figure in the biographical literature on the comedian. See especially Taylor's *W. C. Fields: His Follies and Fortunes*. 313.
23. Fowler, *Minutes of the Last Meeting*, 257.
24. Fowler, 152.
25. Fowler, 152.
26. This story also appears frequently in Fields material. See especially Taylor, *W. C. Fields: His Follies and Fortunes*, pp. 264-65; Fowler, *Minutes of the Last Meeting*, 204-5.
27. *Henry the IV, Part I*, act 4, sc. 4, lines 75, 119, 127-28.
28. This is another oft-reported incident. See especially Alva Johnston, "Profiles: Legitimate Nonchalance – II," *New Yorker*, February 9, 1935, p. 26; Taylor, *W. C. Fields: His Follies and Fortunes*, 150-51.
29. Taylor, *W. C. Fields: His Follies and Fortunes*, 259.
30. Taylor, 161.
31. *Henry the IV, Part I*, act 3, sc. 3. lines 25-28.
32. The sketch "Feathered Friends," from the record album *W. C. Fields on Radio: With Edgar Bergen & Charlie McCarthy* (Columbia CS 9890), n. d.
33. Jack Grant, "THAT NOSE of W. C. Fields," *Movie Classic* (February 1935), 56, 60.
34. Fowler, *Minutes of the Last Meeting*. 222.

WILL CUPPY:

Somewhere Between Benchley & Groucho

BACK IN THE GOLDEN AGE of humor books (from the late 1920s until the early 1950s), when pantheon wits like Robert Benchley, James Thurber, and S.J. Perelman were producing their signature works, there was another singular satirist who more than held his own with such fast company. Named Will Cuppy (1884-1949), this factual funnyman's métier is a dark comedy which flirts with nihilism. His agenda is baldly stated in such Cuppy book titles as, *How to Be a Hermit* (1929), *How to Tell Your Friends from the Apes* (1931), and, *The Decline and Fall of Practically Everybody* (1950).

His short comic essays, ranging from natural history to the history of man, would involve massive amounts of research. A visit to the "Will Cuppy Papers" at the University of Chicago reveals the humorist might fill hundreds of note cards for a single essay of no more than a 1,000 words. Thus, there is frequently a dry, darkly comic professorial air to his satire. For instance, in "The Tiger" essay from his "*Apes*" text, Cuppy writes, "Young normal Tigers do not eat people. If eaten by a Tiger you may rest assured that he was abnormal. Once in a while a normal Tiger will eat somebody but he doesn't mean anything by it."

Cuppy frequently, moreover, uses his fact-based humor to satirize human behavior at its darkest, such as his "*Decline and Fall*" comic treatise on "Alexander the Great": "[His opponent Darius] had chariots armed with scythes on each side for mowing down his enemies. These did not work out since Alexander and his soldiers refused to go out and stand in front of the scythes. Darius had overlooked the fact that scythed chariots are effective only against persons who have lost the power of locomotion and that such persons are more likely to be home in bed than fighting battles in Asia."

Cuppy's smart aleck heckling of history and/or authority is reminiscent of his comedy contemporary Groucho Marx (1890-1977), particularly in the academic satire "Horse Feathers" (1932), in which the mustached Marx Brother is president of Huxley College. Fittingly, when the "*New York Times*" reviewed Cuppy's *How to Become Extinct* (1941), their literary critic drew a direct line between the satirists. The catalyst was a Cuppy footnote chronicling how herpetologists had recently decided that the boa constrictor should have a new name. The humorist's response – "I have decided that it should not. Two can play at that game"—had the "*Times*" reviewer observing, "Somehow the judicious reader is apt to hear the tone of Mr. Groucho Marx in a statement like that" (December 6, 1941).

Of course, one might as well call Groucho Cuppy-like, because the print humorist had the same razor wit from his earliest work. My favorite such folly-of-man Cuppy crack occurs in the preface to his "*Apes*" text. He states, "I grant you there are plenty of old-fashioned and pretty ineffective ways to tell one's friends from the Apes. What could be simpler, for instance, when you are at the zoo? The Apes are in cages. Yes, but when you are *not* at the zoo, what then?"

Or, if one wanted to get more specific with the Cuppy-Groucho chronology of wit, one might key upon the following Marx movie gem from *Monkey Business* (1931, co-scripted by S.J. Perlman), in which an insulted woman complains to Groucho, "I don't like this innuendo." He responds, "That's what I always say. Love flies out the door when money comes innuendo." Six years earlier, in an unpublished letter to an old friend (journalist and future Libertarian pioneer, Isabel M. Paterson), Cuppy wrote the following romantic advice, "Your boyfriend probably has some libidinous fixation on you which complicates it, too. Where the libido flies in the window, logic flies out the door" (the Cuppy-Paterson Correspondence, folder 1, the Herbert Hoover Presidential Library, West Branch, Iowa). Examples such as these suggest Cuppy needed little period prompting from the most vociferous of the Marx Brothers. But for readers now unaware of Cuppy, the parallels with Groucho provide an immediate take upon the "voice" of this print humorist.

Yet, if anyone influenced Cuppy's work it would have been Robert Benchley (1889-1946). There was no other humorist Cuppy admired more. Indeed, in the extensive aforementioned correspondence with Paterson, Cuppy's high regard for Benchley could surface in some curmudgeonly comic ways. Both Paterson and Cuppy had book section columns in the Sunday *New York Tribune* (and its successor, the *Herald Tribune*). Thus, in one undated letter [circa 1925] to Paterson he complained, "Do you mean to tell me that you have not yet printed the [praising] masterpiece I wrote about Robert Benchley?   [Paterson's column periodically included long excerpts from Cuppy's letters.] Save it, by all means, until everybody else has reviewed it [Benchley's latest book]" (Cuppy-Paterson Correspondence, folder 1).

In another Cuppy letter to Paterson [circa 1929], the humorist acidly defended Benchley: "Harry Hansen wrote a review of the [latest] Benchley book which [is unique] for sheer godamed [sic] filthy ignorance and insensitiveness to all that is lowest in the animal creation…. Such [people] should not write reviews of funny books" (Cuppy-Paterson Correspondence, folder 2). Cuppy was hardly alone in considering Benchley the comedy gold standard. For example, in one of James Thurbers' casuals (short essays) for a January 1926 *New Yorker* he observed, "… one of the greatest fears of the humorous writer is that he has spent three weeks writing something done faster and better by Benchley in 1919."

What provoked such Benchley passion in Cuppy, and how had he seemingly influenced the humorist? Benchley's earlier MO, like Cuppy's, often assumed a professorial tone, best exemplified by the series of short subject films Benchley did from the late 1920s until his mid-1940s death. Often drawn from Benchley's own essays, starting with such pioneering sound shorts as *The Treasurer's Report* and *The Sex Life of the Polyp* (both 1928), these mini-movies featured the humorist as a lecturer whose material either gets the best of him, and/or simply amusingly derails his details. Paradoxically, while Benchley clearly set the precedent, the names of his cinema short subjects eventually carried Cuppy-like "How to" titles, such as the Oscar-winning, live-action short film, *How to Sleep* (1935).

As previously suggested, however, the Benchley academic persona, whether on the printed page or in pictures, usually had a more gentle comically befuddled aura about it than did Cuppy's. For instance, in the Benchley essay "A Trip to Spirit Land," he observes, "In all the recent talk about spirits and spiritism (by 'recent' I mean the past three hundred and fifty years) I have maintained what amounts to a complete silence, chiefly because I have been eating crackers a great deal of the time and couldn't talk…." Though amusingly absurd in its rambling, the piece still manages to satirically undercut its serious subject matter, which Cuppy also accomplishes with his blunter comic bludgeoning.

Benchley's "Spirit" essay is from his book, *No Poems Or Around the World Backwards and Sideways* (1932). Starting in the 1920s, Benchley's essay collections always had inspiringly amusing titles, something Cuppy successfully emulated, from his aforementioned *How to Tell Your Friends From the Apes*, to my personal favorite, *How to Attract the Wombat.* (1949). Cuppy would also have appreciated the *No Poems* portion of Benchley's title, because Cuppy's writing, both in his correspondence and comic essays, is peppered with negative cracks about verse. For example, in a short *Decline and Fall* piece on Frederick the Great, Cuppy reveals the leader eventually "became a poet. His poems were very silly, even for poems."

Cuppy's more attack mode professorial persona was simply grounded in *Decline and Fall* text, "It's easy to see the faults in people, I know, and it's harder to see the good. Especially when the good isn't there." That line would never be confused for a Benchley axiom, though it would not be out of place coming from Groucho. Benchley blunted/ softened his questions about the modern world by being self-deprecating. For example, in another piece from *No Poems*, he confesses, "It is the inanimate enemies who have me baffled. The hundred and one little bits of wood and metal that go to make up the impedimenta of our daily life… the shoes and pins, the picture books and door keys, the bits of fluff and sheets of newspapers … every one bent on my humiliation, and working together, as one great team, to bedevil and confuse me.…"

In ironic contrast, to paraphrase a line from *poet* Dylan Thomas (1914-1953), Cuppy did "not go gentle" into his satirical reveries. And if there was any comic paranoia involved (á la Benchley's aforementioned comments on inanimate objects) Cuppy was comically out to blame humanity. In both his correspondence and his essays there were even periodic references to an oblique "Hate Cuppy Movement." Sometimes he applied the comment with a blanket conspiracy broadness, such as the actual bad timing of the *Hermit* book being published precisely when the Stock Market crashed in 1929, and the *Extinct* text's first appearance coinciding with the Japanese attack on Pearl Harbor (1941). Or, Cuppy could zing an individual with a "Hate Cuppy" agenda, as he did when a reader once complained about the humorist's proclivity for satirizing Aristotle. In Cuppy's rebuttal, "Aristotle, Indeed!," he comically plays the "Hate" card, and then defensively observes, "I don't doubt that Aristotle thought more in actual footage… than any other person… however, any prize he deserves for so doing should be for quantity, not quality, as a

Groucho Marx (right) shish kebabbing education as president of Huxley College
in *Horse Feathers* (1932).

great deal of it [his writing] was spinach" (reprinted in Cuppy's *Extinct* text).

Cuppy's only concession, or satirical subterfuge, in his hard line against humanity, is to often filter his digs through comments on natural history. For example, in an essay allegedly about "The Ant," from his *Wombat* collection, he writes: "Ants operate by instinct instead of intelligence. Intelligence is the capacity to know what we are doing and instinct is just instinct. The results are about the same." If that subtextual bite was not clear enough, his statement had the following footnote: "But we do it on purpose."

With paradoxical appropriateness, however, for a humorist with such a low opinion of humanity, the masses generally seemed to miss this satirical point. Cuppy was forever comically complaining, as he does in his *Wombat* preface, fittingly entitled "Are Wombats People?," how readers were always unbelievably asking him, "Why don't you write about *people*, Will?" Sometime Cuppy illustrator William Steig (1907-2003) put it more bluntly in an undated [circa 1941] letter to the humorist: "This book [*How to Become Extinct*] is better than the "Apes" book – it will make a hit. Dopes laugh at your stuff, too, though not for the best reasons – they think the author is crazy & are thrilled at their own discernment" (Cuppy Papers, University of Chicago).

Steig, the celebrated *New Yorker* cartoonist and later award-winning children's author (including creating the character Shrek), could be penciled in as an important comic artist influenced by Cuppy. Steig illustrated both the *Extinct* and the *Decline and Fall* texts, and his entertainingly extensive correspondence with Cuppy reveals an often kindred spirit as well as someone acknowledging the impact of an older, artistically stimulating artist. The following letter excerpt is also typical of how Steig constantly provided the insecure Cuppy with positive reinforcement: "And when any Tom, Dick, and Harry laughs at your stuff & says you are very good, he is laughing at something, not intended, that he has chosen to discover. Dear Cuppy, please don't be unhappy – because I identify with you to such an extent that when you suffer I suffer" (circa 1936, Cuppy Papers, University of Chicago).

This constant neediness on Cuppy's part, a trait also front and center in the Paterson papers, is just one of several dysfunctional components which, when coupled and/or contrasted with his biting wit, makes the humorist an even more compelling figure. That is, under all his dark comedy bravado was a tortured artist. Indeed, Cuppy's real story rivals his iconoclastic satire. For instance, through the years, he conducted his attacks on humanity from a series of metaphorical safe house hideaways, starting with a *twelve-year* powder at the University of Chicago. In a later obscure 1930s interview on his professional student status he confessed, "Deciding after [college] graduation that I knew nothing whatever about anything, I hung about campus for the next seven years, taking courses in practically everything, with or without credit, as the spirit moved me" ("History of DeKalb County, Indiana: 1837-1937," where Cuppy was born and raised).

Though Cuppy's classic humor books would come later, this extra-inning, cloistered college life provided him with his eventual professorial persona, even to the signature touch of generously sprinkling his essays with comic footnotes. After knocking about in New York for several years, he became a practicing hermit for most of the 1920s, living in a shack on Jones Island, just off Long Island's Atlantic-side South Shore. Affectionately calling his dump, "Tottering-on-the-Brink," the recluse wrote his reviews and comic essays at a safe distance from "the City," only venturing into New York out of necessity. The comic culmination of this experiment was the bestseller, *How to Be a Hermit.*

Though Cuppy's correspondence with Paterson from this period occasionally notes his escape from "Hicksville" (his Auburn, Indiana, hometown), his haven by the sea is essentially celebrated as the anti-New York, without urban distractions (á la social interaction) and city noise. In his later *Apes* text he faulted psychologists who suggested "something amiss with a bookish old recluse who does not enjoy the combined yawpings and yowlings and yammering of the entire brute [urban] creation while he is trying to get some... writing done." But Cuppy was more subtextually comic when he addressed the same subject, as was his habit, via the animal kingdom, "There are worse things than rabbits. Rabbits are among the few remaining vertebrates which neither bark, sing, whistle, play the piano, lecture nor invent new machines to make more of the same or other loud noises. They should be encouraged" ("Consider the Lettuce," from the *Hermit* book).

Sadly, while you can take the "bookish old recluse" out of the city... sometimes the city follows you home. By 1929, Jones Island had become Jones Beach State Park, and with a major bridge from the mainland, Cuppy's hermitville had been invaded by noisy tourists. Made to abandon his full-time "Tottering-on-the-Brink" residence, he found a new sanctuary in a Greenwich Village apartment (at 130 West 11th Street). His small fourth floor walk-up soon resembled an explosion at your local library. Other than occasional off-season forays to his Jones Island shack, Cuppy seldom left his apartment. He also continued his long-standing hermit hours in the Village, writing and reading/researching at night and sleeping during the day.

Food was often ordered in, and communication with a small circle of friends and/or publishing-related people was largely limited to correspondence and late night phone calls. In an undated [circa 1930] newspaper article entitled, "That's Why I Never Married!," the humorist blamed his lifelong bachelorhood upon "scientific determinism": "As you know, statistics show that a certain number of people get married each year and the rest don't. Well, I got in the wrong bunch of statistics" (Cuppy Papers, University of Chicago). But his correspondence with Isabel Paterson documents their flirtation with the institution of marriage.

Cuppy was capable of witty interaction with the masses when needed, such as his short-lived talk show on NBC radio (1933, in which he discussed his pet peeves), or periodic book signings. But the "Hate Cuppy

Movement" was always in the back of his mind, such as Cuppy's description of a certain shopper who did *not* buy his book: "Where on earth do such people come from and how do they get into bookstores? He was a large, fat, brutish-looking man… [with] close-set, malevolent eyes. There was that intangible something about him that immediately proclaims the … homicidal maniac…" (*Author's League Bulletin*, December 1929).

The manner in which Cuppy's sharp tongue covered a tortured psyche (revealed in his unpublished letters) anticipates the later humor books of pianist/composer/actor Oscar Levant (1906-1972), whose signature line was, "There's a thin line between genius and insanity [pause] I have erased that line." In Levant's *Memoirs of an Amnesiac* (1965) and *The Unimportance of Being Oscar* (1968), he comically bares his Cuppy-like neurotic, hypochondriacal, humanity-baiting, self-declared genius core. Had Cuppy also been able to reveal his much earlier similarly brilliant bittersweet private ramblings with such cathartic bestselling success, he might not have taken his own life. But the humorist eventually reached that place where there are no road maps home. Seemingly caught in the crawl space of life, Cuppy took an overdose of sleeping pills, and died on September 19, 1949.

In an earlier Levant book, *A Smattering of Ignorance* (1942), he had revealed to a friend a normally well-hidden vulnerability which might have also doubled as a Cuppy axiom on humanity, "Well, you know I hate 'em 'till they say hello to me."

GROUCHO LOST & FOUND:

His *Other* Letters

IN 1967, SIMON AND SCHUSTER published the immediately celebrated *The Groucho Letters: Letters From and To Groucho Marx*. The catalyst for the publication had been the wave of publicity concerning the earlier request by the Library of Congress for Groucho's correspondence. Not surprisingly, when a delightfully amusing book by a certifiable American legend has been further ennobled by a stamp from on high (*Newsweek's* review stated the Groucho correspondence was already "enshrined in the Library of Congress"[1]), the man and his work are not so much reviewed as commemorated. Such was the case with *The Groucho Letters*.

There is no denying the entertaining nature of the collection. For instance, in a letter to author E.B. White, Groucho observed, "I write by ear. I tried writing with the typewriter but I found it too unwieldy."[2] But as in this example, there is often a self-consciously polished nature to this eclectic collection of correspondence which focuses on the famous (including intellectuals like T.S. Eliot and entertainers like Brother Harpo), as if it were being salted away for future publication. The close of the book's Introduction, by family friend and author Arthur Sheekman, even brings this self-consciousness to mind. Sheekman recycles the comedian's famous one-sentence letter to the scandal sheet *Confidential Magazine*, after it made libelous accusations about him. The Groucho "warning" was, "If you continue to publish slanderous pieces about me, I shall feel compelled to cancell [sic] my subscription."[3] Thus, while the work is not without personal insights, *The Groucho Letters* is best treated as an entertainment volume, in the tradition of such Groucho books as *Beds* (1930), *Many Happy Returns* (1942), and *Memoirs of a Mangy Lover* (1963).

Just how removed the collection was from more ordinary Groucho correspondence was not, however, fully brought home to this author until doing research for his book *The Marx Brothers: A Bio-Bibliography* (Greenwood Press, 1987). The State Historical Society of Wisconsin (Madison) proved to have an unrecognized bombshell—a collection of a hundred-plus Groucho letters, dated from 1928 to 1971, written to a noncelebrity and longtime Chicago family friend, plastic surgeon Dr. Samuel Salinger. The correspondence is a further bonus since *The Groucho Letters* is largely limited to correspondence written after 1940.

Marx Brothers stage mother and initial manager Minnie had moved the clan from New York to Chicago in approximately 1910. The then young team (Groucho was twenty) needed a home base which was more geared to bookings in small-time, heartland vaudeville, of which they were still very much a part. Between this move and the team's 1920s big-time return to New York, the Marxes made the acquaintance of Salinger, purportedly through his earlier medical practice. (There is no evidence that any of the Marxes had need of Salinger's specialty.)

The Marx Brothers in 1946's *A Night in Casablanca* (left to right, Chico, Groucho, and Harpo, with Zeppa having left the team).

While history has left very little background on why a friendship developed between the doctor and a comedian whose favorite role would eventually be that of a quack doctor (Dr. Hugo Z. Hackenbush in *A Day at the Races*, 1937[4]), correspondence between the two provides a time capsule worth of insight and humor not generally available in any other Groucho literature. The comedian's correspondence with Salinger, written with less an eye toward history, often reveals an honesty and earthiness not to be found in *The Groucho Letters*. In fact, a reader familiar with the Madison letters is little shocked by the ribald commentary of *The Marx Bros. Scrapbook*, the controversial 1967 book complied by Richard J. Anobile. Groucho received co-author billing but attempted to stop distribution of the book when he discovered his salty taped interviews were *not* to be laundered first.

Most importantly, the Madison letters simply provide very startling revelations—revelations which shatter some long-established Marx Brothers background. Indeed, the most prominent example even manages to undercut the legitimacy of the most comically celebrated aspect of the published letters—the conflict over the use of the name Casablanca in the Marxes's *A Night in Casablanca* (1946).

The film was an independent production distributed by United Artists, with the Marx Brothers receiving a percentage of the profits. While this comic tale of hidden Nazi loot was not the Marxes at their best, the general critical consensus was that it was just good to have them back following their "retirement" as a team after *The Big Store* (1941). The now celebrated critic James Agee summed it up best in his *The Nation* review: "The worst they might ever make would be better worth seeing than most other things I can think of."[5]

The film has become most famous, however, for the series of letters Grouhco purportedly wrote to the Warner Brothers legal department concerning the studio's supposed contesting of the title use of Casablanca. The issue was whether Warners, because of its earlier classic film *Casablanca* (1942) had exclusive rights to titular use of the city. The question generated a great deal of comic interest both in 1945, when the film was in preproduction, and in 1967, when some of Groucho's Library of Congress correspondence was published in book form, with the comedian's responses to Warners opening the volume. (Not surprisingly, his Warner Brothers comments were also frequently highlighted in reviews of the book.)

Groucho's Warner letters are indeed humorous, fluctuating from comic outrage to outrageous comedy. For example, he asserts in one that if Warner Brothers has exclusive rights to *Casablanca*, then the Marxes had a similar claim to Brothers, because "Professionally, we were brothers long before you were."[6] (For a period publication of this letter—in a slightly varied style—see the December 22, 1945, issue of *The Saturday Review.*[7]) *But* in a startling May 31, 1945, letter to Salinger, Groucho revealed:

> We spread the story that Warners objected to this title purely for publicity reasons. They may eventually actually object to it, although I don't think so… My hunch is that any court would throw out such a case as an absurd one… At any rate, the publicity has been wonderful on it and it was a happy idea. I wish they would sue, but, as it is, we've had reams in the papers.[8]

Besides rather baldly suggesting that comic manipulation was not something limited to Groucho's screen character, the letter represents actual evidence that at least in this incident, comic correspondence was polished for public consumption rather than a private dialogue. Ironically, Warner Brothers would eventually lodge a formal complaint, but it was settled quickly in arbitration.

As if this revelation were not enough, the May 31, 1945, Madison letter also puts the kibosh to another celebrated legend of Marx Brothers folklore. Granted, it is neither as unique as the *Casablanca* hoax nor does it directly dispute one of the published Library of Congress letters, but it still scrambles a time-honored account of why the Marxes consented to return for *A Night in Casablanca.*

Bad boy Chico, because of his ongoing gambling debts, is invariably blamed and/or credited for bringing the team out of retirement. "Chico needs the money" was the popular anthem born of the period. Again, Groucho's letter reveals something entirely different:

> The first thing I'm asked when I play [World War II] service camps is, "When are you fellows [the Marx Brothers] going to make another picture?… This was one of the reasons for my return to the screen… so I am doing this [*A Night in Casablanca*] partly for my bank roll and partly for the boys—and when I say "the boys," I'm not referring to Harpo, Chico, and Gummo.[9] [Gummo had never been part of the team's hayday, and was replaced by Zeppo, who eventually left for being underused.]

In entertainment circles it is popular to pinpoint a specific scene or action and say, "This alone is worth the price of admission." If that statement were paraphrased for the Madison collection of Groucho correspondence, it would without doubt be applied to the *Casablanca* letter. But besides their bombshell revelation nature, the letters have seven additional characteristics which recommend them: they are funny; they reveal the more earthy, everyday Groucho; they also disclose times of poignancy; they exhibit the exuberance of early film acclaim; they portray Groucho as the private egalitarian; they show his writing kinship with Arthur Sheekman; they hold a possible beginning idea for a future book of Groucho correspondence.

First, like everything Groucho wrote, these letters are full of humor, too. It is a comedy range which runs from the civilized frustration of his published essays (and letters), to an earthy private sexuality which the general public knew little about until late in his life (and even then often blamed on his approaching senility). An example of the first was inspired by a 1934 country vacation:

> As you know I am up in the Maine woods, and it is lovely. Theres [sic] a thrilling piece of news, and one that will probably set your heart to palpitating wildly. I am up in the woods. Hundreds of thousands of people are at this very moment up in the woods and writing to their friends that they are up in the woods. This is as insipid a line as anyone could write. If it is written to anyone who is in the city, it could only make them angry or envious, and if it is written to someone in the woods, it could only be received with apathy and boredom. At any rate, I am up in the woods.[10]

In contrast, Groucho's Madison letter humor was just as likely to be chauvinistically ribald. Thus, while on a 1928 tour shortly after recovering from an appendectomy, Groucho wrote,

> I get plenty of time here [Boston's Metropolitan Theatre] to woo the festive muse, and also to feel any unlucky ladies who happen to be on the bill. It's the only kind of exercise you can possible get, and unquestionably the best …. You can gather from these remarks on sex… that the scars of

nature are rapidly healing up, and I will soon be back on the happy humping grounds....[11]

The second characteristic expands upon the last quotation in a new direction. While the level of comedy in the Madison letters varies, the language itself is always surprisingly frank, and often of a sexual nature. Consequently, these letters provide a fascinating and rare look at the more casual conversation of Groucho—supplying a voice for the already documented early carnal lifestyles of the young Marxes (see especially Hector Arce's authorized biography *Groucho*, 1978, which is also the best book treatment of the team). Thus, in a 1928 letter to Salinger, Groucho noted that Harpo was returning from Europe that day "and I am sure that one of the things he won't declare at the Customs Offices will be a slight dose of Mussolini Gonorrhea."[12] In another letter Groucho likened relearning Marxes' stage production of *Cocoanuts* (for its 1929 film adaptation) to "the thrill of a warmed over pot roast, and giving in to a dame that you were through with many years ago...."[13]

Third, the refreshing everyday earthiness of the language notwithstanding, the Madison letters also occasionally allow one a rare and poignant look at the darker moments in Groucho's life. For example, the letter he wrote shortly after the death of his legendary mother (from a cerebral hemorrhage, September 13, 1929), the architect of the team's success, is both elegant and unique, seeming to be the only period commentary by any of her sons which has survived:

> The swiftness of the entire happening makes it a little terrifying. In the afternoon she was at the theatre watching a rehearsal joking and laughing. Four hours later she was gone. The only grain of comfort, if there can be one, was the fact that it was merciful.... It's a thing we all have to face, but to each one it's a harrowing experience.[14]

There was no doubt added trauma present for Groucho in the death of his mother. As oldest and favored son Chico later observed, Groucho "was always trying to be the good son [in their childhood], while I was busy being the bad one—and yet Minnie always forgave me and loved me and was never that way with Groucho."[15]

Fourth, because Groucho's correspondence with Salinger begins so early (the 1920s), some letters provide an excellence sense of the team still trying to come to grips with celebrity. Thus, in late 1930, after the phenomenal early sound film successes of *Cocoanuts* (1929) and *Animal Crackers* (1930)—their first two commercial movies—a Groucho letter to Salinger concerning the eleventh-hour negotiating taking place to book them into the London Palace nicely captures the pleasant craziness of it all:

> We have made such absurd demands in the way of financial concessions that no manager with a spark of manhood in him could possible comply with our insane requests. We are doing this purposely, as we do not care to go, but if we have to we will sell ourselves as dearly as possible. [16]

Needless to say, the Marxes went to London. Indeed, they were such a hot property that Paramount renegotiated their film contract on shipboard, before they left for England.

Fifth, as befits correspondence with a noncelebrity, Groucho's private celebration of the individual (at lease the *male* individual, sometimes obscured by his public persona's misanthropy) is better showcased here than in any of his other writings—private or public. Thus, in one 1931 letter to plastic surgeon Salinger, who had recently authored a book on his specialty (Groucho preferred calling it "plastered surgery"), the comedian comically questions alterations to the "extraordinary proboscis" of prominent Americans (Fannie Brice's earlier, well-known "beak" operation being his example). But Groucho subsequently makes more general his comic warning:

> You and your medical brethren should be very careful with your knives, lest in time you erase all individuality from this country, and make us a race of straight faced citizens with all the personality of so many smoked white fish…. Employ your scalpel economically and only in times of great emergency, and by so doing you will help to retard the standardization that is rapidly smothering what was once supposed to be a free nation. [17]

Moreover, the Madison correspondence as a whole seemingly was made possible by a celebration of individualism. Groucho bitterly hated anything smacking of a yes-man mentality, and his letters to Salinger frequently find him thanking his friend for constructive criticism of the comedian's work in film, radio, and television. Amusingly, however, sometimes Salinger could go too far even for the *democratic* Groucho:

> Dear Quack [Salinger],
>
> I read your customary insulting letter with the customary amount of indifference.... I once made the mistake of telling you that you were one of the few people I know who didn't hesitate to tell me the truth whenever I acted or wrote. This, however, can be carried to excess. It seems to me that sometime in the past five years I must have done something that was good. But I attribute the whole thing to your spleen....[18]

In contrast, the letters to Groucho in the book collection are generally anything but critical of the mustached one. In fact, T.S. Eliot's fawning thank-yous over having *two* Groucho photographs to frame (for home and office) and David Susskind's closing "I love you" are enough to give a cynic diabetes.[19] How ironic is it when an iconoclast becomes an old and celebrated icon?

Before moving from the subject of a democratic Groucho, one must also sample the contents of a letter penned during the production of *Monkey Business* (1931). Besides demonstrating Groucho's ongoing scorn for the pompous and the petty, it is also a fascinating earthy documentation of the film colony's party-time small talk during its golden age:

> Von Sternberg with baggy pants and a cane [was] trying awfully hard to forget that he was born in Brooklyn and not Vienna [he had christened himself with the Von]. The place was afire with repartee, wiseys, who was the best director, what their [sic] next part was going to be, who was humping who [sic], why this supervisor was fired, why Carl Laemme Jr. [sic, Laemmle, head of Universal Production] was going to displace Thalberg [MGM production head] as the little Napoleon of the silver screen, and all the claptrap that goes to make a Hollywood conversation one of the dullest on earth.[20]

Sixth, one of the Madison letters provides comic insight into the writing controversy surrounding Groucho and author friend Arthur Sheekman, who also wrote the Introduction to *The Groucho Letters*. That is, official Groucho biographer Hector Arce (a friend and co-author with the comedian of *The Secret Word is GROUCHO*) convincingly states that both *Beds* and *Many Happy Returns* were done in an uncredited collaboration with Sheekman.[21] Of course, that sort of arrangement was typical for this time. It would be years before the credit "with such-and-such" became an acceptable admission.

While the relative contribution of each man is not known, their comedy writing styles are similar, something indirectly borne out through their close friendship, their work together on comedy sketches, and the fact that Groucho had substituted for Sheekman in writing the latter's Chicago newspaper column. But nothing directly documents their common comic spirit better than a letter to Salinger which they co-authored. Though the letter is primarily Groucho, the Sheekman interjections are so close to the Groucho persona that one is sometimes confused as to just who is writing/dictating.[22] Moreover, the letter fairly oozes a joyous, comic camaraderie that is a silly yet somehow significant commentary on the secret of their writing together. Interestingly enough, the letter begins with Sheekman at the typewriter and Groucho up and talking, a set-up they would reverse as the note progressed. This was a working style which Groucho and Norman Krasna later used in their collaborations for the 1937 screenplay *The King and the Chorus Girl* and the 1948 Broadway play *Time for Elizabeth*.

Seventh and most ironically, the seed for the more self-consciously polished *The Groucho Letters*, with a "name cast" of correspondents, was quite possibly first planted in a 1931 Salinger-Groucho exchange. That is, Salinger must have queried Groucho about a collection of their letters, because the comedian replied:

> Its [sic] too bad that these letters aren't better literature
> than they are, because then someday in the distant future
> when one of us becomes famous [Groucho is being
> modest], they could be published in two volumes in a
> cardboard box and called, The Doctor looks at the actor,
> of footlights and tonsils, and no one would buy the books
> [the sales of Groucho's *Beds*, from the previous year, 1930,
> had not been large, a probable reaction to the onset of the

depression], except your friends and my friends, which makes a total of three sales in all. At any rate its [sic] a fine idea and one that should be given very little thought.[23]

These, then, have been the seven most important revelations of the Madison collection, but countless other comments of interest remain. One such is Groucho's almost embarrassed beginning with the soon-to-be-celebrated *You Bet Your Life*—"It's not too distinguished a set-up, but you know me, I have no shame.[24] (This anticipates *Newsweek's* famous initial response to Groucho's *You Bet Your Life* career move: "Marx fans mourned that it was like selling Citation to the glue factory.) But in three years another Groucho letter would movingly observe, "to come up with a spectacular [solo] success after all these years I find enormously satisfying."[25]

Thus, for the Marx Brothers aficionado and/or the student of comedy, these forgotten letters provide a line-by-line attraction. Granted, their earthiness could offend some. But the bottom line is that these unpublished letters give the readers refreshing new perspectives on an old subject—Groucho Marx. And the better the understanding of an artist, the richer is one's appreciation of his art. Besides, the letters are funny, something that becomes lost in an amazing number of comedy studies. And perhaps that humor is the ultimate message of the collection—that even the private, less-polished man behind the public persona was just as obsessed with being funny.

(Originally appeared in *Studies in American Humor*, Summer/Fall 1986; Wes D. Gehring Copyright.)

NOTES

1. Paul D. Zimmerman, "Epistles of Groucho" (review of *The Groucho Letters*), *Newsweek*, April 3, 1967, 94.
2. Groucho Marx, *The Groucho Letters: Letters From and To Groucho Marx* (New York: Simon and Schuster, 1967), 133.
3. Groucho Marx, *The Groucho Letters*, 10.
4. Groucho Marx "The Role I Liked Best..." *Saturday Evening Post*, May 8, 1948, 115.
5. James Agee, *A Night in Casablanca* (review), *The Nation*, May 25, 1946, 636.

6. Groucho Marx, *The Groucho Letters*, 14.
7. Groucho Marx, "The Customers Always Write" ("Trade Winds" column), *The Saturday Review*, December 22, 1945, 20.
8. The Groucho letter dated "May 31, 1945," in "The Groucho Marx Papers," Box 1, Folder 3 (Correspondence with Dr. Samuel Salinger, 1928-1939), State Historical Society of Wisconsin Archives, Madison, Wisconsin.
9. Groucho letter, "May 31, 1945."
10. The Groucho Marx letter later dated "1934, July" in "The Groucho Marx Papers," Box 1, Folder 1.
11. The Groucho Marx letter dated "Dec 6 30," in "The Groucho Marx Papers," Box 1, Folder 1.
12. The Groucho Marx letter dated "1928," in "The Groucho Marx Papers," Box 1, Folder 1.
13. The Groucho Marx letter incorrectly dated "1930?" in "The Groucho Marx Papers," Box 1, Folder 1.
14. The Groucho Marx letter labeled "Death of his mother," in "The Groucho Marx Papers," Box 1, Folder 1.
15. Maxine Marx, *Growing Up with Chico* (Englewood Cliffs, N.J.: Prentice-Hall, Inc., 1980), 172.
16. The Groucho Marx letter dated "Dec 6 30."
17. The Groucho Marx letter dated "1937," in "The Groucho Marx Papers," Box 1, Folder 1.
18. The Groucho Marx letter dated "December 13, 1945," in "The Groucho Marx Papers," Box 1, Folder 3.
19. Groucho Marx, *The Groucho Letters*, 156-57, 223-24.
20. The Groucho Marx letter later dated "1931, April?" in "The Groucho Marx Papers," Box 1, Folder 1.
21. Hector Arce, *Groucho*, (1979; rpt. New York: Perigee Books, 1978), 169, 272.
22. The Groucho Marx letter dated "1931 May?" in "The Groucho Marx Papers," Box 1, Folder 1.
23. The Groucho Marx letter dated "1931."
24. The Groucho Marx letter dated "October 3, 1947," in "The Groucho Marx Papers," Box 1, Folder 3.
25. "Master Marx," *Newsweek*, May 2, 1949, 53.
26. The Groucho Marx letter dated "December 11, 1950," in "The Groucho Marx Papers," Box 1, Folder 3.

VONNEGUT &

A War By Any Other Name

WHEN KURT VONNEGUT WAS WRITING *Slaughterhouse-Five*—published in 1969 and adapted to the screen in 1972—his classic novel about World War II, filmmaker Harrison Starr asked him if it was an anti-war book. When Vonnegut answered, "I guess," Starr shared his cynical slant on this nontraditional genre: "Why don't you write an anti-glacier book instead?" After all, he might have added, it would have the same effect.

Ironically, it is a cynical truism with which Vonnegut agreed (and included) in the opening pages of *Slaughterhouse-Five*, but sometimes one has to underline the madness and just look back, even if, as the novelist kiddingly reminds us, we risk the fate of Lot's wife. Yet, Vonnegut was after a catharsis, for, as a young prisoner of war, he had survived the Allies' senseless fire-bombing of Dresden—the subject of the book. Not surprisingly, all major wars produce poignant commentaries against armed conflict. That being said, several circumstances stack the deck in favor of World War I being the greatest fiction and film tutorial in any anti-war movement. In fact, even Vonnegut credited Erika Ostrovsky's book about a veteran of that conflict, *Céline and His Vision*, as being pivotal for his own text.

So, what is there about World War I? Critic Deirdre Donahue, in a review of Jacqueline Winspear's 2006 novel, *Messenger of Truth*, observes, "The extraordinary carnage of World War I did not just kill men. The violence destroyed accepted ideas about valor, duty, class, human behavior, and whether the future even mattered."

As a film professor, it is difficult to avoid this legacy in teaching an assortment of movie classes. For instance, arguably the watershed anti-war novel, Erich Remarque's *All Quiet on the Western Front* (1928, WWI from a German soldier's perspective), soon was adapted (1930) into an equally memorable American movie of the same name by director Lewis Milestone. Though *Quiet* often surfaces in my World Film History course, Stanley Kubrick's 1957 adaptation of Humphrey Cobb's 1935 novel, *Paths of Glory*, is a staple of my World Film History II class. While *Quiet* chronicles the shattering universal horror of war, the catalyst for *Paths* is an even more insidious take on war's insanity. That is, a French general orders his soldiers on a suicidal attack that results in overwhelming casualties… and then has the audacity to demand that a randomly selected trio of men be tried for cowardice. Inspired by real events, at a time when faulty French military leadership threatened mass mutiny on the Western Front, Kubrick and star Kirk Douglas never have been better in depicting man's inhumanity to man—what became the central theme of Kubrick's career.

The film history classes also explore various national cinemas, including the influential "Australian New Wave" pictures of the 1970s and early 1980s. The central movie in this movement is director Peter Weir's *Gallipoli* (1981), about the ill-fated World War I British operation in which young idealistic soldiers from Down Under were used as so much cannon fodder in a hopeless battle against the Central Powers. Given that Weir's storytelling allows the viewer to connect with the two protagonists (Mel Gibson and Mark Lee) long before they enlist makes the movie's French New Wave influenced freeze-frame conclusion—a shot similar to Robert Capa's celebratedly chilling Spanish Civil War photo of a still-standing soldier at the instance of death—one of cinema's most moving moments.

Though each of these movies still sets the standard for anti-war pictures by way of World War I, maybe the most metaphorically poetic examination of the subject is director Jean Renoir's *Grand Illusion* (1937, whose very title tells the tragic story of most wars). Focusing on Allied prisoners (including Jean Gabin, a French Spencer Tracy), and the cultured Prussian flyer turned commandant (Erich von Stroheim), this movie's sympathetic elegy for human frailty is yet another example of Renoir's democratic mantra that "everyone has his reasons." The gifted director was not excusing the wasteful tragedy of war, but rather sensitively spreading the blame among all countries and classes.

The horrors of World War I surface in yet another way, as movie artists long have been aware of a phenomenon which took cinema critics and historians, like *Newsweek* writer Rick Martin, years to articulate: "The men with broken faces [were] fitted with masks to hide their

Vonnegut's time-tripping Billy Pilgrim (Michael Sacks) caught in World War II during the 1972 adaptation of *Slaughterhouse-Five*.

hideous scars." Early 20th-century medical advances meant many men who normally would have died on the battlefields of the First World War survived—but with rather shocking appearances. This grizzly fate became the foundation for horror cinema's rebirth during the 1930s. Director Abel Gance underscored this development when he remade his anti-war film

J'accuse (1919) as *That They May Live* (1938), in which disfigured World War I veterans literally rise from their graves to protest the gathering storm of yet another world war.

More recently, writer-director Bill Condon's exquisite film adaptation *Gods and Monsters* (1998, from Christopher Bram's novel *Father of Frankenstein*), examines the lingering impact of World War I upon filmmaker James Whale, the director of the seminal *Frankenstein* (1931) and the equally significant *Bride of Frankenstein* (1935). As with Gance, Whale was a World War I veteran.

Whether anti-war literature makes any more sense than anti-glacier material remains to be seen, but at a time when a still bumbling mankind now is making those glaciers disappear, maybe it finally is time to get serious about an anti-war world.

CONTROVERSIAL AND/OR TRAGIC

THE LAST RIDE:

The Death of James Dean

THE FRIDAY MORNING OF September 30, 1955, began early for budding film star James Dean. The twenty-four-year-old actor, who had thrown himself into three successive film productions, *East of Eden* (1955), *Rebel Without a Cause* (1955, though not yet released), and *Giant* (to open the following year, 1956), was now just enthusiastically embracing his first break from filmmaking in more than sixteen months. The multitalented Dean's latest passion was racing sports cars, though this fascination with speed dated from his Hoosier childhood. Indiana, then and now, is a state most synonymous with the Indianapolis 500. And no one was ever a bigger fan than Dean. Indeed, one of his goals his freshman year of college was to someday race in the 500. Moreover, as a teenager growing up on a farm just outside of Fairmount, his favorite means of transportation was a motorcycle—a speeding motorcycle. Naturally, when Dean later graduated to sports cars, he continued his habit of helter-skelter haste. When passengers complained, the actor said, "I've got to go places in a hurry. There just isn't time."

While Dean had done some professional racing early in his brief Hollywood career, he had been banned from participating in the sport by *Giant* director George Stevens for the duration of the lengthy, expensive shoot. Thus, once Dean's scenes on the film were completed, he was raging to race again. By this time, the young man had become positively poetic about the subject of speed: "It's the only time I feel whole." Consistent with his fervor, Dean had gone "Hollywood" with his first pricey purchase—a silver Porsche 550 Spyder. This model was already making a name for itself on racetracks in both Europe and America. Dean paid for the car with a check for approximately $3,000 [nearly $30,000 today] and by trading in his white Porsche 356 Speedster.

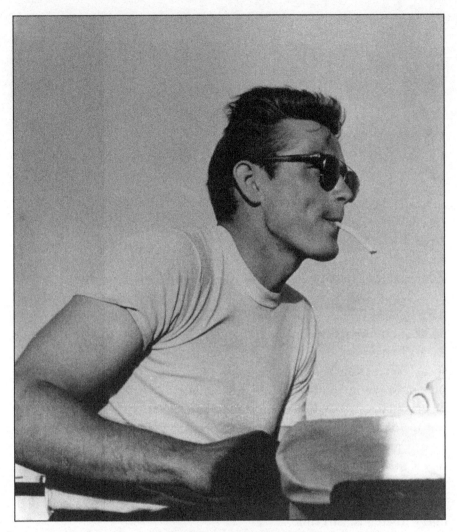

James Dean near the end (1955).

The high-dollar amount paid by Dean for the Spyder was unlike the normal frugality exercised by the actor, whose tightness rivaled the comic cheapness of one of America's then most popular comedians, Jack Benny. Dean seldom picked up a check and usually avoided any ostentatious displays. Consequently, this atypical financial behavior further underlined the hold racing had on him. Dean so related to this symbol of speed that he had had his own provocative nickname, "Little Bastard," painted in red on the Porsche's tail.

Metaphorically, of course, speed defined Dean's acting, too. As one biographer noted, "There was about Dean a sense of urgency, a desire to get to the top of the acting profession as rapidly as possible. He didn't want to be bothered with such details as technique." This was the reason he had dropped out of the University of California at Los Angeles and had minimized his involvement with Lee Strasberg's Actors Studio, which had been cofounded by *East of Eden* director Elia Kazan. Coupled with this "urgency" was a proclivity to take chances, both as an actor and as a racer. Dean's tendency to constantly push the proverbial envelope was entertainingly exciting and dangerous. And it was a key reason why many people saw him as a "Little Bastard."

On the highlighted last day of September in 1955, Dean was driving to a Sunday race in Salinas, California, located three hundred miles north of Los Angeles. This was familiar territory for the actor, since it was the hometown of novelist John Steinbeck and the setting for much of his book, *East of Eden*, with some of the screen adaptation actually being shot there. After the race, Dean planned on a short vacation in San Francisco. Leaving his small Sherman Oaks rental cabin in the San Fernando Valley before eight in the morning, Dean drove his late-model Ford station wagon to Competition Motors, where the actor had purchased the Porsche. A pivotal part of his Salinas racing entourage, master mechanic Rolf Wütherich, was already doing some final fine-tuning on the sports car. The eternally impatient Dean attempted to help, but as was the case when he was a boy at the local motorcycle shop in his native Fairmount, the mechanic waved him into the waiting room.

Wütherich was Dean's preferred mechanic at Competition, with the sales agreement for the Porsche contingent on Wütherich crewing for the actor in his forthcoming races. Emblematic of Dean's circle of friends, the mechanic was yet another colorful character. Gifted with movie star good looks to rival even those of Dean, Wütherich's past included a stint as a teenaged German fighter pilot in the final days of World War II, when the Third Reich's armed forces were largely composed of boys and senior citizens.

The two men were soon joined at Competition Motors by the other two members of the Salinas contingent, Bill Hickman and Sanford Roth. Hickman was a stunt man and sometime character actor in his mid-thirties. Dean had met him during the production of director Samuel Fuller's Korean War film, *Fixed Bayonets* (1951), in which both actors had bit parts. Their friendship was cemented when they discovered a mutual fascination with fast cars. Hickman's greatest claim to fame now would be his later work as a stunt driver in the celebrated chase sequence in *The French Connection* (1971). At that time, however, Dean knew Hickman best for his work as Clark Gable's mechanic in the Indianapolis 500 racing film *To Please a Lady* (1950). (With a portion of *Lady* being filmed on location at the Indianapolis track, this had been a major media event in Indiana. And naturally, Gable's devil-may-care character took racing chances in the picture.)

Roth was a photography friend to Dean. In the transplanted Hoosier's myriad of interests, photography ranked behind only acting and racing, and maybe bullfighting. Moreover, despite Dean's alleged angst over the phoniness of fame, he flirted with hypocrisy in his obsession to have his every mood and movement photographed. Roth was then working on a Dean photo layout for *Collier's* magazine. But the actor also liked the idea of having him document the racing trip, showing off another side of his life. Dean had met the photographer during the making of *Giant*, when Roth had been hired by Warner Brothers to shoot publicity stills. Although Roth's later notability is directly attributed to his association with Dean, he was no stranger, even then, to the famous. Prior to his work with this young movie star, Roth had done photo essays of such eminent subjects as Pablo Picasso, Albert Einstein, Marc Chagall, and Jean Cocteau. Dean enjoyed being included in such heady company. Plus, it enabled Dean to not only pick Roth's brain on the subject of photography (the actor had an inclination for choosing friends and associates based upon what he might learn from them), he could also quiz Roth about his celebrated subjects.

While the actor had many friends and contacts, remaining on a friendly basis with him could sometimes be an iffy proposition. He was what might be called a "user," forever scrambling to feed a gargantuan appetite for knowledge and success. His need to constantly find new mentors probably dated from his mother's attempt to immerse her child in the arts, from dance lessons to art classes. Coupled to this hungry mind, however, was a fragile psyche, dating back to his mother Mildred's early death in 1940, when Dean was only nine years old. These combined to saddle the actor with a mercurial personality. He might be the most brilliant of companions, from entertaining his friends with an inspired impersonation of Marlon Brando or Charlie Chaplin, to performing various comic dialects. Indeed, he might even impersonate Brando imitating Chaplin, or the Tramp doing the king of Method acting. But this could quickly turn to sullen rudeness, or late-night calls and visits, when being alone was more than Dean could handle.

Later that last September morning in 1955, the actor's father, Winton Dean, and a visiting uncle, Charles Nolan, stopped at Competition Motors. Dean's relationship with his father had long been strained, starting with the death of the boy's mother. At that time the young widower had sent his child back to Indiana, where Dean would be raised by Winton's sister and brother-in-law, Ortense and Marcus Winslow. Consistent with this lack of father-son rapport, Winton had turned down his son's invitation to attend the Salinas race. Winton and Charles, however, had come to the dealership to see the young man off.

As anxious as the actor was about starting this mini-adventure, the foursome of Dean, Wütherich, Hickman, and Roth did not leave the Los Angeles area until about two o'clock in the afternoon. They had been delayed by Wütherich going home to get cleaned up, Dean giving his uncle a test ride (Winton refused a similar offer), and a late breakfast at a local restaurant. The four men would caravan to the race in two cars. Sadly, Dean had already made a fatal decision that morning—he would drive the Porsche to the race, with his mechanic riding shotgun. The original travel plan had all four men riding together in the actor's station wagon, with the sports car in tow on a trailer. But Dean believed he needed more time behind the wheel of the new Porsche, which he had purchased just two weeks before. The hectic schedule of being a rising movie star had not afforded him enough driving time. Plus, his surrogate parents, the Winslows, had been visiting from Indiana. Wütherich seconded Dean's change in plans, given that it would also be beneficial to have more miles on the car before the race, not to mention a final monitoring of the powerful but sensitive Porsche Spyder engine. Of course, the new travel arrangement was fueled by the fact that Friday was a beautiful summer-like day. Had the weather been bad, the topless Porsche would have been banished to the trailer. Thus, the movie star's acting buddy Hickman and photographer Roth followed the streaking sports car in the more pedestrian Ford.

Historically, Dean literature suggests the Hoosier-born actor had a death wish. Certainly, he had a fascination with the macabre, from a well-publicized *LIFE* magazine photo in a coffin, to a friendship with the sexy television horror movie hostess known as Vampira, who might have stepped out of a Charles Addams cartoon. (As an addendum to the coffin story, he had told the undertaker that when the lid came down, it pressed on one's nose.) The star also gravitated toward deadly sports, from automobile racing to bullfighting. Indeed, as a New York actor Dean enjoyed doubling as a matador when he jaywalked in busy midtown, using his coat like a cape on speeding taxis. But be this as it may, Dean savored being outrageous. It was no coincidence that many of rock and roll's soon-to-be pioneers, starting with Elvis Presley, emulated the provocative poser known as the original rebel. Moreover, there was a bravado about Dean the person that might simply be equated with the aura of invincibility associated with youth. In fact, the actor was said to have once admonished someone who had attempted to drag race with him and was nearly injured, "You can't do the things I'm doing. I can flirt with death and come through—you can't." Dean's uncle and surrogate father, Marcus Winslow, had a definite opinion on the subject of Dean's alleged death wish, calling it "a bunch of crap." This was also the strong view of Marcus, Jr. (Dean's cousin/"brother") when I interviewed him.

Certainly Dean's immediate plans for the future necessitated, if not living forever, at least sticking around for a reasonably lengthy lifetime. He had just signed a long-term contract with Warner Brothers. He also was set to portray boxer Rocky Graziano in the film *Somebody Up There Likes Me*, which was to be followed by a loose biography of Billy the Kid, titled the *Left-Handed Gun*. Both pictures were ultimately made (in 1956 and 1958 respectively) with Paul Newman finding fame as the title character of each production. (In television's New York-based live production beginnings, Dean and Newman had often competed for the same parts.) The Hoosier-born actor also planned to form his own production unit, in collaboration with his *Rebel* director, Nicholas Ray. Dean's immediate 1955 plans, after competing in several races, were to return to his favorite city, New York, and star in several television specials, including a series of Shakespeare plays. The ambitious actor also believed television would be the perfect medium in which to work in his long-term goal of becoming a director. Both Ray and Kazan had encouraged these aspirations by way of their collaborative filmmaking styles. Consequently, instead of someone with a death wish, Dean might be called a rebel *with* a cause.

The only addendum to death is that the actor feared any long-lingering illness, such as the cancer that ultimately killed his mother. Death by inches was just not Dean's style. This also helps explain why he was so drawn to both bullfighting and Ernest Hemingway's artistically concise take on the subject in *Death in the Afternoon* (1932): "The only place where you could see life and death, i.e., violent death now that the wars were over, was in the bull ring." While the actor had no plans to "check out" early, he also believed, as did Hemingway, that a life without dangerous ritual was not worth living. Ironically, this flies in the face of Dean's new type of screen antihero, a vulnerable cross between the rebellious Marlon Brando persona and the psychologically troubled Montgomery Clift— both of whom Dean idolized. A final footnote on death and Dean must acknowledge his curiosity factor, with the actor noting, "if you're afraid to die, there's no room in your life to make discoveries."

The fact that the real Dean was more provocatively adventuresome than his screen persona merits a brief consideration of the evolving American hero in the early 1950s. For the young actor, as for much of the world at this time, Hemingway set the standard. This was never more true than with his work *The Old Man and the Sea* (1952), where baseball legend Joe DiMaggio represents a microcosm of America that fortifies the novel's title character, who states, "I must have confidence and I must be worthy of the great DiMaggio who does all things perfectly even with the pain of the bone spur in his heel." But while DiMaggio today remains an enduring figure of what Hemingway once described as "grace under pressure," early 1950s pop culture had another "J.D." factor in addition to DiMaggio through which to filter hero (or more precisely, antihero) worship.

J.D. Salinger wrote his watershed work *The Catcher in the Rye* in 1951. This tour de force chronicling the comic alienation of young Holden Caulfield could be called a blueprint for the Dean screen persona that would follow. Had Salinger sold the novel's rights to Hollywood, Dean playing Holden would have been inspired casting. Both Dean and Caulfield have now come to symbolize the estranged youth of post-World War II affluence, fighting the inherent phoniness of a society lost in consumer decadence. Whether one's preferred iconic "J.D." factor is James Dean, J.D. Salinger, or Joe DiMaggio, there is little debate that the antiheroic configuration has now been in ascendancy for some time.

This transition was driven, in part, by another strain of early 1950s American history, the dark chapter known as the McCarthy Era, with the hunt for supposed communists in government by the House Un-American Activities Committee and U.S. Senator Joseph McCarthy. Suddenly the long-heralded inherent wisdom of the populist people seemed easily hoodwinked by demigods such as McCarthy. American pop culture responded with the derailing of a host of traditional folk heroes, from the clay feet of the Ruthian Roy Hobbs (a character "as American as a figure in a Norman Rockwell magazine cover") in Bernard Malamud's classic baseball novel *The Natural* (1952), to the corrupted homespun rustic

Lonesome Rhodes (Andy Griffith) of director Elia Kazan's *A Face in the Crowd* (1957).

As Dean and company sped toward Salinas that last day in September 1955, it is unlikely, however, that anyone was thinking of McCarthyism. With the Senate's censure of the controversial politician late the preceding year, he probably seemed like ancient history. Moreover, when the young actor got close to a competition he tended to obsess about the said event. The situation was further intensified this time because it was both a new car and a new racing category—the Porsche Spyder's more powerful engine put Dean among the premier drivers. Indeed, enough novelty was involved that the actor's mechanic simply wanted him to be competitive, learn the ropes, and *not* push for a win. For someone with a warrior mentality such as Dean, however, this was not the kind of racing advice he wanted to hear. Tragically, the actor decided to apply his go-for-broke philosophy to the sports car even before the race. Years after the accident, Wütherich confessed that the studio had paid him to say that Dean had been going the speed limit at the time of the accident. "I'd tried to tell Jimmy since we left Hollywood… that he couldn't run such a new machine in that manner—like a monkey beating on something without considering what he might break," Wütherich remembered. "Jimmy would say the way to win was to go for broke… [He] drove like a crazy person. I said, 'Ease up.' He wouldn't hear me because he was out of view of anyone he supposed was watching to make sure he didn't get in trouble. 'Ease up!' I told him."

At approximately 3:30 that afternoon, both Dean and Wütherich in the Porsche and Hickman and Roth in the trailing Ford were stopped for speeding. Dean became upset by the ticket, given that his home studio had recently pressured him into making a National Safety Council driving commercial with actor Gig Young. But he was polite to the patrolman, who did not recognize either the name or the face of the young star. The officer was, however, interested in the Porsche, and they talked briefly about the sports car.

On the road again, Dean soon returned to his speeding ways. Of course, in his defense, the pre-interstate route from Los Angeles to Salinas, first on Highway 99 and then on Highway 466, represented a lengthy day of driving, even at normal speeds. In the roughly two hours remaining in Dean's life, his racing foursome would make one more brief stop, at a place called Blackwell's Corner, where Highway 466 met Route 33. The actor had recognized a fellow driver's sports car at this combination gas and food store. The racer in question was Lance Reventlow, the son of Woolworth heiress Barbara Hutton. As Dean drank a Coke, he showed Reventlow his speeding ticket and complained, "I just done a road safety film. Some fucking journalist is going to love to pick that up." Paradoxically, he then bragged that he had just had the Porsche up to 130 miles per hour.

Though this might have been an exaggeration, something the actor was famous for (a tall-tale trait he traced to his grandfather), later calculations by authorities suggest Dean must have been driving at a highly dangerous speed. To clock the distance between where he was stopped for speeding and the fatal accident site, Dean would have needed to average roughly 75 miles per hour, even without the Blackwell's Corner pit stop. Factor in this bull-session break, and "he must have been hitting 90 to 100 most of the time." Moreover, several Dean biographers have documented a near head-on collision shortly before the accident, when the actor's risky pass on the two-way highway forced an oncoming vehicle off the road.

The irony of the fatal crash, just minutes later, was that Dean was not at fault. As the Porsche flew down Highway 466, a college student in a 1950 Ford approached the highway's Y-turn intersection with Route 41. The young man about to accidently change Hollywood history had a name that might have graced a filmland adaptation of *Tobacco Road*—Don Turnupseed. As Turnupseed started to turn left from Highway 466 onto Route 41, he paused, as if he had finally seen the Porsche. Sadly, this was not the case.

Several circumstances aggravated the situation. With the late afternoon's setting sun, Dean's small, silver, extremely low-to-the ground sports car was all but invisible. Thus, Turnupseed proceeded to turn directly into the path of the Porsche. And because the Ford's stutter-effect stop at the intersection had fooled both Dean and Wütherich, the actor made no attempt to brake until it was all but meaningless. Plus, his high rate of speed gave the young movie star no insurance space to avoid the accident.

The resulting crash was more of a one-way demolition derby. The tank-like Ford was not badly damaged; Turnupseed walked away from the accident. In contrast, the Porsche was crushed like a soda can. The lightweight aluminum sports car, sans bumper and with a rear engine, offered no protection for its riders. In a twisted tribute to the Porsche's "flying" speed, the car had become airborne, performing several horrific cartwheels. Wütherich was thrown from the vehicle and suffered multiple injuries, including a serious skull fracture that would necessitate several surgeries in the months to come. Dean essentially died on impact from a broken neck; his body was pinned in the Porsche by a steering wheel that had caved in both his chest and forehead. Wütherich later claimed he believed that the actor had briefly survived the crash, since he had heard the release of air coming from Dean. This was undoubtedly, however, some macabre body function that had nothing to do with life. Dean was dead.

As with most tragedies, paradoxes abound. The last words of this now screen immortal were poignantly desperate: "He's gotta see us." The flat northern California farmland that was the backdrop for Dean's final drive was also surprisingly similar to the level countryside of his beloved north-central Indiana, a fact the actor even noted that final September day of 1955. (Consistent with this thinking, in 1959 Alfred Hitchcock would shoot the crop dusting Indiana portion of *North by Northwest* near this same area of California.) When the trailing Hickman and Roth eventually caught up to the accident, Roth's concluding photo shoot with Dean documented the actor's grisly death. After a lengthy rehabilitation, Wütherich fully recovered, only to die in a 1981 automobile accident. But the greatest irony of Dean's death was that while his brief life had ended, the legend was about to begin. The paradox was caught in a later darkly comic observation by Humphrey Bogart—an observation not inconsistent with the harsher changing Method mores of the time, "It was a great career move."

(Originally appeared in *TRACES of Indiana and Midwestern History*, Spring 2005; Wes D. Gehring copyright.)

HOLLYWOOD'S DILEMMA ABOUT POSTHUMOROUS RELEASES

WHEN JAMES DEAN DIED with two movies yet to be released, Warner Bros. Pictures saw catastrophe. Jack Warner bluntly observed, "Nobody will come and see a corpse." He could not have been more wrong. Both Dean films—*Rebel Without a Cause* (1955) and *Giant* (1956)—turned out to be major critical and commercial hits. There is no set pattern as to how an audience will respond to a picture released after the death of its star.

During the first half of the 1930s, celebrated humorist Will Rogers was arguably the most-popular figure in the movies. In fact, he reigned supreme in *every* entertainment medium of the time, from a daily newspaper column widely syndicated across the country to success in radio and on the stage. Moreover, his often politically tinged humor books were bestsellers that helped make him, to borrow a 1926 title, a *Self-Made Diplomat to His President*. Not surprisingly, his 1932 support for Franklin Roosevelt was instrumental in getting the New York governor elected president of the U.S.

Given Rogers' many talents and interests, he had long embraced the infant aviation industry to get him around the country as quickly as possible. In August, 1935, he joined his famous flyer friend Wiley Post in an ill-fated flight to the USSR, by way of Alaska. Their plane crash deaths shocked the nation, with many commentators suggesting that not since the assassination of Pres. Abraham Lincoln had the country been so moved by tragedy.

A nervous 20th Century Fox was sitting on two completed, but unreleased, Rogers films—*Steamboat 'Round the Bend* and *In Old Kentucky*. While no one at the studio seriously considered shelving the pictures, there was concern that the public might find two posthumous releases in poor taste and stay away. Yet, just the opposite occurred. So many fans honored Rogers with their ticket-buying presence that these final movies helped make the humorist the top male box office draw of 1935. (He was only commercially bested by a diminutive newcomer named Shirley Temple.) Indeed, *Steamboat* and *Kentucky* proved so popular that Fox was soon rereleasing earlier Rogers films, such as the 1936 appearance of the 1933 *Dr. Bull.*

The 1937 death from uremic poisoning as a result of cerebral edema of the original blond bombshell, 26-year-old Jean Harlow, constituted a different dilemma for parent studio Metro-Goldwyn-Mayer. The actress died *during* the production of the horse racing picture *Saratoga*, which also starred Clark Gable. MGM was initially afraid it would have to take a loss on the picture. Nevertheless, with the creative use of Harlow's stand-in, Mary Dees—showing merely a shoulder here or a backside there—enough footage was salvaged to release the movie. Despite these distractions, *Saratoga* still manages to be an entertaining picture.

Indeed, the film proved to be both a major critical and commercial success. However, whereas Rogers' fans seemed anxious to generate some sort of loving closure by way of his posthumous films, the box office clout of *Saratoga*, at least in part, was of a more-macabre nature. Period commentators credited the high patron turnout to a genuine viewer curiosity as to whether they could differentiate between the Harlow and Dees footage. While there were undoubtedly many loyal Harlow fans in attendance, too, the movie's commercial success was not necessarily America's finest hour.

At this point, it might seem that any film fatality could be parlayed into a box office hit, but the next example of a major star dying before a movie's release quickly disproves this premise. The victim was Carole Lombard, the country's designated *Screwball Comedy Girl*, the eccentric heroine of such classics of the genre as *My Man Godfrey* (1936) and *Nothing Sacred* (1937). Nicknamed the "Hoosier Tornado," she returned to her native Indiana in early 1942 to kick off America's first war bond-selling rally of World War II. Anxious to return to Hollywood and husband Clark Gable, she canceled her train reservations and booked an airplane flight, which crashed in the mountains near Las Vegas.

Lombard's death occurred a month before the opening of her dark comedy about German dictator Adolf Hitler and the war, *To Be or Not to Be* (1942). Unlike *Saratoga*, where added footage needed to be shot, Lombard's death necessitated some of it being cut. The story had her involved with a flyer (Robert Stack), and director Ernst Lubitsch tweaked a couple of aviation-related scenes he felt audiences might find in poor taste, given that Lombard had just died in a plane crash.

This deleted footage was the least of Lubitsch's worries. Lombard's legion of fans seemed to honor their favorite star by staying away from

Clark Gable and Jean Harlow in *Saratoga* (1937), a film she did not live to complete.

her final film. However, this less-than-stellar performance at the box office cannot simply be blamed upon depressed viewers. A greater factor was no doubt her death in conjunction with the groundbreaking nature of the movie—a pioneering example of dark comedy.

While *To Be or Not to Be* is now a celebrated film (the American Film Institute selected it as one of the 100 funniest movies ever made), it was ahead of its time in 1942. Among its critics, *The New York Times'* Bosley Crowther was scathing in his attack on the picture: "To say it was callous and macabre is understating the case." Ironically, the type of dialogue which most offended him is now routinely quoted as an entertainingly classic example of dark comedy writing. Sig Ruman's comic Nazi criticizes Jack Benny's in-film *Hamlet* performance by observing, "What he did to Shakespeare, we are doing to Poland."

One should hasten to add that the movie was a posthumous triumph for Lombard, with *Newsweek* summarizing it best: "Lombard has never been better... Her Maria Tura is an attractive, intelligently humorous characterization that is all too rare on the screen and will be rarer from now on." Still, Crowther's 1942 take on dark comedy as being in poor taste was probably a better "reading" of period audiences, because *To Be or Not to Be* proved a disappointment at the box office.

CULT STATUS

Of course, neither Warner nor anyone else could have predicted the instant cult status accorded James Dean with his 1955 death in an automobile accident. As author Derek Marlowe later observed in a 1976 *New York Magazine* piece on the persistence of the actor's hold over the young, "When Dean was killed and *Rebel Without a Cause* was released, the farm boy from Indiana was elected hero by his generation." It's a position—martyred symbol—that young people have kept him in ever since. Youth mourned itself.

Whereas *To Be or Not to Be* had been a groundbreaking dark comedy the public had *not* been able to embrace (indeed, Lombard's death made the genre all the more distasteful, like punishment for making light of serious subjects), *Rebel* was a more-palatable groundbreaker, at least for the young. Here was a family melodrama where the parents, not the children, were causing the pain.

Through the years, melodrama has often made a cottage industry out of martyred mothers, such as *Mildred Pierce* (1945) and the two versions each of "Imitation of Life" (1934, 1959) and *Stella Dallas* (1937, 1990, the latter simply titled "Stella"). In this pro-parents scenario, even grown children continue to cause pain, from the gut-wrenching separation of the elderly couple in the classic *Make Way for Tomorrow* (1937), to kids more concerned about appearances than their mother's happiness in *All That Heaven Allows* (1955).

Rebel, therefore, broadsided the traditional melodrama equation. Each of the young principals (James Dean, Natalie Wood, and Sal Mineo) was fearfully insecure because of the inadequacies and/or absence of his or her parents. Their dangerous teenage activities, such as the film's "chicken run" (staying in a racing car as long as possible before it goes off a cliff), were both a cry for attention and an embracing of something real in a world layered with "phoniness," to borrow a pivotal word from James Dean's literary counterpart, Holden Caulfield, in 1951's *The Catcher in the Rye*.

Unlike Lombard's passing, so jarringly contradictory to her signature screwball roles, Dean's death in a speeding car seemed like yet more evidence that the actor really was that vulnerable character he was playing in the movies. Moreover, his Method acting techniques, from the halting speech to the awkward twists of his expressive body, endeared him to young viewers who said, "That's me." This breakable quality helped make him not a hero, but the then-new "antihero." Holden Caulfield describes a fight he *lost*, "I don't remember if he knocked me out or not, but I don't think so. It's pretty hard to knock a guy out, except in the goddamn movies." Dean's *Rebel* did *not* seem like the "goddamn movies" to his young fans. It was a slice-of-reality torn from their own lives.

Dean's second posthumous release, *Giant*, was also a critical and commercial success, in part because of the almost-religious cult that had by now grown up around this young man. By this time, the year after his death, more than 4,000,000 people in the U.S. alone belonged to James Dean fan clubs, and his likeness was being marketed on every product imaginable. Warner Bros. was flooded with thousands of Dean fan letters each week, many from young viewers who refused to believe the actor had died. One popular myth was that he had survived the automobile accident, but was horribly disfigured. Consequently, he had gone into hiding. America had not seen such public hysteria since the death of Rudolph Valentine, shortly after the release of his last hit film, *The Son of the Sheik* (1926).

Though elements of the Dean phenomenon continue to this very day, rivaled only by comparable cults devoted to Marilyn Monroe and Elvis Presley (a major Dean fan), Dean's public much prefers *Rebel* over *Giant*. While the actor was even more critically acclaimed for *Giant* (receiving an Oscar nomination, as he had for 1955's *East of Eden*), his *Rebel* character is more consistent with the aforementioned youthful method acting vulnerability that has become his trademark. In contrast, *Giant* showcases Dean as a supporting player who is neither as central to the story nor as sympathetic. Indeed, viewers ultimately see his character become a drunkenly racist old man.

Compared to the sudden shooting star quality of Dean's emergence, the next major name performer to die before the movie's release was strictly old school—Clark Gable. Five years after *Giant*, he costarred with Monroe in *The Misfits* (1961). Gable's durability as a romantic leading man might best be defined by the fact that the blonde bombshells of two generations (Harlow and Monroe) would make their last movie with him. Gable died of a heart attack before *The Misfits* opened. (Monroe committed suicide the year after its release.)

Like Lombard's *To Be or Not to Be*, numerous critics praised *The Misfits*, but it was a commercial disappointment. Although starring the mainstream Gable, in some ways the picture owed more than a little to the Method acting revolution that produced Dean. Three of Gable's costars (Monroe, Montgomery Clift, and Eli Wallach) had logged time with the New York Actors Studio that helped spawn Dean. Even the story, about an aging cowboy (Gable) in the modern antiheroic West (the wild mustangs they are tracking are to be sold to a dog-food manufacturer), aspired to the realism so central to the Actors Studio.

This was not, however, the kind of picture a traditional Gable fan wanted to see, even with Monroe's compassion for the horses resulting in his last-minute freeing of the animals. Those who skipped the movie missed a tour de force performance from Gable, who had decided to do many of his own stunts in the grueling pursuit of the mustangs, which quite possibly contributed to his death from a heart attack shortly after the production shut down.

Another posthumous swan song from a second major star during Hollywood's golden age occurred in 1961 when Gary Cooper died before the release of *The Naked Edge*. There was a certain irony in his outliving Gable by a few months, since Cooper had long ago established "The King" as the screen rival he most wanted to best at everything. (In pre-World

War II Hollywood, after the death of Rogers, Gable was the dominant box office star—thus the title of "The King.")

Regardless, the public response to *The Naked Edge* was not unlike the box office take for *The Misfits*—disappointing. Again, as Gable did in his final role, much of *The Naked Edge* has Cooper playing against type. The suspense thriller has his screen wife (Deborah Kerr) thinking he is guilty of murder. Still, one might have assumed greater returns for both pictures, given the coverage accorded their deaths. Indeed, Cooper's lingering death (from cancer) had even given the movie industry time to honor him in 1961 with a lifetime achievement Academy Award, which was accepted on his behalf by distraught close friend James Stewart. (Cooper died less than a month later.)

The third 1930s superstar to have a posthumous film release in the 1960s was Spencer Tracy. *Guess Who's Coming to Dinner* (1967) reversed the mediocre final commercial showings of his two illustrious contemporaries. Of course, *Dinner* had the box office boost of a then-controversial mixed screen marriage (between Sidney Poitier and Katharine Houghton). Moreover, the picture also featured Tracy's nine-time costar and off-screen love Katharine Hepburn, though the public was not aware of their real-life relationship until long after his death.

While there are some who would opt for crediting the film's ultimate commercial success to controversy, many viewers (including my family) attended *Dinner* out of homage to the silver screen's greatest couple—Tracy and Hepburn. While Gable and Cooper had flirted with playing against type in their last pictures, *Dinner* gave Tracy and Hepburn fans a final moving dose of what had most attracted them in the past—a love story between two strong individuals willing to work hard at making a relationship endure. When Tracy ultimately gives his speech on why Poitier and Houghton deserve their chance at being a couple, his poignant references to Hepburn reverberate well past the *Dinner* storyline. One remembers a montage of memorable Tracy/Hepburn moments, starting with *Woman of the Year* (1942) and best highlighted with *Adam's Rib* (1949) and *Pat and Mike* (1952). By the end of Tracy's talk, Hepburn is not the only one with tears in her eyes.

One's passion for Tracy's performance is further fueled by knowing the production background for *Dinner*. The actor was in such poor health that he could not pass the all-important studio physical that would guarantee insurers picking up the tab if he failed to make it through the production. *Dinner* was only able to proceed when Hepburn and director

Stanley Kramer waived their salaries in the event of Tracy's death. At the time, Tracy said this about Kramer, who was also responsible for the actor's previous three films: "I tell him my life expectancy is about seven and a half minutes and he says, 'Action!' He's some kind of a nut or saint. Or both."

Dinner would go on to become a major critical and commercial success, snagging 10 Oscar nominations. Both Tracy and Hepburn would be included in the tally, although he would not live to know that. Fifteen days after finishing his portion of the movie, he was dead of a heart attack. Though Tracy did not win an Oscar for his performance, at that time no major category Academy Award statuette had ever been given posthumously. The unofficial Hollywood take on the subject was *Oscar was for the living*. Consistent with this, Hepburn later credited her Academy Award for *Dinner* as really being for her beloved Tracy.

Other prominent performers have since died before their movies were released, but none match the stature of Rogers, Harlow, Lombard, Dean, Gable, Cooper, and Tracy. Three more recent deaths, however, merit noting for what might be called provocative reasons. First, Peter Finch's posthumous best actor Oscar for *Network* (1976) finally reversed Hollywood's tradition of reserving Academy Awards for the living. Second, Natalie Wood's 1981 death during the production of *Brainstorm* (released in 1983) triggered Hollywood's longest quandary to date over whether to shelve a film permanently or proceed with a revised story. Third, the dilemma of Oliver Reed's dying during the shooting of *Gladiator* (2000) was solved by state-of-the-art technology. Another actor was filmed in the remaining scenes, with computer graphics later making him appear to be Reed! Hollywood's acceptance of such an idea was evidenced by Reed's posthumous Oscar nomination for best supporting actor, though he lost to Benicio Del Toro (for *Traffic*).

If one were to garner any posthumous postulates from this article it would be that the most popular of these focus films showcased a star in a typical role. The commercial disappointments (which involved Lombard's *To Be or Not to Be*, Gable's *The Misfits*, and Cooper's *The Naked Edge*) all had stars pushing the envelope with regard to their established personas. Dean's sudden emergence as a new Method acting meteorite might seem to be the exception, but one must remember his rebel image was already strongly established in the only starring feature that opened during his lifetime, *East of Eden*. (Even the aforementioned melodrama-breaking precedents of *Rebel Without a Cause* have antecedents in "East of Eden.")

While *The Misfits* was a commercial disappointment, Gable's and Monroe's last lines on screen offer a haunting foreshadowing and metaphorical relevancy:

> **Monroe:** "How do you find your way back in the dark?"
> **Gable:** "Just head for that big star straight on. The highway's under it, and it'll take us right home."

Drawn to darkened theatres to watch our favorite movie stars, the comfort zone they give us is predicated upon preestablished behavior. This is merely a variation upon the bedtime ritual synonymous with small children, as the repeated reading of the same stories provides a consoling constant in a world so often seen as chaotic. Thus, we like our film favorites (especially in last roles) to be as constant as the North Star.

THE LAST PATRIOTIC DAYS OF CAROLE LOMBARD

IN THE DAYS AFTER JAPAN'S surprise attack on Pearl Harbor and Germany's subsequent declaration of war on America, President Franklin D. Roosevelt considered the high cost of waging a war both in Asia and Europe. To help fund the war effort, he immediately thought of the hugely successful war-bond rallies during World War I that were spearheaded by such Hollywood stars as Charlie Chaplin, Douglas Fairbanks Sr., and Mary Pickford. Roosevelt had firsthand knowledge of the rallies because he had joined those performers (and actress Marie Dressler) in a Washington, D.C., Liberty Loan Drive on 14 April 1918 when he was assistant secretary of the navy. Roosevelt also kept in mind his association with Hollywood in the 1930s, when he frequently called upon movie stars to attend his annual birthday celebrations, which were used as ambitious fund-raisers to battle against infantile paralysis.

Because of these past successes, it was only logical that the president turned to the film capital at the start of the war. Fittingly, the government contacted Metro-Goldwyn-Mayer, whose advertising slogan at the time was "more stars than in the heavens." MGM head Louis B. Mayer suggested that a new war-bond campaign be headed by one of the studio's reigning stars, such as Clark Gable or Mickey Rooney, the top two box-office draws in America for 1941. All things being equal, Rooney seemed the more logical choice. In addition to being the number one box-office attraction of 1941 (as well as 1939 and 1940), he was also a friend of the president, having entertained at the White House during the aforementioned birthday fund-raisers. Plus, Rooney enjoyed performing before a live audience, which was pivotal to a bond campaign's success.

Gable won the honor, however, because presidential adviser Harry Hopkins believed the bond drive should be launched from heartland America. (Gable was originally from Ohio; Rooney had been born in Brooklyn.) Roosevelt concurred, adding that Gable's sex appeal would probably sell more bonds than Rooney's youthful enthusiasm. What they had not anticipated was Gable's lack of confidence at appearing before a live audience. He turned Hopkins down, stating, "I'll help you in any way I can, other than personal appearances. But I hate crowds and I don't know how to act when I'm in one. Besides, I'm no salesman."

Gable's wife, film star Carole Lombard, told Hopkins she would be able to change her husband's mind. Lombard promised Gable she would accompany him and help out. When that did not work, she played a patriotism card, telling him what an honor it was to be asked to kick off the war-bond campaign. But Gable turned the tables on her by answering, "Right, Maw [his nickname for Lombard], consider yourself asked." When it was clear she could not convince her husband otherwise, Lombard accepted Gable's offer, though she was still hopeful he would accompany her.

Carole Lombard selling war bonds in Indianapolis the day before her death (1942).

Roosevelt and Hopkins were both pleased with his new development, feeling that a high-profile female star such as Lombard might sell even more bonds than a man. Moreover, the president still remembered and greatly appreciated Lombard's 1938 endorsement of both his administration and income tax in general, despite her paying more than 85 percent of her salary in state and federal taxes. ("I have no kicks at all," Lombard had said at the time. [The] fact is I'm pretty happy about the whole thing ... I enjoy this country. I like the parks and the highways and the good schools and everything that this Government does.") Of course, the topper to Lombard's selection was that she was from the heartland state of Indiana. In fact, the Hoosier connection became the official reason given for Lombard's involvement in the project. "The honor of being the first state to have a Defense Bond rally on a state-wide basis since the war began was accorded Indiana because the Hoosier state led in the Liberty Bond sales, on a per capita basis, in the first world war," noted the *Indianapolis News*.

Consistent with this position, it was logical that Lombard would lead the mid-January bond drive back in Indianapolis. The continuity with World War I was further accented by booking a second famous Hollywood Hoosier to join Lombard in the state capital: Will H. Hays, the former censorship czar of American films who had been in charge of selling Indiana's Liberty Bonds during the previous war. Hoosier pride became a selling point for Lombard. When she spoke at Indianapolis's Cadle Tabernacle on the evening of 15 January 1942 (after a full day of patriotic activities), she concluded her speech with these words, "As a Hoosier, I am proud that Indiana led the nation in buying Liberty Bonds in the last war. I want to believe that Indiana will lead every other state again this time – and we will! We won the last war. And, with your help, we will win this war!"

Once Lombard was convinced that Gable would not accompany her, she asked her mother Elizabeth Peters, to join her on her patriotic adventure. As with several other period screen actresses, Lombard was extremely close to her mother, who often doubled as her daughter's best friend and companion. Peters immediately accepted the invitation with the understanding she would make a brief side trip to their Indiana hometown of Fort Wayne.

To celebrate the trip, Lombard outfitted her mother with a new Beverly Hills wardrobe, assuring her she was the sexiest mother in America. Peters kidded back that maybe she would find a Hoosier millionaire back in Indianapolis. The two were also accompanied by

Otto Winkler, an MGM press agent and a friend of Gable and Lombard. Though Lombard was not associated with MGM (it was Gable's home studio), she was acting upon the request of a husband who also headed the actors' division of the Hollywood Victory Committee. Under these circumstances, it was natural for the studio to provide a press agent as a buffer – not that Lombard ever needed a buffer at any time in her life.

The trio of Lombard, Peters, and Winkler left Hollywood aboard the City of Los Angeles train on Monday, 12 January 1942. A short stop in Salt Lake City enabled Lombard to test her bond-selling skills, as a crowd had gathered in anticipation of her Chicago-bound train. Always a passionate and patriotic person, she easily took to this whistle-stop opportunity to hone her speaking skills, becoming a flag-waving hit. Upon reaching Chicago on 14 January, Lombard discussed her one-time fear of public speaking, just prior to a WGN radio broadcast. But what comes through in her words is a pep talk-like enthusiasm for defense and the Hollywood Victory Committee, "Years ago I used to be afraid to make speeches, but when you've got bonds to sell, and the country the way it is [patriotically involved], you go right ahead. [It's the] least you can do … Well, it's terrific. This is the first unity Hollywood ever had. We're to have from 10 to 15 [war-bond] shows on the road at one time … From now on it's sell a bond, sell a bond, sell a bond. You finish a picture and before you get off the [studio] lot, it's [waving a commanding finger] 'Pittsburgh by 4 o'clock [for a bond rally]' and off you go again. It's terrific!"

Although always devoted to her country, Lombard had during the 1930s displayed isolationist tendencies, even threatening to chain Gable to a barn door if he attempted to enlist. All that changed with the Japanese attack on Pearl Harbor. She still "thought women probably could have done a better job of ruling the world," when she whooped as only Lombard could whoop and headed east. ("She could sell anything" was Gable's take on the subject.)

Lombard and Winkler stayed in Chicago for several hours, doing bond-related publicity, while Peters went on by train for a brief stopover in Fort Wayne. Lombard biographer Larry Swindell has the actress and agent then flying to Indianapolis and reconnecting with Peters on Thursday, 15 January, when the latter arrived by train. Other period accounts, however, have the trio arriving together by rail early Thursday afternoon, where they were met at Union Station by Indianapolis mayor Reginald H. Sullivan and other dignitaries. Thus, Lombard and Winkler must have stayed over in Chicago Wednesday night and then taken an

Indianapolis-bound train the following morning. Somewhere along the way Peters joined them.

Regardless, Lombard, who likened her sales-pitch style to a "barker at a carnival," had an overbooked Thursday. Her first official act was a two o'clock flag-raising ceremony at the Indiana Statehouse, where governor Henry F. Schricker introduced her as "the little Hoosier girl who made good in Hollywood." The actress was the last of several speakers on a cold, windy Indiana winter day. She concluded her short, impassioned speech with the dramatic direction, "Heads up, hands up, America! Let's give a cheer that will be heard in Tokyo and Berlin!" The crowd went wild, with "one voice above the others calling, 'Carole, the victory girl,' as she made the victory sign with her fingers against the background of the Stars and Stripes."

The aforementioned "heads up" conclusion to Lombard's speech might have been inspired by Chaplin's then famous war-related address that closed *The Great Dictator* (1940), in which he encourages the heroine to "look up, Hannah, look up [and have faith]!" Though many period movie critics faulted Chaplin for stepping out of character to deliver it, the speech was popular with the public, and the comedian was frequently asked to repeat the address. Given that Chaplin was the most high-profile artist in prewar Hollywood, it makes sense that Lombard might have been influenced by the film, especially as the high point of her teen years was a 1924 screen test for the comedian's *Gold Rush* (1925). Regardless of its source, the close of Lombard's speech displayed the passion the actress brought to every activity. She was most articulate on this subject in a 1938 *Motion Picture* magazine article, telling an interviewer, "I'm intensely interested in and enthusiastic about everything I do, *everything*. No matter what it is I'm doing … I give it all I've got and I love it … If I don't love what I'm doing I don't do it."

The flag-raising ceremony outside the statehouse lasted until shortly after half past two, when Lombard and the other dignitaries moved inside to the rotunda for a furious round of bond sales. With a long line already formed since early morning, the actress had her work cut out for her. Patriotic buyers received a bond receipt bearing her picture and autograph, which she signed "Carole Lombard Gable." The actress also had a smile and a ready quip for every customer, such as the man who asked, "Where's Clark?" "Oh, he's home working," Lombard replied. "Someone in the family has to work, you know." She was surprised only that it had been a man who first asked about her matinee-idol husband.

Lombard gave a "ringing laugh" when a mother with a sleeping baby told the actress that the child, for whom she was buying the war bond, was Carole's namesake. With that, the actress took time to pat the baby gently and say, "Why, bless her heart."

The original sales goal for the rotunda rally had been $500,000, though Schricker hoped to reach $1 million. But when Lombard asked for a total after almost an hour of steady trade, she was pleased to discover sales already were well above $1 million. "We'll make it two," she laughed, and turned back to business. Amazingly, when the final figures were tabulated later in the day, her bond sales had done just that. This phenomenal tally was not limited to just a "meet the movie star" mentality. Lombard knew sales. She limited autographs to the red, white, and blue bond receipts. The actress also directed a legion of salesgirls with entertainingly knowing tips, such as, "The fellow in the brown suit will go five hundred [dollars for a bond] – kiss his bald head and tell him it's from me!" For a time Lombard even mounted a table in order to be seem and spy additional customers. (In today's dollars the figures are worth 10 times those numbers.)

At half past three Lombard went briefly to her hotel (Indianapolis's Claypool) to raise a large flag to the top of the thirty-six-foot staff in the lobby. This action officially opened recruiting booths there for the army, navy, and marines. A brief stop in her hotel suite revealed dozens of roses sent by her husband. The actress explained to impressed visitors that it was their custom, when apart, to bombard the traveling partner with large quantities of the flower.

Lombard was then almost immediately whisked away to the governor's mansion for a tea and reception both for the actress and the women members of the Indiana Defense Savings Staff. Press coverage reveals that "so irresistible was the spell cast by Miss Carole Lombard ... that, though it was supposed to be a completely social affair, guests began taking orders for defense bonds for each other." This was no small accomplishment given that everyone was already a member of the Defense Savings Staff. Perhaps part of this success came from Lombard's brief opening comments at the tea, "Ladies, you are doing a magnificent job." Journalist Florence Webster Long later reported, "Never did a public speech make more of a hit than her seven-word classic." Of course, Lombard seldom limited her insightfulness to such brief statements. For example, when asked at the same tea what women could do best to help win the war, she responded, "I think morale work is the most important just now. That is, until a regular women's army has been organized, as we've been promised it will be. I think it's particularly important for women to … concentrate on taking care of their own homes and their own families the very best they can."

That evening Lombard was a featured speaker at the aforementioned Cadle Tabernacle. More than twelve thousand Hoosiers turned out for a war rally that began at seven o'clock with patriotic and popular music provided by bands from both Indiana and Purdue Universities. In Lombard's star-turn speech, she movingly observed that everybody in the country knew what the war was going to cost. "But the peace it will bring is priceless," she said. "We know what an enormous task lies ahead … [But] as Americans, we have the rare privilege of deciding for ourselves the direction we are to take. We have made that decision."

Again, there was an impressive audience response, which she then topped by leading the crowd in a rousing rendition of the national anthem. It was the perfect conclusion to a perfect Lombard day. As one Hoosier journalist observed, "Carole Lombard never scored a greater success on the screen than in her latest role as saleswoman for Uncle Sam." The actress herself observed, "I have never been entertained more perfectly than today in Indiana. And I've never been so convinced that the American people are really united in this crisis."

With Lombard's Hoosier bond-sales assignment at a close, she put all her sizable energy toward getting back to her Hollywood home and Gable. (Her husband had encouraged her to return as soon as possible.) The prearranged return schedule had the trio of Lombard, Peters, and Winkler leaving Indianapolis for California by train on Saturday, 17 January. But Lombard was never a prearranged sort of woman. Plus, as the actress explained to *LIFE* magazine photographer Myron Davis shortly after making flight arrangements, she could not handle three more days on a "choo-choo train."

Lombard was used to getting her way, but the decision to fly back was strongly challenged by both of her traveling companions. First, Winkler was responsible to the government for getting the actress on a train. Officials had concerns about putting bond talent on planes – because of the chance of both general mishaps and war-related sabotage. Second, Lombard's mother was deathly afraid of flying. Third, Peters was a numerologist, and all the signs for this flight were bad, she warned. In numerology, three is a hard-luck number. The trio's DC-3 plane would be Flight 3 from New York. They were a party of three. And Lombard was thirty-three years and three months old. Not surprisingly, Peters put up a stiff fight, as did Winkler. Although he was no numerologist, he both wanted to follow the government directive and get some sleep – Flight 3 was scheduled to leave Indianapolis shortly after four in the morning on Friday, 16 January. Ultimately, the stocky, well-liked press agent served as a sort of referee between the dueling daughter and mother. With no agreement reached, he suggested a coin flip. The actress won.

Period accounts reveal, however, that the argument continued at the Indianapolis airport. Numerous witnessed overheard Peters continue to warn her daughter, "Carole, we musn't take that plane." Winkler again used the rest-routine request, noting there were no sleeping accommodations on their projected seventeen-hour flight. But Lombard said, "I'll curl up and take a pill and pff, I'll be asleep." Even the aforementioned *LIFE* photographer gently entered the dispute in support of Winkler, telling the actress she looked tired. Lombard dismissed his concern with a wave of her hand and the comment, "When I get home, I'll flop in bed and sleep for twelve hours."

Sadly, that never happened. Early that Friday evening, shortly after refueling at Las Vegas, the plane carrying Lombard, Peters, Winkler, and nineteen other occupants crashed in the Sierra Nevada mountains. There were no survivors. America was stunned. Among the scores of tributes that followed Lombard's shocking death, President Roosevelt's telegram to Gable was the most movingly articulate, "Mrs. Roosevelt and I are deeply distressed. Carole was our friend, our guest in happier days. She brought great joy to all who knew her and to the millions who knew her only as a great artist. She gave unselfishly of her time and talent to serve her Government in peace and war. She loved her country. She is and always will be a star, one we shall never forget nor cease to be grateful to."

Of the many comments made by Hollywood friends, most were along the lines of a stunned Walter Pidgeon: "I am too shocked to express anything but the deepest grief." But there were two memorable exceptions. Errol Flynn stated a poignant and almost poetic sense of loss, "Carole Lombard's tragic death means that something of gaiety and beauty has been taken from the world at a time they are needed the most." James Cagney honored her as a fallen war hero. "Carole Lombard died doing her job for her country. Every one of us is proud of her," said the actor.

In the days and weeks following Lombard's death, Cagney's patriotic perspective dominated, as in the *New York Herald-Tribune*'s statement, "For all her identity with the somewhat unreal goings-on of celluloid comedy, she was a thorough-going patriot." The *Washington Times-Herald* opined, "It must be no small consolation for Clark Gable that she gave her life for her country."

As Hollywood linked Lombard's high-energy work ethic to her Indiana background, calling her the "Hoosier Tornado," the actress's patriotic, egalitarian nature was associated with a populism inherit to the nineteenth state. For example, a syndicated Hollywood article shortly after her death explained the grief felt by her blue-collar film friends. "Miss Lombard not only was loved but respected as a straight-shooter. Every grip [set mover], every property boy, every commissary waitress adored her, for she had the common touch, the common speech and never for a minute forgot they were fellow workers." Thus, the movie star simply called Pete by her working-class friends and Maw by her husband, in death found the name patriot.

(Originally appeared in *TRACES of Indiana and Midwestern History*, Spring 2002; Wes D. Gehring Copyright.)

STRANGE FRUIT:

And a Pioneering Trilogy

"STRANGE FRUIT"—BETWEEN 1880 and 1950 "The Negro Holocaust" occurred—an estimated 4,000 plus (exact figures vary) black men, women, and children were murdered by lynch mobs. A victim might also be either tortured before the hanging, or set aflame during this abomination. So what was Hollywood doing during the latter sound era portion (1930-1950) of this barbarism? Given this period was largely dominated by the Depression and World War II nationalism, the film industry's dream factory was primarily concerned with mind candy escapism. Plus, Hollywood's 1934 censorship code would not allow such racist-directed cinema.

However, a few films subtextually attacked the phenomenon, just as the South African science fiction film *District 9* (2009) encaged other world aliens to suggest the seeds of Apartheid and the Holocaust are more dormant than dead. Regardless, three such earlier films indirectly attacking "The Negro Holocaust" were Fritz Lang's *Fury* (1936), John Ford's *Young Mr. Lincoln* (1939), and William Wellman's *The Ox-Bow Incident* (1943). Sometimes it takes a foreign artist to best address another country's transgressions. Such is the case with Lang, arguably Germany's greatest filmmaker. Moreover, as a Jew when Hitler came to power, Lang was sensitive to intrinsic hate and persecution.

Fittingly, *Fury* was his first American film. An Everyman (Spencer Tracy) is wrongly accused of kidnapping. When a lynch mob fails to get Tracy out of custody, they set fire to the jail. Their victim manages to escape and goes "underground," in order that a trial will convict the alleged murderers en masse. He eventually cannot go through with it, but not before a frightfully visceral in-film trial documentary showcases how hatefully entertained the mob is by their actions.

The director later told Peter Bogdanovich (*Fritz Lang in America*, 1967) that to really make a film about lynching, "One should have a white woman raped by a colored man ... [and] still prove lynching is wrong." However, *Fury* was as close as MGM would let him go. Indeed, the studio even cut a scene of a black couple listening to the trial on the radio and nodding in agreement when the District Attorney noted the country's unconscionable number of lynchings. Whether in Europe or America, Lang said, "[when people] become a mob ... they have no personal conscience anymore."

This is clearly born out in *Young Mr. Lincoln*, when a fictionalized story has the future president (Henry Fonda) defending two young men wrongly accused of murder. Almost immediately he was to face down a jailhouse lynching party. Lincoln succeeds by defusing the mass back into being people. He calls out different *individual* mob members and appeals to their basic humanity. The sequence anticipates the scene in Harper Lee's 1960 novel *To Kill a Mockingbird*, when Scout Finch assists her father Atticus in stopping a similar lynching scenario. She talks directly to a mob acquaintance and helps thwart a hanging by drawing out individual tolerance.

Interestingly, Lang's and Ford's personal philosophies about people were mirror opposites. Lang helped orchestrate 1920s German Expressionism—a movement anchored in fatalistic chaos, a distrust of everyone and a visual motif of a "darkness more than night," to borrow a later phrase describing American film noir. Fittingly, Lang also greatly contributed to this post-World War II nihilistic genre which draws so much from German Expressionism. Lang would *not* have had Tracy save the mob.

In contrast, Ford was a practical populist, versus the idealistic Frank Capra variety, commonly described as "Capra-*corn*." They both felt men were inherently good. However, while a Capra crowd intuitively knew this, Ford felt most people needed cajoling. Indeed, in another *Young Mr. Lincoln* scene, the title character ever so gently threatens violence to get two essentially good people to see things "correctly." Regardless, "The Negro Holocaust" plays subtextually here, both because our subject is the later *Great Emancipator* (surfacing frequently in Ford's work), and that Fonda's personal liberalism came, in part, from witnessing a black lynching as a boy.

The Fonda connection segues into *The Ox-bow Incident*, since the actor lobbied hard to play a cowboy that attempts to stop a lynching. Wellman's adaptation of Walter Van Tilburg Clark's 1940 novel involves

Lincoln (Henry Fonda) entering Illinois' Springfield à la Christ's arriving in
Jerusalem—*Young Mr. Lincoln* (1939).

hanging three suspected rustlers (Dana Andrews, Anthony Quinn, and
Francis Ford—John Ford's brother). Wellman managed to be modestly
less subtextual by including a ragtag black minister in the picture (Leigh
Whipper), who briefly relates seeing his brother lynched—all of which
was *not* in the book. In interviewing Wellman shortly before his death
(1975), he told me that was as far as he could push the studio. Yet, Wellman
(who helped fund the film) managed to have a letter written for the movie
(only referenced in the novel) which Andrews' character had written to
his wife. Read by Fonda after the lynching, it is a moving indictment
of all vigilantism, stating, in part, "[Man cannot] hang people without
hurtin' everybody in the world … 'cause [law] is the very conscience of
humanity. There can't be any such thing as civilization unless people have
a conscience… And what is anybody's conscience except a little piece of
all men that ever lived…."

Sadly, to paraphrase critic Anthony Lane, "One assumes we live and
learn, and history, once comprehended, will not repeat itself." Yet, living

and learning still often results in death, and "lynching" continues today in many forms. *Strange Fruit* indeed.

McCARTHYISM &
THE MOVIES:

Two Genre-Changing Pictures

ANDREW DOWDY ONCE WROTE, "Hollywood wobbled into the fifties ..." (*Films in the Fifties*, 1973). But `50s America, in general, was struggling to stand erect, too. This wobbling factor was tied to a paranoid post-atomic climate of fear, coupled with a hysteria-producing wave of communist witch-hunting now simply synonymous with "McCarthyism." (Put another way, everyone in `50s America but Edward R. Murrow and Rocky Marciano were afraid to clear their throats for fear of being branded a "commie" or a "pinko.") "McCarthyism" was fanned by the House Committee on Un-American Activities (HUAC) Hollywood hearings, which resulted in an equally shocking abomination by the studio establishment—the creation of an industry-wide blacklist of artists with leftist resumes.

Suddenly company policy in filmland was preaching the standard "better-dead-than-Red" anti-intellectual mantra in movies like the *Red Danube* (1949, with Janet Leigh), "I Married a Communist" (1950, with Robert Ryan), *My Son John* (1952, with Robert Walker), and *Big Jim McLain* (1952, with John Wayne). Yet, an unwritten law of art suggests that political and social upheavals are invariably reflected by comparable watershed changes in creative endeavors. Granted, any historical perspective teaches us no activity, whether artistic or otherwise, is created in a vacuum. The events of the day, any day, have an impact upon the creative process. Nevertheless, dramatic societal events can fuel equally radical transition in art.

Two such examples of a cinema rebirth during the volatile Cold War `50s are classic examples of seemingly standard genre films: Fred Zinnemann's legendary Western *High Noon* (1952, with Gary Cooper),

Gary Cooper and Grace Kelly in *High Noon* (1952).

and Robert Aldrich's celebrated film noir adaptation of Mickey Spillane's
Kiss Me Deadly (1955, with Ralph Meeker as Mike Hammer). But other
than the shocking conclusion to *Deadly*, these two movies keep their
meaningful leftist Cold War commentaries subtextual, as opposed to the
shallow surface red-baiting of the aforementioned films. (Both movies
were assisted in their flying under the radar perspectives by the nature of
each production. *High Noon* was independently produced, and the career

of its only star, Gary Cooper, was in decline. *Deadly* was a low-budget "B" movie with a cast of essentially unknowns.

High Noon was produced by problem film guru Stanley Kramer, later most famous for his cinematic attacks upon racism, *The Defiant Ones* (1958, with Tony Curtis and Sidney Poitier), and Guess *Who's Coming to Dinner* (1967, with Poitier, Spencer Tracy, and Katharine Hepburn). *High Noon* was scripted by the already blacklisted writer Carl Foreman as an allegory about that very subject. Cooper plays a sheriff whose marriage to a Quaker (Grace Kelly, in her first significant screen role) forces his retirement from law enforcement. But when Cooper learns a gunman is returning to town for revenge, his crisis of conscience necessitates he put his badge back on … despite Kelly's threat to leave him.

So far this "man has got to do what a man has got to do" is nothing new for the Western. One could trace the genre's juxtapositioning of the civilizing pacifist female love interest versus the gun-toting justice-serving cowboy back to Owen Wister's precedent-setting Western novel *The Virginian* (1902, with Cooper actually starring in the first sound film adaptation of the novel, 1929). What made *High Noon* unique in the genre's history was the absence of a populist foundation—the people do not rally around the hero—and that Cooper's marshal was almost antiheroic in his displays of vulnerability.

Scripter Foreman's message was subtextual but clear; just as the fear of blacklisting made one's Hollywood "friends" evaporate, when Cooper needed support his neighbors also disappeared. Thus, he faced an apparent death sentence when his nemesis, Frank Miller (Ian MacDonald) and three accompanying henchman confront him at high noon. While blacklisting did not necessarily mean a physical death (though it was the catalyst for several suicides and other premature passings), the betrayal factor was worse than in Cooper's cowtown. That is, while the sheriff simply had to deal with cowardly friends, the blacklist frequently involved cowardice *and* collaboration—naming names before HUAC. However, the most sympathetic of Cooper's failing friends, a former mentoring marshal (Lon Chaney, Jr.), aptly summarizes the moral malignancy of McCarthyism, "People gotta talk themselves into law and order before they do anything about it. Maybe because down deep they don't care. They just don't care."

The anti-Western nature of Cooper's character was a revelation for the time. While this was still Gary tall-in-the-saddle Cooper, his marshal was completely de-glamorized. There is no masking of his fear, and Cooper's handsome countenance is shot as if to accent every facial stress line of his fifty-plus years. In a brief moment alone, he even puts his head down as if to weep. And when he has a knockdown, drag-out fight with his former deputy/ally (Lloyd Bridges), the barely victorious Cooper looks more like the loser. *High Noon* takes *the* American genre, and it's most iconic actor, and shatters basic Western myths of invincibility.

However, like Clint Eastwood's similar deconstruction of the classic Western forty years later in the *Unforgiven* (1992, after he had become the face of the genre), Cooper ultimately reverts to type and manages to vanquish all his villains. But he does not forget or forgive the hypocrisy of the town. *High Noon* ends with the marshal throwing his badge in the dust and forever leaving *Hadleyville*—a name not unlike another two-faced town in American literature, Mark Twain's *Hadleyburg* (from "The Man That Corrupted Hadleyburg," 1899).

Just as *High Noon* was a pioneering anti-Western, Aldrich's *Kiss Me Deadly* jumped the film noir tracks. Pop culture cinema historian Peter Biskind goes so far as to call this installment of Spillane's Hammer the genre's obituary: "The age of the private eye had ended" (*Seeing Is Believing*, 1983). *Deadly*'s split from traditional noir is even more dramatic then the genre-changing developments of *High Noon*. Cooper is still the sympathetic quiet "man of few words" cowboy on a mission to do what traditional Westerners forever attempt—sacrifice for the common good. The then revolutionary twist was both showing a vulnerable hero/antihero, and an unworthy community. In contrast, whereas the defining noir detectives of Raymond Chandler (Philip Marlowe) and Dashiell Hammett (Sam Spade) were, in the words of Chandler, "tarnished knights" in "mean streets," á la urban cowboys with a Western code, Hammer was as mean as his name, and those aforenamed streets. Consequently, while the Cold War subtext for *Deadly* mirrors *Noon*—"people … just don't care"—Meeker's Hammer (unlike Cooper) is not someone for whom most viewers can root. Granted, the narrative initially seems to point in a standard noir direction. Meeker meets a seemingly unstable sexy blonde (Cloris Leachman in her film debut), and with her predictable murder he becomes obsessed with solving the case. But unlike honorable Spade and Marlowe, or Jack Nicholson's retro noir private eye in *Chinatown* (1974), Meeker's motivation is merely money. Even late in the movie, when federal authorities reveal he has stumbled into the theft of a nuclear device, Hammer still asks, "What's in it for me?" So while Cooper's character is a tragic reminder of how far the modern ('50s) world has fallen, *Deadly* even denies the viewer the lingering hope/idealism of an old school hero. Meeker's Hammer is as selfishly shallow as everyone else. The noir filmmaker/critic Paul Schrader satirically describes this Hammer as "a midget among dwarfs" (*Film Noir Reader*, 1996).

Of course, the greatest departure from the ˋ50s subtextual messaging of both movies is the apocalyptic conclusion of *Deadly*, when the purloined object of everyone's desire, an atomic age "Pandora's Box," turns out to be "the bomb." But to momentarily back up the noir bus, one needs to briefly rewind the *Deadly* narrative. The naked-under-a-trenchcoat blonde (Leachman) Hammer picks up at the story's beginning, an escapee from a mental institution, eventually turns out to have been a scientist held against her will by government agents. This sacrificial lamb was not crazy but rather the keeper of a terrible secret; she knows the whereabout of the "great whatsit?" (the nuclear device).

The clue Christina (Leachman) gives Hammer, though he initially does not realize it, is in a medieval-like sonnet by Christina Rossetti (1830-1894) with the haunting opening line, "Remember me." Auteur historian Jean-Pierre Coursodon has called the refrain this picture's "Rosebud" (*American Directors, Volume II*, 1983). Regardless, it is perversely fitting that a looking backwards poem holds the key. Because, once it is solved by the self-serving Hammer, the most pervasive fear from the Dark Ages occurs—a man-made apocalypse.

Deadly also links its cautionary Cold War story to even earlier tales from ancient literature, from Greek mythology's aforementioned Pandora's box to the Bible's story of Lot's wife's refusal to heed another warning. Except in the case of *Deadly*, when the film's metaphorical Lot's wife (Gaby Rogers) murders her way to opening this new age radioactive Pandora's box, it means universal annihilation. Hammer and company's blindly selfish obstinacy represent an indictment of a scientific community whose technological expertise outstripped its sense of morality. In a broader sense, noir filmmaker/critic Martin Scorsese has added, "[Director] Aldrich's [*Deadly*] point, an important one during those McCarthy times, was: 'The end never justifies the means.'"

Aldrich's contempt was not limited to society in general. He and his scriptwriter (A.I. Bezzerides) wanted to depict their "utter contempt and loathing for the cynical, fascist private eye [named Hammer] (*The Rough Guide to Film Noir*, 2007). Merely adapting Spillane's Hammer to the screen represents instant noir slumming, compared to the idealistic Marlowe/Spade models. But Aldrich heightened Hammer's despicable quotient (and the era itself) by changing the "great whatsit?" In Spillane's novel the contents of the elusive container were merely drugs. However, by making it a radioactive package, a saga of greed damning several souls is transformed into Armageddon for *all* of humanity.

That being said, as with many other Aldrich films, where a central character is less than admirable, from Burt Lancaster in *Vera Cruz* (1954), to Bette Davis in *What Ever Happened to Baby Jane?* (1962), a never better Meeker seems to have an intensified form of being. Aldrich's visceral cinema is further electrified by the stylized realism of every shot. *Deadly* was later a major influence on the "French New Wave." Indeed, one of the principle architects of the movement, Francois Truffault, wrote, "It is not unusual to encounter a new idea with each [*Deadly*] shot. In this movie the inventiveness is so rich that we don't know what to look at—the images are almost too full, too fertile. Watching a film like this is such an intense experience that we want it to last for hours" (*The Films In My Life*, 1975).

Ironically, despite such period praise from Truffault and other European artists, *Deadly* was a largely neglected and/or unappreciated "B" movie upon its initial release in the United States. In contrast, *High Noon* was a modest "A" picture with box office staying power. Besides becoming one of 1952's top grossing movies, it won several Academy Awards: Best Actor (Gary Cooper), Film Editing (Elmo Williams, Harry Gerstad), Best Song (Dimitri Tiomkin and Ned Washington's "Do Not Forsake Me, Oh My Darlin' "), and Best Scoring of a Dramatic or Comedy Picture (Dimitri Tiomkin). *High Noon* also received Oscar nominations for Best Picture (losing to Cecil B. DeMille's *The Greatest Show on Earth*), Best Director (Fred Zinnemann lost to John Ford's "The Quiet Man"), and screenplay (Carl Foreman lost to Charles Schnee's *The Bad and the Beautiful*)

High Noon`s anti-blacklisting subtext is now generally acknowledged as having cost the film the Oscar statuettes for Best Picture and Screenplay, with DeMille's circus movie considered one of the weakest features to ever win the top prize. After completing his *High Noon* script in 1951, Foreman was blacklisted following his testimony before HUAC. The writer had refused to either confirm his political affiliations or name names. (Kramer and company had to fight to just keep Foreman's name on the completed film.) Going into self-imposed exile in England, Foreman's many later honors would include being awarded the title "Commander of the British Empire" (1970). Sadly, the blacklist also prevented Foreman from receiving Oscar credit for co-writing the acclaimed *Bridge on the*

River Kwai (1957). Not until 1985 was Foreman posthumously awarded his *Kwai* statuette.

The "cost" of the blacklisting is impossible to quantify, but Foreman would later write, "Every time I sat down at the typewriter, bitter and aggrieved feelings intruded upon my screen work. I wanted to write angry letters rather than a script" (*The Inquisition in Hollywood*, 1979). Yet, movies like *High Noon* and *Deadly* deserve ongoing recognition for bucking the Hollywood system at arguably the nadir of its existence.

The ongoing legacy of both movies assumed some predictable and not so predictable directions. *High Noon* entered the language as a phrase synonymous with *any* principled confrontation. (Foreman later even used the title as the name of his production company.) Paradoxically, while *High Noon* gave the genre a new vulnerable antihero, Cooper's lone sheriff so resonated with the general public he was soon redefined as a classic Westerner. Even more ironic, future anti-heroic cinema cowboys, such as Clint Eastwood's *Man With No Name* figure in Sergio Leone's "spaghetti westerns" had much more in common with Meeker's selfish Hammer.

What fueled *Deadly* as a later model for French New Wave (1960s) directors like Truffant, and New American Cinema (1970s) filmmakers like Scorsese, skipped the political subtext. Both these movements were obsessed with a dark antiheroic take on mankind. Moreover, they were often drawn to counterculture auteurs like Aldrich, whose films were frequently nihilistic, and showcased a distinct visual and/or thematic patterns consistent with despair. In contrast, *High Noon* was difficult to champion along auteur lines, beyond the broad problem film ties of Kramer the producer. And Cooper's character remained old school noble.

An unusual auteur twist, related to *High Noon*, involves the French New Wave critics' (turned filmmakers) pioneering recognition of director Howard Hawks. The politically conservative Hawks and John Wayne were bothered by Cooper's *High Noon* hero asking friends for help (and presumably the anti-McCarthy subtext). For them a Western protagonist was a grace under pressure loner. Thus, in *Rio Bravo* (1959) they created an unofficial anti-*High Noon* picture, in which another beleaguered marshal (Wayne) faces a comparable evil gang without either requesting assistance, or even breaking a sweat. But in an ironic flaw to their argument, Hawks allows his Wayne hero to be assisted by a drunk (Dean Martin), a kid (Ricky Nelson), and a handicapped old geezer (Walter Brennan). The paradox comes from the fact that Cooper's character turns down unsolicited assistance from a similar motley *High Noon* crew ... because his idealistic marshal feels he would be unfairly putting them at risk.

In the eyes of Hawks and Wayne, *Rio Bravo* is somehow a more "patriotic Western." Whatever one's take on the subject, this often entertaining film also found a popular audience and inspired the similar Hawks/Wayne follow-up film *El Dorado* (1967). But lest anyone think *High Noon* is knee-jerk blasphemy to the political right, its central theme of duty despite community betrayal is at the heart of Don Siegel's original conservative *Dirty Harry* (1971, with Clint Eastwood). In fact, Eastwood's Western marshal-like contemporary cop even replicates Cooper's close to *High Noon*—*Dirty Harry* ends with Eastwood's title character disgustedly throwing his badge in the dust, too.

Movies are modern man's own special brand of mythology, and two of its most iconic figures are the rugged cowboy and the private eye. While *High Noon* and *Deadly* helped change how pop culture saw these two characters (spurred on by period politics), they remain quintessential figures in any movie-made deity. But strangely enough, one could make a final link between the Cooper-Meeker dichotomy by way of classical Greek mythology. For instance, some Cooper biographers, such as René Jordon, have likened the actor's betrayed *High Noon* victim to Prometheus (*Gary Cooper*, 1974). As a benefactor of mortals, Prometheus stole fire from Zeus and gave it to mankind. For his championing of the people, Zeus had him bound to a rock while an eagle daily ate his liver ... only to have it grow back by the following morning, for the eagle to pluck once again. Zeus' punishment for mortals was to gift Pandora, Greek mythology's first woman on earth, with a beautiful box (actually a large ornate jar). Pandora was warned not to open the jar/box under any circumstances. But Zeus knew her great curiosity would make this command impossible to keep (not unlike the story of Eve and the apple). When the container was opened, all imaginable evil was unleashed.

Moreover, beyond this *High Noon* / *Deadly* connection of Prometheus and Pandora, the movie narratives end with implications consistent with these Greek myths. Bitterness will undoubtedly eat at Cooper's ex-marshal for the rest of his days. And when *Deadly*'s Gaby Rogers opens the radioactive container/bomb, a world-ending evil is suggested. If there are any questions regarding this interpretation, keep in mind Rogers' character is sometimes called Gabriel. In Christianity, Gabriel is a messenger of God who doubles as an angel of death. Gabriel is also implied to be the figure who will blow the trumpet beginning the end of time. Though a "he" in the Bible, moderns frequently portray Gabriel as a female, as in the guilty pleasure noir/horror film *Constantine* (2005).

Ultimately, the beauty of *High Noon* and *Deadly*, as in all art which taps into universal truths, is that a viewer could miss every metaphorical McCarthy era Cold War subtext (with its revisionist tweaking of two genres), and still savor the films on a purely mind candy entertainment level. To paraphrase humorist Will Cuppy, "Entertainment is recognized, even by the glummest among us, as a thing to be desired in all the arts."

LONESOME RHODES &

1957's *A Face in the Crowd*

THERE ARE COUNTLESS neglected films that need to be resurrected. A prime candidate is Elia Kazan's *A Face in the Crowd* (1957). Kazan arguably was America's most creative Broadway and Hollywood force in the mid 20th century. He directed Tennessee Williams' game-changingly controversial *Streetcar Named Desire* on Broadway (1947-49), and adapted it to film (1951). He won Best Director Academy awards for *A Gentleman's Agreement* (1947, which attacked American Anti-Semitism) and *On the Waterfront* (1954, about union corruption and possibly his defense on why he named names for the House Committee on Un-American Activities during the McCarthy era's Communist witch hunts). Moreover, he helped create the naturalistic realism called Method acting. Of course, Marlon Brando's acclaimed demonstration of the technique in both versions of *Streetcar* (as well as in *Waterfront*) sometimes kiddingly was called the "itch-and-scratch" style.

Regardless, *A Face in the Crowd* becomes more timely with each passing year. Written by another HUAC-friendly witness, Budd Schulberg, its importance lies in the simple but terrifying Marshall McLuhan phrase, "The medium is the message." Besides this pioneering warning about the power of media to sell anything and create cookie-cutter political candidates, the film also is a cautionary tale about the U.S.'s love affair with the crackerbarrel populist-the charismatic, folksy man of the people.

Crowd chronicles the story of an Arkansas hobo (Andy Griffith) soon to be christened "Lonesome Rhodes." Fluctuating between down-home humor and biting disregard for the calcified status quo—which he undercuts with horse-sense solutions—the meteoric surge of TV personality Rhodes seems like a budding Will Rogers, or an Arthur "Old Redhead" Godfrey. (The latter possibly was a key inspiration for the

169

character.) Rhodes' rapid rise is orchestrated by captivated small-town radio personality Marcia Jeffries (Patricia Neal).

The narrative slickly reverses the standard Frank Capra populist blueprint of *Mr. Deeds Goes to Town* (1936), or *Mr. Smith Goes to Washington* (1939). That is, the Capra template has a cynical leading lady so sure the populist figure is a hoax that she helps institute some sort of mid-film humiliation, and then discovers he is the real corny deal. From then on, her loving direction successfully brings his common sense to the common man.

In contrast, Neal's naïve faith has her lovingly choreograph Rhodes almost immediately into a powerful "aw shucks" national phenomenon. However, this apparent cure-all populist turns out to be more of a Huey Long wannabe.

Consequently, Neal's character continues to reverse the Capra pattern by personally bringing down Rhodes. When one TV broadcast concludes, with end titles rolling, he ridicules the viewers to his entourage, since his

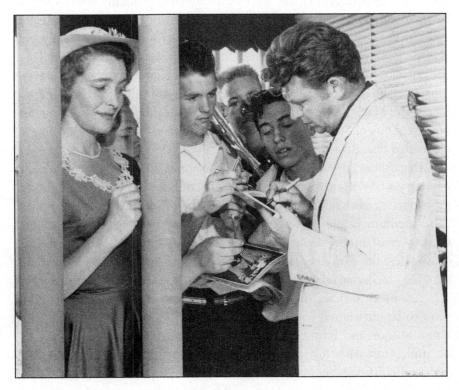

False populist Andy Griffith and Patricia Neal in *A Face in the Crowd* (1957).

microphone is off. Yet, unbeknownst to him, Neal switches it back on and his hypocrisy is revealed cost-to-coast. However, the film ends suggesting the powers that be either will resurrect him and/or create other similar demigods selling products and politics interchangeably. Besides being so prophetic, today the film packs an added chill because Griffith now is so associated with the idealized populist, á la his later *Andy Griffith Show* (1960-68). His Mayberry marshal is an America Solomon, the most benevolent of homegrown autocrats.

With 24/7 media coverage of The U.S.'s seemingly 24/7 political campaigning, the increasing danger of this "Lonesome Rhodes" factor seems ever on the rise. Indeed, before Glenn Beck self-destructed a few years ago, he sometimes was stamped, sans a reference, as a "Lonesome Rhodes." Of course, *A Face in the Crowd* goes back to television's early days, when the small screen was just beginning to mesmerize the public with grandfatherly Godfrey types. Indeed, Godfrey regularly had two shows in TV's top 10, yet, off the air, he was not someone to cross.

Coincidentally, Rhodes had many parallels with Godfrey. They both had neighborly-nicknamed on-air personas which engagingly could mock sponsors and sell any product in a folksy manner yet play powerbroker in private. For example, Godfrey's friendship with Pres. Dwight Eisenhower even had the entertainer recording public address spots—never broadcast—in case of a nuclear war. Ike felt Godfrey's demeanor would calm a panicked public. However, most importantly, Rhodes, like Godfrey, had a single incident which blindsided him. While Godfrey's was not so dramatic as Rhodes', he never fully recovered from firing one of his most popular TV regulars on-air.

That being said, Rhodes also had additional precedents. In the early 1950s, a regional New York kiddie show host made derogatory remarks about his little fans when he also thought his mic was off. Plus, a key Rhodes tip to a possible presidential candidate about ditching his cat and getting a dog undoubtedly was drawn from vice-presidential candidate Richard Nixon's famous 1952 "Checkers" TV speech. Nixon was denying any misappropriation of campaign funds but closed by stating he would not give up Checkers, the family dog, given to him by supporters.

While *Crowd* showed how easy it was to remake and sell everything from a Geritol-like product to wannabe presidents, 1957 had two other memorable movies with the same TV marketing message: Charlie Chaplin's *A King in New York* and Frank Tashlin's *Will Success Spoil Rock Hunter?* Today, every year feels like 1957, except now the warning often appears to apply more to political products. Satire can be a savior here, but it would help if the human herd seemingly did not so need this empty prattle and/or follow if just as easily.

(Reprinted with permission from *USA Today Magazine*, January, 2017. Copyright © 2017 by "The Society For the Advancement of Education, Inc. All Right Reserved.")

OH, WHY COULDN'T IT HAVE BEEN ROBERT?

I take Life as it comes, and although I grouse a great deal
and sometimes lie on the floor and kick and scream and
refuse to eat my supper, I find that taking Life as it comes
is the only way to meet it.

– Robert Benchley[1]

IF ONE'S CHILDHOOD CAN BE most marked by a single event,
Robert Benchley's was forever changed by the July 1, 1898, death of older
brother Edmund, an early casualty of the Spanish American War. Besides
the natural tragedy attached to any young person's death, especially one
so promising as the intelligent, handsome Edmund (fresh from early
West Point graduation), there was additional pain. In her extreme grief
over the death of her favorite son, Benchley's mother Jennie had asked,
"Oh, why couldn't it have been Robert?"

After this chilling statement, which soon entered the folklore of the
family's hometown (Worcester, Massachusetts), eight-year-old Benchley
could not have had a more attentively smothering mother. The humorist's
son Nathaniel (namesake of Edmund Nathaniel) states that Jennie tied
his father's shoes "until he was ready to go to high school."[2] A more telling
example for a future humorist was Jennie's reprimanding of a Sunday
school teacher for scolding her son when he played the class clown.
Indeed, comedy psychologist Mary K. Rothbart suggests it is much more
common to have a parent inhibit a youngster's sense of humor by teaching
when *not* to laugh.[3]

Benchley was reared in a middle class, matriarchal home. His father
Charlie was a lifelong mayor's clerk whose paycheck was always collected
and strictly budgeted by his wife. Charlie was neither ambitious nor

forceful, content to let his wife make the decisions. With the death of Edmund, the Benchley home would now revolve around the younger child.

Jennie's long-term attention/protection resulted in a closeness between mother and son which is fully fleshed out in Benchley's diaries as a young adult.[4] This is largely a neglected source (especially the comic entry foreshadowing of his later essays), other than Nathaniel's fleeting references in *Robert Benchley, A Biography*, which later authors had to use as a primary source before the family donated the diaries to Boston University.

In Benchley's diaries his special affinity for his mother often suggests the entries are those of a younger person. For instance, a 22-year-old Benchley wrote, "Mother and I walked downtown and did some New Year's shopping ... it was a beautiful day for walking with one's mother."[5] Later in the same entry he added, "Mother and [childhood sweetheart and future wife] Gertrude were beside me, so I may say I have never enjoyed a theatre party more in my life." Though admittedly banal comments, they are representative of the loving reverence granted Jennie in the diaries. Moreover, extensive research on Benchley shows this position is reinforced both in his correspondence home at Boston University and in my interview with the humorist's daughter-in-law and Nathaniel's widow, Marjorie – executor of Benchley's Boston University papers.[6]

Fittingly, Benchley often mirrored his mother's influence throughout his lifetime of writing, despite the seeming disparity between a modest New England upbringing and the sophisticated later world of a pivotal early *New Yorker* writer. Though this might not seem particularly striking, it is important for four reasons. First, the extent of this influence has not previously been examined, and in our culture, "the personal life of a comedian or clown is often considered to be something special."[7] This fascination with the clown's background is possibly an outgrowth of the secret of why clowns have always sustained society. They comfort us comically in our short lives with their resiliency – both physically and spiritually.[8] Thus, Charlie Chaplin's "Little Fellow" thrives on every pratfall, just as his shuffling film-closing gait (after a comic compendium of life's adversities) symbolizes the triumph of human spirit. Along the same lines, society seems most fascinated with the clown biography that reveals tragic roots – the resiliency to provoke laughter despite personal sadness. This might include the Oliver Twist-like childhood of Chaplin, the young runaway W. C. Fields, Groucho Marx's early hurt over his mother's preference for Chico, and Stan Laurel's lifelong fear he would lose his mind like his comic hero—English music hall great Dan Leno. Consequently, Benchley's comedy success, despite his mother's numbing plea when her favorite son died, is the stuff of comic legend – humor's version of the phoenix. Moreover, the plea and Benchley's early lack of maternal attention (compared to his brother) has more recently became the stuff of fact. That is, studies have shown that elementary school aged children with a marked sense of humor (which Benchley demonstrated) are more likely to have had, in McGhee's words, "a lack of prior maternal babying and protectiveness."[9]

Second, while the examination of early archrival material is not scientifically methodical in terms of comedy theory, it does, in this case, provide valuable insights on a unique comedian/author whose career is surprisingly underresearched. In fact, by examining early documents like Benchley's diaries, one goes a step beyond the most prevalent (though also non-methodical) comedy theory approach to the professional comedian—establishing interviews with the already established comic figure. For instance, in *Make 'Em Laugh: Life Studies of Comedy Writers*, one is especially taken with the chapter interview of Norman Lear.[10] It not only suggests that Lear grew up in a home atmosphere not unlike *All in the Family* (his most famous television creation), but that the earthiness of his language is reminiscent of his more controversial characters. Again one sees the comedy influence of childhood stress, especially when Lear relates the funny/sad story of keeping score during his parents' arguments. But while the Lear interview is data recalled from a distant past filtered through fame and fortune, the Benchley diaries are pre-success period reflections in close proximity to his childhood. If the Lear interview is valuable, then the Benchley diaries offer an opportunity for even further insights.

Third, though rarely explored, Benchley's mother was a comically eccentric person. Marjorie Benchley's favorite example was: "Jennie hated trees because they lived longer than people."[11] Once, when struck by an ice truck, her only response had been the comic non-sequitur, "They say I dented a fender."

Jennie's views are reminiscent of the comically peculiar traits of James Thurber's maternal grandmother, who "lived the latter years of her life in the horrible suspicion that electricity was dripping [from empty sockets] all over the house."[12] I am reminded of Thurber's grandmother whenever I read Benchley's "Three men in the dog house," which revolves around Jennie's belief that when one sees three or more men travelling by buggy, they are drunk."[13] One might reason with her, but she remained forever convinced they were "up to no good."

Appropriately, as McGhee (1979) has observed, numerous "Interviews with comedy writers and comedians have shown that professional humorists typically had strong and consistent models of joking and clowning in one or both parents ... "[14] They also, like Benchley, were invariably closest to their mothers, even if the parent had not been overly protective in the pre-school years.

Fourth, psychologist/comedy theorist McGhee stated in an earlier article that at seven or eight years of age children gain a more perceptive sense of humor in which "newly acquired cognitive capacities play a central role in generating humor in response to stimulus discrepancy [comedy of incongruity]."[15] This is precisely the age at which comically eccentric Jennie Benchley began giving increased attention to her surviving son. Indeed, her admonishment of Benchley's Sunday school teacher comes at this time and involved a child's early example of comic cognitive skills; the boy had changed a hymn.

Jennie's increased attention to her son also paralleled an inflation of her eccentrically superstitious nature. Remembering incidents from her oldest son's last day at home, she decreed that family members could no longer use the expression "good-bye" when parting, kiss in the bathroom, or watch a departing form of transportation into the distance.

In discussing this with Marjorie Benchley, she declared, "Benchleys are [still] very superstitious." For instance, she related that at a recent (1990) airport parting, she affectionately left—with no waiting. Marjorie also revealed that her humorist father-in-law, with whom she was very close even prior to marrying Nathaniel, did not attend their marriage ceremony because he was afraid he would jinx it. After his close involvement in several previous weddings which all ended in divorce, he was taking no chances. Disappointed, husband-to-be Nathaniel sat Marjorie down and explained his father's "superstitious thing." The rest of the family did not treat this behavior as anything unusual.

With these factors in mind, Benchley's mother's boyhood influence surfaces in four ways in the diaries—an influence most fitting for a future self-depreciating antiheroic author (as was the statement which generated the total attention). Materials drawn from the diaries are *not* meant to be seen as funny but rather as early evidence of how his mother would affect him.

Robert Benchley (left) and the idealized Edward who died shortly after this picture was taken.

First, while his essays seldom display the domineering wife/mother figure of antiheroic colleague Thurber, such as the Mr. and Mrs. Monroe stories from his *The Owl in the Attic* (1931), Benchley's pieces frequently suggest a bewildered little boy quality—someone in need of and/or used to a parental guiding hand. For instance, his diaries often anticipate his celebrated later piece, "My White Suit" (1936), which recently was reprinted in *Gentlemen's Quarterly*.[16] Benchley feels he never looks quite right in his white suit, fearing, among other things, he did not put it on correctly. Fittingly, his diaries record motherly clothing suggestions—the 23-year-old Benchley observing, "went on a search for another necktie to replace my green one, which with my purple shirt disturbed Mother."[17] Man/child Benchley had childishly bright tastes. An earlier adult entry describes a pink swimming outfit. (After all, this was a child who had had his shoes tied by his mother until he was a teen.)

In a second direct motherly influence, Benchley reflected his mother's strong pacifist feelings, an outgrowth of her older son's military death, which was reported to the family on the Fourth of July. Thus, "Oh, why couldn't it have been Robert?" was uttered in front of a family audience. Regardless, Nathaniel Benchley does note his father's later diary thoughts on the brink of World War I: "… I can't make it seem possible that they [Europe] will fall so fast back into the middle ages after having come so far."[18] Benchley's future comedy essays would generally avoid issues like war, especially after he was a well-established humorist. But early examples do exist, such as the piece "A substitute for war," which satirically suggests calling a town meeting under the slogan, "Fight your neighbors first. Why go abroad for war?"[19]

While Jennie could also be darkly cynical about war, à la the later 1970 *M*A*S*H** (she opposed the Red Cross because they simply patched people up to return to war), her pacifist nature surfaced in less obvious ways. Edmund's death made her distrustful of all officials, from mailmen to passport workers. And Benchley's antiheroic comedy often builds on his persona's general paranoia around any official or authority figure: "I feel that my modest demands on his time may, unless tactfully presented, be offensive to him and result in something, I haven't been able to analyze just what, perhaps public humiliation."[20] This is a kindred spirit to entries in the diary like, "The surf was great … and if I hadn't been watched by two [horn-blowing] life guards … I would have had the time of my life."[21]

Third, the eccentric Jennie was serious about helping the needy while maintaining their sense of self-worth. Appropriately, the period after her older son's death (when Benchley received increased attention) parallels the birth of what is now called the "Progressive Era" (1900-1920, a period of generally liberal political activity, eventually culminating with women receiving the right to vote). Jennie reflected the times in her concern for the poor. Benchley often assisted her when she donated food and assistance to the needy. At one point he even considered a career in social work. As a young adult he was involved in both the Big Brother program and volunteer work for the Urban League.

Ironically, at a community Christmas gathering to which the young Benchley accompanied his mother, the gift he was to receive in a children's exchange was misplaced. Jennie was so upset by her son seemingly being forgotten that she avoided such exchanges in the future. Thus, Benchley's "education" about the have-nots also had its poignant side. Indeed, Benchley would later confess in a comic essay that he had an:

> instinctive habit … of putting myself in the place of anyone
> I am watching. I haven't been at a fight for more than three
> minutes before I begin indulging in one of my favorite
> nightmares. This consists of imagining that I myself am
> up in the ring facing the better of the two men.[22]

Jennie's sensitivity for the individual lived on in a Benchley comedy persona so disarmingly pleasant and self-deprecatingly funny (versus comically undercutting others) that one feels an innate kinship with him. To illustrate, for his blundering "little man"; "hockey is a great big sport now, and I can remember when its only function was to humiliate me personally."[23] Even as a critic in the theater, Benchley worried about putting actors out of work. This concern contributed to the amusing carryover use in the reviews of his antiheroic persona—which comically softened any negative criticism. For example, "I always know that a play is clumsily written if I can detect passages in it I myself might have done."[24]

The start of the Depression also found the humorist contributing ten percent of his royalties from *The Treasurer's Report and Other Aspects of Community Singing* (1930) to the Actors Equity's Unemployment Relief Fund. (He would have further mixed feelings later about being both a critic and a performer. Did it compromise his position as a reviewer?)

His diaries have direct links to this concern for the poor and to maintaining self-dignity. They are *serious* commentaries about his responsiveness. Thus, on an early job assignment as a reporter he was to write about an unusual low-income divorce case where the couple still lived in close proximity to each other. Benchley described it as "the most unpleasant assignment I have had, for I felt it was none of my, or the paper's business … [I] walked up and down in front of the house before I could get up nerve."[25] Benchley's heightened sensitivity to the poor (and to "progressive" issues in general) is equally obvious in another entry:

> I made beginnings on my first great literary success – a powerful, yet cynical and very cleverly written sketch which I think I shall call "The Socialist." Just why I chose to write about that I can't say, only ever since fall [1912, Benchley had just turned 23] I've wanted to write about men that wrap themselves up in newspapers to sleep in the park.[26]

No other single quote from his diaries better demonstrates why Benchley would later feel ambivalent about the great success of his generally non-issue-oriented comedy essays, or more pointedly, his work as a "mere"—but highly paid—film comedian. This entry, therefore, is not without a certain two-part tonal irony, despite Benchley's relatively tender age at the time of writing.

First, besides his real concern for the poor, he also wanted to be a successful writer. Jennie had made him aware of the plight of the poor. His own upbringing had been modest, with even his Harvard education being provided by a family benefactor. In fact, at the same time he was dreaming about this street person project, Benchley could only afford to live at the New York City YMCA. Second, despite his antiheroic persona, Benchley the humorist exerts a certain control through his writing (as do all successful comedy authors). McGhee observes, "The child or adult who is consistently joking or clowning maintains control of most ongoing social interaction by creating circumstances to which others are obliged to react ... [it] is not only socially acceptable, but usually lavishly rewarded."[27] Thus, adjectives from the entry like "powerful" or "cleverly written" are a rare instance of Benchley letting the power trip of humor show through. As a later essay on boyhood tennis reveals, he understood this principle early—winning means getting your "opponent to laughing so hard that he is unable either to serve or get the ball back. (A good-natured opponent is almost a necessity in this form of play."[28]

It is sad but not unexpected that late in life he would complain (in an unpublished 1941 letter to his wife): I am "mad at myself for getting into such a financial spot that I couldn't turn it [a high salary for being cast in a mediocre film] down."[29] The letter went on to say he was going to reduce his future Hollywood professional ties and return to increased writing. Just the opposite transpired. He publicly retired from writing in 1942, devoting all his time to the less satisfying but more lucrative film acting. Evidently, Benchley's scarcity of money memories could not resist Hollywood's easy cash.

These, then, have been the four main mother-son connections in the Benchley diaries. But a peripheral area merits mentioning. Jennie's emphasis on strong family values, especially her intense attention to children, might be called a final tie between the two, as demonstrated by the diaries. At first glance, this might seem ludicrous. After all, Benchley's writing career frequently kept him away from his Scarsdale, New York-based wife and children (Nathaniel, born in 1915, and Robert, born 1919). And his occasional discrete affairs recently found a biographer of Benchley close friend Dorothy Parker condemning him as a hypocrite, since his screen persona sometimes played upon being a family man.[30]

Seemingly more damaging would be examples of his humor which makes children the butt of his jokes. For example, in "Kiddie-Kar Travel" he observes, "In America there are two classes of travel – first class, and with children."[31] But in defense of his humor which focuses on youngsters, he generally makes himself the antiheroic butt of the essay, which is in fitting with his self-deprecating style. For instance, in "Museum Feet": a complaint contracted by over-zealous parents," he notes, "The sad thing about a trip through a museum with the children is that you start out with so much vigor and zip … Daddy will show … [them] everything and explain everything. And what a sap that makes of Daddy before the day is done!"[32]

His children were also an affectionate presence in his comic criticism for *LIFE*: "The most popular review which has appeared in this department in recent years was the one dictated by our six-year-old son on the circus. … So far, we have heard no charges of log-rolling against him …"[33]

Though it did not make his film short subject, Benchley's *How to Raise a Baby*, the original script included a comically touching antiheroic father's Bill of Rights on being included in early child rearing: "There is also a feeling in some quarters that the father is temperamentally unsuited to take part in the character training until the child is old enough to talk back, but this … is a mistaken notion."[34]

As with many Benchley scripts, this one draws some inspiration from his earlier published essays, such as "How the Doggie Goes."[35] But the best fatherly "research" is found in Benchley's unpublished diaries. For example, "The baby's bottle having been dropped and smashed at 5:30, it was the father's care to keep him [Nathaniel] engaged in conversation until the milk-man came at 6:45."[36]

Fittingly, Benchley's mother remains pleasantly present in the diaries after the humorist becomes a father. She also continues the caring family tradition with her son: "Mother came down to see the Baby [Nathaniel] just after his bath and she and I went down town together. She took me into the Boston Store and blew me to [purchased for Benchley] some under-drawers and shirts and socks."[37]

Benchley's generally warm antiheroic stance on children seems all the more pronounced when compared with a comedy contemporary of truly anti-youngster tendencies—S. J. Perelman. For example, in "Billiards and Their Prevention" (1929), Perelman says, "I am 25 years old and hate children, in that respect I am different from billiards; although I cannot say for sure whether billiards hate children, as I never asked them."[38] And in "Frou-Frou, of the Future of Vertigo" Perelman observes, "After a quick look into the nursery, I decided to let my blond child go to hell her own way, as they do in America."[39] Not surprisingly, one Perelman biographer observed, "Like so many temperamental men of genius, he found children tiresome nuisances."[40] Unlike Perelman and other self-centered artists, however, Benchley did not seem to see youngsters as competitors for attention.

This is not the place to belabor what has been called the greatest difficulty of the biographer as noted by Woolf, "By what standard … is he to judge the morals of the dead?"[41] But any mention of Benchley's marital infidelity should be coupled with the stacks of amusingly warm letters and telegrams home, one of which was described as "my fun for the day."[42]

Housed at Boston University, these often neglected letters deal with universal family matters, including money and taxes, "I wish the Government would die; and the children's achievements, The [Harvard] Class of 1908 will soon be famous as having had Nat Benchley's father in it."[43]

Fittingly for this mother-focused essay, the best Benchley letter showcasing the humorist as amusing father was written to Jennie. Describing a family vacation abroad, Benchley the comic-tourist surfaced: "Everything around here is Roman ruins and we have got so that we don't stop to look at anything later than 1200 A.D."[44] In 1932 Benchley took Jennie on another European family vacation, and the octogenarian insisted on taking her bicycle!

Though the written word is hardly a substitute for a loved one's presence, there seems to have been genuine love of family present, which is emphasized further by conversations and correspondence with his daughter-in-law Marjorie. As one of his biographers observes, none of "the ladies who adored him, really influenced Benchley's feeling about his family. It was clear always that his family came first."[45]

The special attention Jennie Benchley gave to a young impressionable son after her unfortunate comment had an ongoingly positive influence on his life and humor. But the story has a final, unusual twist, a quixotically indirect statement of forgiveness. Bookworm Benchley's eventual self-claimed favorite novel was Evelyn Waugh's dark comedy *A Handful of Dust* (1934). The book contains a passage eerily close to his own mother's comment at Edmund's death. The heroine's (Brenda) lover and young son share the same name (John). Thus, there is initial uncertainty when she is told that John is dead, followed by joy when it turns out to be her son—"Oh, thank God."[46] The work is considered Waugh's greatest novel, and Benchley often recommended it to friends. Thurber later included the title in a reading list for his daughter.[47]

Though critics have sometimes differed in their interpretation of Brenda's character, Waugh's definitive biographer has recently been most convincing in portraying her in a positive light.[48] This empathy for another dominant mother, despite her Jennie-like pronouncement, is consistent with Benchley's forgivingly close relationship to his own mother. (The novel's understanding tone possibly had increased poignancy given Jennie's death at a near-parallel time – 1936). The child's death in *A Handful of Dust* generates an anthem of "It wasn't anybody's fault," an apt description of the novel's dark humor. Waugh's work is based on the funny/sad plight of the directionless individual in the absurd modern world—a stance in tune with Benchley's life and comic art. (Fittingly, *The New Yorker* magazine is even used in *A Handful of Dust* as an arbiter of style.)

Benchley's affinity for the novel might also have been enhanced by an additional factor. Waugh's *A Handful of Dust* succeeds in a way long expected but never realized by Benchley. In most of Waugh's books, his "intention is simply to entertain" (a description applicable to Benchley's essays), but *A Handful of Dust* goes beyond this – "the result is both moving and reflective in a way outside most farce's range."[49]

Regardless of hypothesis, the novel's "It wasn't anybody's fault" applies equally to traumatically rash statements, untimely deaths, and the tongue-in-check Benchley motto which opens this essay: "I take life as it comes. ..." His embracing of this work, as with his comedy, suggests if "you can't go home again," part of home (a mother's influence) can be forever with you.

(Originally appeared in *HUMOR: International Journal of Humor Research*, 1993, Vol 6-3; Wes D. Gehring copyright.)

NOTES

1. Robert Benchley, *No Poems or Around the World Backwards and Sideways* (New York: Harper and Brothers, 1932), 230.
2. Nathaniel, Benchley, *Robert Benchley, A Biography* (New York: McGraw Hill, 1955), 30.
3. Mary Kay Rothbart, "Laughter in Young Children," *Psychological Bulletin* xx, 1973, 252, 253.
4. Robert Benchley, in *The Robert Benchley Collection* (unpublished), Box 5, Special Collections, Mugar Memorial Library, Boston University.
5. Robert Benchley, Diary Entry January 1, 1912, in *The Robert Benchley Collection*, Box 5.
6. Wes D. Gehring, "Marjorie Benchley Interview," October 20, 1990, author's files.
7. Howard R. Pollio, and John W. Edgerly, "Comedians and Comic Style," in *Humor and Laughter: Theory, Research and Application*, eds. Anthony J. Chapman, and Hugh C. Foot (London: John Wiley and Sons, 1976, 215-242.
8. Enid Welsford, *The Fool: His Social and Literary History* (New York: Farrar and Rinchart, 1935), 314-315.
9. Paul E. McGhee, *Humor: Its Origins and Development* (San Francisco: W. H. Freeman and Company, 1979), 192.
10. William Fry, and Melanie Allen, "Norman Lear," in *Make 'Em Laugh: Life Studies of Comedy Writers* (Palo Alto, CA: Science and Behavior Books, 1975), 13-41.
11. Gehring, Marjorie Benchley Interview.
12. James Thurber, *My Life and Hard Times* (1933 rpt. New York: Bantam Books, 1947), 41.
13. Robert, *After 1903—What?* (New York: Harper and Brothers, 1938), 232-233.

14. McGhee, *Humor and Its Origins and Developments*, 190.

15. McGhee, "On the Cognitive Origins of Incongruity Humor: Fantasy Assimilation Versus Assimilation," in *The Psychology of Humor* (New York: Academic Press, 1972), 68.

16. Robert Benchley, "My White Suit," *Gentleman's Quarterly*, July 1990), 181. The original essay appeared in Benchley's *My Ten Years in a Quandry and How They Grew* (Garden City, New York, 1936), 302-304.

17. Robert Benchley, Diary entry dated February 13, 1913.

18. Nathaniel Benchley, 70.

19. Robert Benchley, *Of All Things!* (Garden City, New York: Garden City Publishing, 1921), 122.

20. Ibid., 10.

21. Robert Benchley, Diary entry dated July 13, 1911.

22. Robert Benchley, *20,000 Leagues Under the Sea or David Copperfield* (Garden City, New York: Blue Ribbon Books, 1928), 34.

23. Ibid., 49.

24. Robert Benchley, "Drama and Some Forty-Niners," *LIFE* (humor magazine, not the later pictorial), June 16, 1921), 876.

25. Robert Benchley, Diary Entry, January 25, 1916.

26. Robert Benchley, Diary Entry January 1, 1912.

27. McGhee, *Humor: Its Origins and Developments*.

28. Robert Benchley, *From Bed to Worse Or Comforting Thoughts About the Bison* (New York: Harper and Brothers, 1934), 208.

29. Robert Benchley, *The Robert Benchley Collection* (unpublished 1941 letter), Box 11, Folder 8 (family correspondence), Special Collections, Mugar Memorial Library, Boston University.

30. Marion Meade, Dorothy Parker: What Fresh Hell Is This? (New York: Villard Books, 1988), 322.

31. Robert Benchley, *Pluck and Luck* (New York: Henry Holt and Company, 1925), 6.

32. Ibid., 209.

33. Robert Benchley, "The Younger Literary Set," *Life*, May 3, 1923, 20.

34. Robert Benchley, Original 1938, Script, "How to Raise a Baby," in *The Robert Benchley Papers* (unpublished), Box D, Archives of the Performing Arts, Doeheny Library, University of Southern California (USC), Los Angeles.

35. Robert Benchley, *No Poems or Around the World, Backwards and Sideways*, 14-21.

36. Robert Benchley, Diary Dated September 6, 1916, Box 5 (Boston University).

37. Robert Benchley, Diary Dated February 19, 1916; Box 5, (Boston University).

38. S. J. Perelman, *Dawn Ginsbergh's Revenge* (New York: Random House, 1940), 102.

39. S. J. Perelman, *Look Who's Talking* (New York: Random House, 1940), 45-53.

40. Dorothy Herriman, S. J. Perelman: A Life (New York: Simon and Schuster, 1986), 193.

41. Virginia Woolf, "Eliza and Sterne," in *Granite and Rainbows: Essays* (New York: Harcourt Brace Jovanovich, 1986), 176.

42. Robert Benchley, 1928 Letter, in The Robert Benchley Collection (unpublished), Box 10, Fold 9 (Boston University).

43. Robert Benchley, Letters dated September 3, 1944 (unpublished), Box 11, Folder 11; Letter dated June 28, 1933 (unpublished), Box 10, Folder 13, (Boston University).

44. Robert Benchley, Letter dated July 7, 1929 (unpublished), Box 10, Folder 9 (Boston University).

45. Babette Rosmond, *Robert Benchley: His Life and Good Times* (Garden City, New York: Doubleday, 1970), 109.

46. Evelyn, Waugh, *A Handful of Dust* (1934 rpt. Boston: Little, Brown and Company, 1962), 162.

47. James Thurber, Letter in *Collecting Himself: James Thurber on Writing and Writers, Humor and Himself* (1949); rpt. New York: Harper and Row, 1989), 45.

48. Martin Stannard, Evelyn Waugh: The Early Years, 1903-1939 (New York: W. W. Norton, 1987), 361-362.

49. Kenneth McLeigh, *Arts in the Twentieth* Century (New York: Viking Penguin, 1986), 191.

GENRES AND/OR DIRECTORS

ACROSS GENRE LINES:

Five Key Factors For
Road Pictures

THE ROAD STORY was nothing new when Cervantes wrote what is often credited as the first novel, *Don Quixote* (1605/1615). And road pictures have been a movie staple since the early silents, such as Charlie Chaplin's nomadic Tramp forever shuffling down yet another dusty road. Indeed, my favorite examples of the phenomenon fall under the genre umbrella of personality comedian, be it the ongoing misadventures of Chaplin's "little fellow," Bob Hope and Bing Crosby teaming up for all those "road pictures" (seven between 1940 and 1962), Steve Martin and John Candy persevering through *Planes, Trains & Automobiles* (1987), and so on.

The beauty of the road picture, however, is that variations exist in all genres. For instance, romantic and screwball comedy have many classics of the form, including Frank Capra's much celebrated *It Happened One Night* (1934), in which Clark Gable's babysitting reporter eventually falls in love with the story's runaway heiress (Claudette Colbert). The first movie to win all five major Academy Awards (Best Picture, Actor, Actress, Screenplay, and Director), it has been an unofficial blueprint for many romantic road pictures ever since, such as Rob Reiner's neglected *The Sure Thing* (1985, with John Cusack).

Obviously, the road picture is also a given for the Western, America's most mythic genre, whether one is talking about John Wayne's Odyssey-like journey to find a niece kidnapped by Indians in John Ford's *The Searchers* (1956), or Paul Newman and Robert Redford being the object of an entirely different sort of chase in George Roy Hill's *Butch Cassidy and the Sundance Kid* (1969). Another watershed Western by Ford telegraphs its road picture status by its very title, *Stagecoach* (1939, which made Wayne a star).

How about trolling deep dish art cinema for road pictures? One need go no further than the modern father figure for the genre, Sweden's Ingmar Bergman. Arguably his two greatest films embrace the picaresque form: *The Seventh Seal* and *Wild Strawberries* (both 1957). In the former, a knight returning from the Crusades encounters death and drags out the inevitable by a prolonged chess match with the grim reaper. In *Wild Strawberries*, an elderly professor reviews his past on an extended car trip to receive an honorary degree from his old university.

If one moves to the world of fantasy, what's more famous than Dorothy's (Judy Garland) adventures on the Yellow Brick Road of *The Wizard of Oz* (1939)? A feminist out for a new age melodrama would be hard pressed to top Ridley Scott's *Thelma & Louise* (1991), with title characters Susan Sarandon and Geena Davis excelling at standard road movie shtick. The catalyst for "New American Cinema" was anchored in two road pictures, Arthur Penn's gangster/western/dark comedy *Bonnie and Clyde* (1967, with Warren Beatty and Faye Dunaway), and Dennis Hopper's tale of alienated youth, *Easy Rider* (1969, with Peter Fonda and a brief star-making turn by Jack Nicholson). In the mood for an epic war movie which doubles as a darkly comic anti-war movie? Go no further than Francis Ford Coppola's *Apocalypse Now* (1979), in which Martin Sheen journeys up-river after Marlon Brando in a Vietnam War take upon Joseph Conrad's *Heart of Darkness*.

Travel is also at the heart of Sci-Fi fantasy, with George Lucas' *Star Wars* (1977) and the rescue of the princess (Carrie Fisher), actually being inspired by Ford's *The Searchers*. Taking Sci-Fi fantasy in a different direction, all cinematic variations of H.G. Wells' *The Time Machine* (1895) are essentially "road" pictures. But thanks to Wells, who actually coined the term "time machine," one could travel (through the years) without leaving your home … or, at least where "home" used to be.

But what do these and so many other genre variations of the road picture have in common? First, they allow our central character(s) an ever changing backdrop for plot twists, from the apocalyptic horrors of the near future in the *Mad Max* movies, to the comedy inherent in Pee-wee Herman (Paul Reubens) tracing his stolen bike to the Alamo in Tim Burton's *Pee-wee's Big Adventure* (1985). Personality comedy road trip pictures also have the instant bonus of memorable comic clashes between the funny man persona and his backdrop. For instance, seeing Chaplin's Klondike-bound Tramp skidding around a glacier in *The Gold Rush* (1925) is delightfully incongruous, just as the traditional garb of Laurel &

Clark Gable and Claudette Colbert beginning a journey to love in *It Happened One Night* (1934), maybe cinema's most romantic title.

Hardy is amusingly out of place on their trek through cowboy country in *Way Out West* (1937).

Second, along similar lines, the road movie allows our hero or heroine to interact with a constantly changing cast of characters. Wayne's cowboy in *The Searchers* encounters every Western type, including Indians, cavalry, settlers, outlaws, Texas Rangers, and a Mexican profiteer. Sci-Fi fantasy does this character smorgasbord one better by literally taking the viewer out of this world, such as the intergalactic Western-like frontier bar scene from *Star Wars*.

In Ruben Fleischner's dark comedy horror picture *Zombieland* (2009), Woody Harrelson' road trip (with friends) across Southwestern America, after some sort of zombie apocalypse, necessitates they come in contact with random survivors, sexy hucksters, Bill Murray playing himself … not to mention *every* variety of zombie. Regardless, in all these and other road movie scenarios, once the story has milked all the entertainment value from said characters, the films, to borrow a song title from the nomadic *The Wiz* (1978), go into an *Ease on Down the Road* mode. Because there are always new characters and/or plot twists *down the road*.

A third component shared by road pictures is a parallel *inward* journey. Characters hit the highway for a myriad of reasons, including escape, adventure, and assorted quests. But if the stories are artfully done, the movies will also showcase character self-discovery ... which ideally impacts viewers, too. Garland's Dorothy learns the importance of home and family in *The Wizard of Oz*. Gable and Colbert discover two takes on love in *It Happened One Night*. She grows up, and he realizes a romantic gift for nurturing. Bergman's knight and professor, two figures facing death, ultimately take actions which help others, easing their own acceptance of the end. Wayne's "Searcher" assumes a modicum of tolerance. But more importantly, he stoically accepts a wanderer's fate, ironically paralleling the curse he has inflicted upon one of his Indian enemies. That is, because Wayne's Ethan has shot out the eyes of a dead brave, and Native American custom suggests the warrior will forever blindly wander in the spirit world. This wandering now will be Wayne's real world sentence.

These and other nomadic cinema protagonists have grown, in part, through the new characters and settings they have experienced on the road. Like the old axiom that travel broadens one's education, suddenly encountering different values forces one to re-evaluate and/or better articulate core beliefs. Though more startlingly obvious in fantasy, such as Dorothy in Technicolor Oz, or Alice's equally surreal "trip" in Wonderland, where everything is topsyturvydom, even the most realistic road movie figures, such as Cusak's hitchhiking college student from *The Sure Thing*, are forever changed by their journey.

Fourth, though personal enlightenment is a central element to the successful road movie, this learning curve is often attached to a "buddy picture" mentality. These films are frequently just as much about with whom one travels, versus the people and places encountered on the way. Of course, many such pairings begin with the old adage, "familiarity breeds contempt." For example, transportation woes force two opposite personality types to travel together, such as Martin and Candy in *Planes Trains & Automobiles*, or more recently, Robert Downey, Jr., and Zach Galifianakis in *Due Date* (2010).

Regardless, over time (and miles) these odd couples find a greater compassion for tolerance and sacrifice. Paradoxically, the end result of such initial forced teamings is often a love story, whether bonding buddies, like Martin and Candy, or the legendary romance of Gable and Colbert in *It Happened One Night*, or Humphrey Bogart and Katharine

Hepburn in John Huston's *The African Queen* (1951). Yet, the joining of some journeying opposites can have a different story trajectory. The duo begins in friendship, only to bicker through some rocky passages, before reaching a greater understanding of self. For instance, this would be the case with *Bonnie and Clyde, Butch Cassidy and the Sundance Kid*, and *Thelma & Louise*.

Still, whenever the team configuration is applied to the road movie, either as an initially prickly duo, or as bosom buddies, both parties are not guaranteed picture-closing light bulb moments. This is most poignantly demonstrated late in *Bonnie and Clyde*, when Dunaway's fatalistic character asks Clyde how he would change things, if they could magically transport their new found love to some other parallel universe. When Beatty's obtuse reply begins with the suggestion the duo could live in one state, and only rob in another, Dunaway's liquid eyes telegraph her realization that Clyde remains the simple man/child she first knew. The tragic depth of the movie is then anchored in her staying the (violent) course of their love story, despite knowing its outcome.

John Huston excelled at similar road movie stories, in which one participant does not grow from the journey. Seminal examples include *The Treasure of the Sierra Madre* (1948) and *The Man Who Would Be King* (1975). Both pictures are studies in greed and vagabond characters at their worst, with *Treasures'* s Bogart and *King's* Sean Connery paying the ultimate price. But each man's compatriots ultimately survive by learning from the self-centered obsessions of Bogart and Connery.

Naturally, there are also comedic takes upon this screen scenario, where one traveler becomes wiser and his sidekick remains an amusing buffoon. This is normally the case in the Hope and Crosby *Road Pictures*, with old ski nose remaining delightfully dense. This is best demonstrated at the close of the *Road to Utopia* (1946), when the picture returns to a contemporary framing device, in which Hope, Crosby, and their perennial best girl (Dorothy Lamour) are elderly citizens. But for once, Hope seems to have won the romantic battle, because Lamour is his wife. The qualifier comes when their only child drops in—a young Crosby. Poor Hope has been cuckolded for years ... and it has yet to register with him.

A fifth and final road movie factor involves a travelogue element. Just as the draw of a real trip usually involves seeing special sights along the way, a road film getaway generally does the same thing. Granted, this was a greater attraction in less cosmopolitan times. For instance, the first documentary, Robert Flaherty's *Nanook of the North* (1922), about the nomadic life of an Eskimo and his family, was a phenomenon because no one had seen anything like it. Today, there are countless outlets for such imagery, starting with cable television's Discovery channel.

Still, famous backdrops are often an intrinsic part of picaresque pictures, especially in the thriller work of Alfred Hitchcock. This is best exemplified by his quintessential *North by Northwest* (1959, whose working title, *The Man on Lincoln's Nose*, referenced its Mount Rushmore finale). But this Cary Grant cross country chase movie also offers up: murder at the U.N., a crop-dusting death scene in Indiana, and farcical intrigue on Hitchcock's favorite means of transportation—a luxurious train. The director's pivotal early British picture *The 39 Steps* (1935, upon which *North by Northwest* loosely draws), follows another innocent man (Robert Donat) crisscrossing England and Scotland to also prove his innocence.

Cary Grant was novelist Ian Fleming's inspiration for the James Bond character. *North by Northwest* was, in many ways, a Bond-like movie. The Bond films, starting with *Dr. No* (1962, Sean Connery), are the longest running "A" series in cinema history, and as with the Hitchcock thriller, varied provocative locations are equally crucial. Moreover, the Bond movies continue to inspire countless knock-off action thrillers and parodies which are all driven, in part, by travel through exotic backdrops.

Since most genres are awash with road movies, as chronicled by this brief examination of its five pivotal components, any attempt to define the picaresque tale as a genre would prove too unwieldy. The form is most beneficially applied as a descriptive adjective to a pre-existing genre, such as a *road* comedy. Otherwise, film study courts the overkill factor that once inspired the definition of movie censorship as "someone who even sees three meanings in a double-entendre." Regardless, however you choose to "read" your road movie map, may all your film trips be enlightening.

THE POPULIST FILMS OF ROBERT REDFORD

LIKE MOST MAJOR MOVIE STARS, Robert Redford has assayed many parts. The most memorable include his career-establishing outlaw in *Butch Cassidy and the Sundance Kid* (1969), the mountain man *Jeremiah Johnson* (1972), the novice politician in *The Candidate* (1972), the writer in *The Way We Were* (1973), the con artist of *The Sting* (1973), an investigative journalist in *All the President's Men* (1976), a contemporary cowboy in *The Electric Horseman* (1979), a baseball player in *The Natural* (1984), the great hunter and aviator Denys Finch Hatton from *Out of Africa* (1985), the security expert of *Sneakers* (1992), and the TV news director in *Up Close and Personal* (1996).

Also, like most great stars, even his lesser works have their moments, such as the conservative attorney in *Barefoot in the Park* (1967), the reluctant sheriff of *Tell Them Willie Boy is Here* (1969), the mysterious gangster of F. Scott Fitzgerald's *The Great Gatsby* (1974), the flyer in *The Great Waldo Pepper* (1975), a CIA low-level functionary in *Three Days of the Condor* (1975), the warden of *Brubaker* (1980), and the assistant district attorney in *Legal Eagles* (1986).

No major career is without a few clunkers. Two Redford candidates which come readily to mind are *Little Fauss and Big Halsy* (1974) and *Havana* (1990). In the former, he plays a thoroughly unlike motorcycle racer, while the latter work casts him as a self-centered gambler in a picture that tries too hard to be a Cuban *Casablanca*. What is most impressive about Redford's filmography is that the number of true failures is decidedly modest.

Redford's batting average as a director is even higher. Indeed, his greatest critical success has come behind the camera. He won an

Academy Award in his directorial debut on *Ordinary People* (1980), a family melodrama that won the best picture Oscar as well. His direction of *Quiz Show* (1994), a thoughtful examination of the TV scandal of the 1950s, rated a second nomination. Although he has directed just three other pictures, each has been critically acclaimed: the populist fantasy *The Milagro Beanfield War* (1988), the elegiac coming-of-age story *A River Runs Through It* (1992), and a western tale of healing and love reborn, *The Horse Whisperer* (1998).

There are five basic themes that surface in Redford's acting resume. First, the past is preferable to the present. A high percentage of his work has a period setting, and frequently, even the contemporary films are rooted in the past, such as the Old West undercurrent of both *The Electric Horseman* and *The Horse Whisperer*.

Second, the superiority of the past often is tied to a country setting. In the populist tradition of director Frank Capra, Redford's characters draw strength from the land, be it the mountain man world of Jeremiah Johnson or the Montana mountains of horse whisperer Tom Booker. It bears noting that Capra's celebrated *Mr. Smith Goes to Washington* (1939) is based on the story *The Gentleman From Montana*.

Also like Capra, praise for the pastoral past in Redford movies often means contrasting it with a negative modern, urban setting. The dichotomy is showcased most effectively in *The Electric Horseman*, where the everything-for-sale, anything-for-a-buck tradition of Las Vegas becomes synonymous with the film's evil conglomerate, whose exploitation includes Rising Star—the champion stallion that is the organization's logo.

As in *The Horse Whisperer*, the saving of a horse (and pivotal people around it) involves a return to the American frontier. *The Electric Horseman* escape is depicted imaginatively in a scene where Redford's Sonny Steele (in his twinkling, corporate cowboy outfit) rides the stallion out of Caesar's Palace, where he and the horse briefly have appeared on stage, and down the equally twinkling Vegas strip. They seem to represent just one more product for sale in a sea of neon.

Their disappearing act also represents a given for populism. One does what is right simply because it is right, and then moves on. There is no thought of a reward in this life or another. George Washington set a precedent for the genre by walking away from the presidency after two terms. It was the first time in modern Western culture that a leader had voluntarily relinquished his power. At the time, it shocked the world. Even Napoleon wrote about it in his diaries.

Steele then pulls the plug on this one-man light show (both literally and, in terms of his conglomerate connection, figuratively), and man and horse seem magically to disappear. This ingeniously articulates the spell they need to beat the company. Visually and symbolically, the scene on the Vegas strip recalls George Bailey's run down a similar street of pleasure in Capra's *It's a Wonderful Life* (1946). In both cases, such a street is symptomatic of the catalyst for change then taking place in each character.

Third, even when not playing historic figures who have become legends, such as the Sundance Kid or Jeremiah Johnson, Redford often gives characters a mythic aura. No better examples exist than the romantic Denys Hatton in *Out of Africa* or the Arthurian ballplayer of *The Natural*. Fittingly, both characters belong to the past (the 1920s and 1930s, respectively) and are defined by the land, from the swashbuckling flyer swooping over his beloved African plains to a heartland hitter who returns to the farm.

The Natural, however, is more entertaining theatrically in creating this legendary aura. Playing for a team called the Knights, batting with the seemingly Excalibur-like *Wonderboy*, and winning despite the evil intervention of a club owner justifies comparing this pennant race to a quest for the Holy Grail. The way in which Redford's character accomplishes the task—a dramatic ninth-inning homer into the stadium's floodlights that causes the electrical system to short out, flooding the field with a fireworks-like shower of sparks, would seem a special gift from the gods.

Redford often enhances the mythic dimension, even when it involves well-known prior properties. For instance, the classic baseball novel from which *The Natural* is drawn has the central player striking out in the ninth, with his fans assuming he has thrown the game. The best-selling novel from which *The Horse Whisperer* is adapted has a title character who easily gives himself over to an affair, while Redford's "reading" of the part assumes an ethically higher ground.

POLITICAL EVILS

Fourth, taking another page from Capra populism, Redford films often posit that the world's ills are the result of an evil minority. Besides *The Electric Horseman* conglomerate or the crooked owner in *The Natural*, evil for Redford (and Capra) is most synonymous with politics.

Robert Redford about to embrace a true populist direction in
The Electric Horseman (1979).

The political Redford movie, as well as being a Capraesque picture for the 1970s (à la *Mr. Smith Goes to Washington*), is *All the President's Men*. Redford and Dustin Hoffman play investigative reporters Bob Woodward and Carl Bernstein, the men responsible for linking Watergate to the Nixon White House. Though the movie is based upon the Woodward/ Bernstein book of the same name, Redford's involvement in the project started so early he actually influenced the form the book assumed.

In *The Candidate*, he plays an idealistic storefront lawyer, John McKay. His character is asked to run for the Senate against a seemingly unbeatable incumbent. The political carrot from the party campaign manager is that, since his opponent is a shoo-in, McKay can be totally candid in speaking about his ideas, without political gimmicks or dirty tricks.

As in Warren Beatty's later *Bulworth* (1998) the people respond to this seeming oxymoron—an honest politician. However, when Redford's McKay stands a chance of winning, the party packagers move in and the unique individual is lost in the shuffle. When he wins an upset victory, the overwhelmed candidate is reduced to asking his campaign manager,

"What do we do now?" The cynical answer comes in a burst of movie-closing presidential music—"Hail to the Chief."

McKay has become the politician he never wanted to be, where winning, not issues and honesty, is the bottom line. Redford's character has much in common with presidential candidate Grant Matthews (Spencer Tracy) in Capra's *State of the Union* (1948). Both McKay and Matthews are outspoken, charismatic non-politicians who gradually allow the party machine to manipulate them. Matthews ultimately breaks away, but McKay's final position is more darkly nebulous.

One also might include Redford's *Three Days of the Condor*, from the James Grady novel, among his political films, though it is more thriller than Capraesque, made during the conspiracy-obsessed 1970s (fed by Watergate). Redford's character is a low-level reader for the CIA—hunting for ideas the organization might convert to reality. Briefly out of the office, he returns to find his coworkers murdered.

On the lam and searching for answers, he barely escapes assassination twice. Ultimately, he learns the killings were orchestrated by a faction within the CIA. Redford's character finally finds freedom by taking his story of clandestine operations to the newspapers—a traditional safety-valve conclusion for political thrillers. Though *Condor* is not as dark as Beatty's conspiracy film *The Parallax View* (1974), in which the reporter is murdered, both the Redford and Beatty movies play upon a society grown distrustful of the government, and politicians in general.

In *Sneakers*, Redford plays a former political computer trickster now leading an eccentric gang of security experts. The Watergate era prologue propels the movie into a conspiracy story for the 1990s, but, unlike *Condor*, the accent is more on comedy and the heavies do not have ties to Uncle Sam. Indeed, with James Early Jones ultimately playing a reluctant government Santa, the system comes out in a positive light.

A fifth Redford theme is the difficulty of modern love. There is a certain irony in this, given, that his work often looks to the past, and there are a million sappy clichés attached to old-fashioned loves stories. Nevertheless, his characters are so fiercely independent, regardless of the period, that their proclivity to end up alone does not seem inconsistant. In probably Redford's most romantic film, *Out of Africa*, Hatton's need for solitude dooms a traditional relationship with Meryl Streep's farmer/storyteller, Karen Blixen. Granted, he seems to be coming around but his untimely death ultimately fits Redford's loner persona.

There are few lasting Redford movie relationships because his leading ladies often portray equally independent and different characters. In *The Electric Horseman* and *The Horse Whisperer*, he is romantically teamed with two sophisticated East Coast journalists, played by Jane Fonda and Kristin Scott Thomas, respectively. Even though there are lots of sparks, it is realistic that nothing permanent occurs. This is a clear break from the romantic payoff in Capra's populism, wherein the strong-willed heroine sublimates her career to that of the hero.

The ultimate case of romantic opposites in a Redford movie occurs in 1973's *The Way We Were*, where Barbra Streisand's Jewish activist is so taken with his WASPish, apolitical writer that portions of the film entertainingly play as a love story spoof. Predictably, despite all the hearts and arrows, their screen marriage is fated to self-destruct, too.

Years before the bought sexual favors of *Indecent Proposal* (1993), there was little longevity in Redford's early screen couplings. His cinematic alter ego often was portrayed as a womanizer and/or less than romantic. This is the case in *Butch Cassidy and the Sundance Kid, Downhill Racer* (1969), *Tell Them Willie Boy Is Here, Little Fauss and Big Halsy, The Candidate*, and *The Electric Horseman*.

An ongoing joke in *Butch Cassidy* has Paul Newman's Cassidy periodically chiding the Kid's lack of romanticism. For instance, there is the tone of Sundance's invitation to Bolivia for Katherine Ross' schoolmarm: "If you want to come with us, I won't stop you, but the minute you start to whine or make a nuisance, I don't care where we are, I'm dumping you flat." The scene is so patently unromantic that Butch's immediate comment invariably generates a big audience laugh: "Don't sugarcoat it like that, Sundance—tell her straight." Despite Ross being Sundance's girl, the film's most romantic moments are between her and Butch, such as their bicycle ride to the Oscar-winning song "Raindrops Keep Falling on My Head."

If the fact that this once Adonis-like actor's early screen roles are less than romantic runs counter to one's memory, the explanation might come in some dialogue from *The Way We Were*. Streisand's Katie asks his character if he is still a nice boy, knowing Redford's Hubbell has had an affair. He replies: "I never was. I only looked it to you ….When you love someone … you go deaf, dumb, and blind."

While his early audience constantly attempted to put him on a romantic pedestal, his films characters' actions undercut the romanticism. For example, when Katie and Hubbell first sleep together, she is on a romantic high and he is too drunk to know who he is with or what he is doing. Even the very idealized love of *The Natural* between his ballplayer and Glenn Close's earth mother is threatened by two femmes fatales (Barbara Hershey and Kim Basinger).

In recent years, Redford has allowed his characters to be more romantically sympathetic, as in *Up Close and Personal*, with an increased emphasis on feel-good films, but there has been a price to pay. In a 1992 *Esquire* profile, he said, "Some of my earlier stuff, *Downhill Racer, The Candidate*, was bleak, critical of the society. But … when you try to say something that's good about the society … you're tagged as a boy scout."

His ongoingly independent screen persona still dictates, however, that we do not think of him in long-term relationships. Thus, his character dies on a dangerous assignment soon after the *Up Close and Personal* marriage, and his strict personal code negates even an affair at the close of *The Horse Whisperer*. (A 1998 *New Yorker* profile had him seemingly obsessed with *Shane*, a 1953 film where Alan Ladd's cowboy also avoids an affair and a possible breakup of a marriage.)

DIRECTING

Several of the themes synonymous with Redford the actor spill over into his directing career. The most obvious is his embracing of Capra populism, especially as it is defined through his love of the land. This is demonstrated best in *The Milagro Beanfield War*, which centers on the imaginary New Mexico town of Milagro (Spanish for "miracle"), whose poor Hispanic population is threatened with displacement by Anglo outsiders.

Redford does a masterful job of updating the Capra heritage, from focusing on a Hispanic community instead of populism's standard WASP slant to showcasing a collective hero rather than the charismatic individual. Still, basic populist norms endure. Redford observed at the time (1988) in *American Film* magazine: "Most of the heroes in our culture are not aware that they're heroes." This could be the theme for populist movies as to why these heroes seldom have difficulty slipping back into anonymity once their cause has been fulfilled.

Milagro has several other Capra connections, from the evil characters having political roots (starting with a dishonest governor) to a small-town newspaper editor discussing "lost causes"—a key Capra buzz phrase, especially in *Mr. Smith Goes to Washington*. As with many populist movies since *It's a Wonderful Life*, *Milagro* has a fantasy-assisting component, in the guise of an old white-haired, poncho-draped angel, to make the happy ending more palatable.

The Horse Whisperer is a traditional populist vehicle, with an older Redford (the only time he has directed himself) as essentially a cracker-barrel cowboy. Like most such populist oracles, what he says invariably is wise and sometimes witty, such as his casual definition of a "horse whisperer": "I help horses with people problems."

The film is a window to an earlier rational world, where age equals insight by way of accumulated experience. Given time in such a populist past, most problems can be solved. Thus, Redford's character rescues both a troubled horse and its teenage owner, while at the same time he rediscovers his own capacity for love. Indeed, by helping someone or something else, like another rescued horse in *The Electric Horseman*, Redford helps his own often flawed character to right itself.

His third populist-directed film, *A River Runs Through It*, from Norman Maclean's poignantly eloquent novella, is about a boy growing up in rural Montana early this century. The dominating force is a Presbyterian minister father who taught his sons about passion and the nature of grace and art by way of an unlikely source—the techniques of fly-fishing.

All this is comically captured in the story's opening sentence: "In our family, there was no clear line between religion and fly-fishing." Redford later observed in a 1992 interview, "I was caught by the book as soon as I read the first line." This and other winning Maclean passages would be retained in the movie by voice-over narration. In the same interview, Redford coupled his interest in the personal grace expressed by Maclean with the "opportunity to say [via beautiful images from rural Montana] that this is the way our environment was when we took it for granted, and for the most part, it's gone." (The environmental message is a given in all of his populist pictures.)

The essentially new theme Redford brings to his directing is an exploration of the dysfunctional family and how it impacts the youngest member. Variations of this exist in all five Redford-directed films, but is most pronounced in *Ordinary People*, *A River Runs Through It*, and *The Horse Whisperer*. In *Ordinary People*, a wealthy family self-destructs after the drowning death of the older son. The guilt-ridden younger brother (Timothy Hutton), who survived the sailing accident, must also cope with knowing his mother (Mary Tyler Moore) wishes he had been the child to die.

The Horse Whisperer has a somewhat similar scenario. A 14-year-old girl is involved in a dreadful riding accident, resulting in a lost leg, the death of a friend, a severely hurt and traumatized horse, and clinical depression. Her high-powered career mother cannot seem to communicate with her.

River is a less obvious dysfunctional story. There is no early tragedy, and many viewers even are oblivious to a problem. Yet, despite the bonding through fly-fishing, there is a communication block between the father (Tom Skerritt) and his sons, particularly the younger one (Brad Pitt). Whereas the other two films work toward a healing process, the sudden unsolved murder of the younger son late in the movie leaves the viewer and the family shattered, grasping for answers.

This slant on the dysfunctional family is disturbing both because one assumes it is more common and because Redford bravely questions a character type—the enigmatic, stoical patriarch—that still often is celebrated in America. Indeed, it is the type of description used to describe both the real Redford and his favorite screen character—the loner cowboy. (An entertainingly insightful stand-up comic labeled Redford the "Camus Cowboy.")

River is his most intellectually and emotionally stimulating work, both because he saw his own troubled boyhood in the story and because the joint celebration of life and the American wilderness is quintessential Redford. Between his narration and the casting of a young, Redford-like Pitt as the younger son, his presence pervades the picture. Whatever one's favorite Redford film, his provocative exploration of the American experience has resulted—like Capra's work—in solid entertainment and a more realistic populist legacy all its own.

THE MANY FACES OF
MOVIE COMEDY

THERE IS A TENDENCY TO JAM everything comic under one overextended umbrella. I suggest that movie comedies can be examined best by breaking them down into five categories: screwball, populist, black, parody, and personality-driven.

In screwball comedy, the narrative is propelled by the humorous misadventures of people in love, usually fueled by the dominating eccentricities of the woman, as in *What's Up, Doc* (1972). In a populist comedy like *Field of Dream* (1989), the story is rooted in the Frank Capra-like world of hope, celebrating the people's inherent goodness. A black comedy, such as *Catch-22* (1970), does just the opposite, portraying an absurd world with a self-centered, mean-spirited population. In a parody like *Young Frankenstein* (1974), the genre being spoofed—in this case, the horror movie—is the star.

Any competent performer could be cast for this quartet of movie types. In the personality comedy film, though, only one person—a Groucho Marx, Robin Williams, or Jim Carrey—can carry that picture, since it is tailored to that actor's persona. Such pictures are not theme-driven, like other comedies, but, rather, clown-directed.

There are three basic components to the personality comedian approach, besides whatever specific schtick one associates with a favorite clown. First, American comedy always has placed a high premium on physical and/or visual comedy. Besides the obvious pratfalls or sight gags one would associate with comedy giants who came out of the silent era, such as Charlie Chaplin or Stan Laurel and Oliver Hardy, personality comedians often simply look funny.

Through costume, makeup, shape, or fluid contortions of face and body, clowns telegraph the message that this will be comedy. Their funny appearance is a key in the clown genre, even when the comic personality might be more linked to verbal humor. For example, while the machine-gun patter of Groucho is famous, it is more than a little dependent upon the visual. Lillian Roth, the young heroine of *Animal Crackers* (1930), in her 1954 autobiography, *I'll Cry Tomorrow*, best described the total Groucho visual package when she explained why she kept giggling in retakes of a scene they had together: "The line itself wasn't so hilarious, but I knew Groucho was going to say it with the big cigar jutting from his clenched teeth, his eyebrows palpitating, and that he would be off afterwards in that runaway crouch of his; and the thought of what was coming was too much for me."

Another characteristic of clowns is that they generally are underdogs who frequently exhibit comically incompetent behavior. The frustrated clown's inadequacies often are showcased in some basic physical task, such as Laurel and Hardy trying to put a radio antenna on a roof, Woody Allen's bumper car-like attempts to drive an automobile in "Annie Hall" (1977), and Steve Martin relearning how to walk while his body is being inhabited by the spirit of Lily Tomlin in *All of Me* (1984).

A final clown trait is that, as outsiders, they frequently are nomadic. Fittingly, cinema's greatest clown, Chaplin, is linked closely to the picaresque through his alter ego as a wandering tramp and the celebrated imagery of him shuffling down life's highways. Not coincidentally, the inspired teaming of Bob Hope and Bing Crosby was evidenced in a series of "Road" pictures in which the duo comically wander about the globe. Regardless of the comedian, travel allows the clown to find humor in new places and people, be it Harry Langdon's cross-country walkathon in *Tramp, Tramp, Tramp* (1926) or the quest to get home in the Steve Martin-John Candy *Planes, Trains, and Automobiles* (1987). As the latter title suggests, the mode of transportation sometimes can become an end in itself. The machine-oriented Buster Keaton led the way with his own ocean liner in *The Navigator* (1924) and the ultimate nonstop train picture, *The General* (1927).

Moreover, sometimes the appearance of the mode of transportation can add humor to the film, such as Laurel and Hardy's propensity to destroy Model-T Fords. This is best exemplified in *Hog Wild* (1930), when a street car crash squeezes the Ford into an upward bound vehicle ten feet tall ... which is still drivable! Martin and Candy do a variation upon this in *Trains, Planes, and Automobile*—when they essentially destroy a rental car which remains drivable. The Marx Brothers comically destroy a 1940 *Go West* train for kindling. Of course, the comic topper is when the vehicle looks funny from the get-go, such as Buster Keaton's delightful based-in-reality *choo-choo* in 1923's *Our Hospitality.*

While personality humor depends upon a clownish lead, screwball comedy keys upon a romantic couple. Personality comedians have existed since the earliest days of cinema, but the screwball duo (farce American style) arose during the Depression. The old "boy-meets-

Bob Hope breaks up Bing Crosby on the set of the *Road to Bali* (1952)

girl" formula turned topsy-turvy generally presents the zany woman-dominated courtship of the American rich, with the male target seldom being informed that open season has arrived. It is as if to say that, in an irrational world—underlined at the time by the Depression—the only effective way to respond to love is in an irrational manner.

The definitive example is director Howard Hawks' *Bringing up Baby* (1938), with Cary Grant playing an absent-minded professor-scientist and Katharine Hepburn a daffy Connecticut socialite. Grant, when not interacting with rich patrons of the arts to obtain contributions to his museum, is busy assembling the giant skeleton of a brontosaurus. The latter detail is pivotal, since it symbolizes the lifeless future he faces as an academic engaged to a suffocating woman aptly named Swallow.

The *Baby* of the title is a leopard in Hepburn's possession—representing the "life" she can bring to his world. The bottom line in this genre, besides the la-de-da escapism (especially big during bad economic times), is that the screwball woman rescues the male from a life of rigidity. Fittingly, *Bringing Up Baby* ends with Grant realizing he loves Hepburn just after she has caused his symbolic, rigid brontosaurus skeleton to collapse. The movie was remade loosely by Peter Bogdanovich to great critical and commercial success as *What's Up Doc?*, with Ryan O'Neal and Barbra Streisand essaying the star roles, and a then new-to-film Madeline Kahn stealing the show as the life-sucking fiancée.

In cinema's modern era (since 1960), the most celebrated screwball comedy is Steve Gordon's *Arthur* (1981), which showcases a different slant on the danger of a rigid, male lifestyle. Dudley Moore plays a wealthy, wonderfully engaging man/child threatened by another deadly fiancée and a 9-to-5 job working for her fascist father. Unlike Grant, Moore is enjoying life to its fullest, but an arranged marriage looks to change that, until his love for working-class girl Liza Minnelli ultimately solves things.

The blue-collar romantic component sometimes was part of the Depression screwball formula, too. It allowed the decadent escapist slant to have a "Cinderella" factor—romance as a fairytale. Moreover, this screwball mixing of the classes underlines the implosive nature of the genre—opposites (both in personality and personal wealth) attract. The most outrageous example of this phenomenon occurs in *Pretty Woman* (1990), when Julia Roberts' free-spirited hooker rescues corporate raider Richard Gere from a cold, rigid lifestyle and is rewarded with a fairytale conclusion.

During the 1930s' golden age of screwball comedy, there were two dominant heroine types, best contrasted in the work of Carole Lombard and Irene Dunne. Lombard was a dizzy physical force (not above socking her leading man) from the opening minutes of each movie; Dunne was the proper lady (often with musical ties) who assumed an eccentric cover midway into the picture. Lombard was at her best in Gregory La Cava's *My Man Godfrey* (1936), while Dunne was incomparable in Leo McCarey's *The Awful Truth* (1937). Both roles generated Academy Award nominations for the actresses. Yet, one best might summarize screwball comedy, past or present, from a *My Man Godfrey* scene devoid of Lombard. When someone likens the film's socialite scavenger hunt gathering to a mental asylum, Eugene Pallette, playing Lombard's wealthy father, observes, "All you need is an empty room and the right kind of people."

CAPRAESQUE COMEDY

Populism, the third genre of comedy, is another product of the 1930s Depression. The archetypal exemplar is director Frank Capra, especially in his central populist films: *Mr. Deeds Goes to Town* (1936), *You Can't Take It with You* (1938), *Mr. Smith Goes to Washington* (1939), *Meet John Doe* (1941), and *It's a Wonderful Life* (1946). They embrace a patriotically American belief that the superior and majority will of the common man forever is threatened by the usurping, sophisticated, evil few. The implication at the time was that the latter caused things like the Depression. Consequently, this often involves a political agenda, something Capra acknowledges in his 1971 autobiography, *The Name Above the Title*, when he notes the influence of crackerbarrel populist Will Rogers. Fittingly, this usually means appropriating real American populist figures. For instance, in *Mr. Smith Goes to Washington*, when the titular young senator (Jimmy Stewart) arrives in the Capital, he immediately visits the Lincoln Memorial. Later, when he has seen the political corruption and nearly been destroyed by it, he returns to "worship" and gain strength at the memorial. Because of this strength (as well as Lincoln's model), the idealistic Washington freshman is able to fight the most courageous of battles against the most corrupt of political machines.

Through its countless television broadcasts, *It's a Wonderful Life* is populism's most well-known example. Again, Capra uses Stewart as everyman figure George Bailey, pitting him against Lionel Barrymore's evil Mr. Potter. The movie is a microcosm of populism basics, from its celebration of family and traditional values, to its embracing of personal sacrifice for the common good. Capra added a fantasy wrinkle by giving Bailey a guardian angel when the central character turns suicidal.

The fantasy trait is important, because it makes populism more palatable to the viewer who otherwise might find the films too idealistic. (Period critics sometimes kidded the founding father/director by calling his work "Carpra-corn.") Consequently, one of the most celebrated modern populist films, *Field of Dreams* (1989), was a conscious attempt by director Phil Alden to emulate the fantasy populism of *It's a Wonderful Life*. *Field of Dreams* also embraces the Christian connection at the heart of Capra's work: good deeds are rewarded; a higher power looks out for us and second chances can defy even death.

Through the years, countless populist variations have followed the Capra lead. Versatile comedy director and Capra friend Leo McCarey made the acclaimed *Going My Way* (1944) and *The Bells of St. Mary's* (1945), with Bing Crosby's performance as a populist priest winning him an Oscar in the former. Fittingly, Capra reminds us of McCarey when George Bailey is allowed to return to life and retrace the steps of his *Christmas Carol* trip through the hometown that would not have existed had he not been born. *The Bells of St. Mary's* is advertised on a theater marquee he passes, and Bailey underlines the moment by saying, "Merry Christmas, movie house!"

Populism sometimes has been given a new twist by casting a woman in the central role, from the Oscar-winning turns by Loretta Young in *The Farmer's Daughter* (1947) and Judy Holliday in *Born Yesterday* (1950), to Goldie Hawn in *Protocol* (1984). All three owe more than a little to *Mr. Smith Goes to Washington*. Indeed, *The Farmer's Daughter* originally was titled *Katie for Congress*.

More recent examples would range from the Robert Redford-directed *The Milagro Beanfield War* (1988), giving populism an ethnic slant, to Ivan Reitman's more traditionally Capraesque *Dave* (1993), with everyman Kevin Kline suddenly finding himself in the guise of president in a crooked Washington. Today's most consistently populist director is Ron Howard, whose films constantly concentrate on family and/or people learning to work together, from Japanese automotive supervisors in the U. S. in *Gung Ho* (1986), to getting astronauts home in *Apollo 13* (1995).

Populism's mirror opposite is black comedy. Dark humor has three interrelated themes: man as beast, the absurdity of the world, and the omnipresence of death. While populism has man as inherently good, living in a rational world, with a life after death, the black comedy of Stanley Kubrick's *Dr. Strangelove or: How I Learned to Stop Worrying and Love the Bomb* (1964) or *Catch-22* makes mankind out to be a cosmic joke whose slogan best might be "Life's a bitch and then you die."

At its most basic, dark humor skewers society's most sacredly serious subjects—especially death. For instance, what seemingly could be more tasteless than a comedy based on teen suicide? Nevertheless, two of black humor's most inspired efforts do just that—*Harold and Maude* (1971) and *Heathers* (1989). Both are excellent showcases of the genre's dysfunctional family, though Oliver Stone's *Natural Born Killers* (1994) wins the brass ring as the ultimate example, with its in-film "I Love Mallory" attack on 1950s family television.

Suicide is never far from dark comedy—dramatically demonstrating that its disregard for life begins with the individual. Life is full of pain, and suicide provides a way around this, as the title to the *M*A*S*H* (1970) theme song, "Suicide is Painless," dramatically proclaims. That this escape always has been an alternative to life's suffering is underscored by Ernst Lubitsch entitling a pioneering black comedy with William Shakespeare's celebrated wording for suicide, *To Be or Not to Be* (1942). Even Malcolm McDowell's ultimate nasty character in Stanley Kubrick's *A Clockwork Orange* (1971) attempts suicide after the government reprograms his brain, insisting that "I just want to die peacefully, with no pain." On a metaphorical level, suicide is an apt phrase for the literal implementation of the death wish-like tendency of modern man seemingly to rush toward an apocalypse of his own making, such as the inevitable mushroom cloud conclusion of *Dr. Strangelove*. Any and all institutions are suspect in the black humor genre.

Unlike populism, which preaches hope even in death, the message of dark comedy is that there is no message. Thus, the type sometimes is described as "beyond a joke" or "anti-comedy." It accents this on-the-edge nature for its audience ("Am I supposed to be laughing here?") by often fragmenting its narrative, such as in George Roy Hill's *Slaughterhouse-Five* (1972) or Quentin Tarantino's *Pulp Fiction* (1994), and thus making it difficult to follow. But life, of course, is merely a rough cut anyway. As Kafka observed, "The meaning of life is you die."

Like life, dark comedy is disjointed. It keeps the viewer off-balance by shock effects that are both visual, such as the leg protruding from the wood-shredder in the Coen Brothers' *Fargo* (1996), and/or auditory— McDowell's *Clockwork Orange* warbling of "Singin' in the Rain" as he stomps someone.

SKEWING THE FAMILIAR

While dark comedy encourages its life-as-chaos premise with an often less than linear story, parody is very structured. The parodist replicates the familiar pattern of a given genre, auteur, or specific work and at the same time subjects it to a fresh comic twist. These spoofing variations are demonstrated best by Mel Brooks. His *Blazing Saddles* (1974) is a takeoff on Westerns; *High Anxiety* (1977) tweaks the mystery/thrillers of Alfred Hitchcock; and *Young Frankenstein* (1974) affectionately undercuts the classic horror film *Frankenstein* (1931) and some of its sequels, especially *Bride of Frankenstein* (1935).

Unlike dark comedy, which only has come into its own since the modern era, film parody has been around since cinema's early days. The father of American film comedy, Mack Sennett, was at his best when parodying the melodramatic adventure pictures of his mentor, D. W. Griffith. For instance, Sennett's *Teddy at the Throttle* (1916) is a takeoff on Griffith's propensity for the last minute rescue, such as the close of the controversial *Birth of a Nation* (1915).

Whether old or new, parody has a compounding phenomenon. While it usually has a specific target, the spoof film is peppered with eclectic references to other "texts." Although *Airplane!* (1980) makes parody mincemeat of the *Airport* movies, it still has irreverent time for other victims, from an opening credit deflating of *Jaws* (1975), to later send-ups of John Travolta's white-suited dance number in "Saturday Night Fever" (1977) and the beach scene in *From Here to Eternity* (1953).

Ironically, parody receives the least respect of the comedy genres, working as it does from a given structure, à la the pun to a stand-up comedian. Nevertheless, a good spoof merits hosannas as "creative criticism," since the artist must be so thoroughly versed in the subject under attack. If anything, it is harder to be a skewering storyteller.

Ultimately, though, humor is so broad a creature it cannot be overanalyzed. As Jim Leach pointed out in *Film Genre: Theory and Criticism*, "a genre which encompasses the vision of Jerry Lewis *and*

Ernst Lubitsch is already in trouble." My students sometimes worry that decoding comedy will destroy the humor. The best reply is that it better helps the viewer understand not only the comedy but themselves.

STURGES' GREATEST MIRACLE:

Making *The Miracle of Morgan's Creek* a Hit

The *Nation*'s pioneering period critic James Agee was entertainingly impressed by Preston Sturges' ability to slip this farce by Will "Hollywood Hitler" Hays' censorship board: "...the Hays office has has been either hypnotized into a liberality for which it should be thanked, or has been raped in its sleep."(February 5, 1944).

A PRESTON STURGES PICTURE often falls under the label screwball comedy, such as his satirical farces *The Lady Eve* (1941) and *The Palm Beach Story* (1942). Yet, just as screwball films parody romantic comedy while jabbing at a litany of other social subjects, Sturges' pictures also frequently satirize feel-good populism, a genre often associated with director Frank Capra, à la *Mr. Deeds Goes to Town* (1936), or *It's a Wonderful Life* (1946). As *New Yorker* critic Anthony Lane later noted:

> Capra comedies dwell on the gentle irony that the perfection you seek may have been sitting in your own home all along—and *that*, Sturges would contend, is the problem with perfection ... [Sturges'] movies remain a bracing tonic against the sentimental ... [a comic red flag] to caution us against the [populist] perils of overestimating human nature ... (September 14, 1998).

Fittingly, in terms of an artist (Sturges) is predisposed to skewer populism, casting the squeaky clean Eddie Bracken as the male lead of *Miracle* enhances one's satirical possibilities. Sturges, arguably Hollywood's greatest author of witty dialogue (which helped him win a screenplay Academy Award for *The Great McGinty*, 1940, and simultaneous Oscar writing nominations for *Miracle* and *Hail the Conquering Hero*, 1944), was also an enthusiastic fan of the slapstick go-getter populist-like *silent* film comedian Harold Lloyd. However, with slapstick intact, Sturges would later satirize the comedian's Horatio Alger-like persona (with Lloyd coming out of retirement to star) in *The Sin of Harold Diddlebock*, 1947, later re-edited and re-released as *Mad Wednesday*, 1950. Interestingly, the year before making *Miracle*, Bracken confessed in an interview:

> I do best as the serious guy—like Harold Lloyd used to portray, for instance, who is constantly involved in comic situations—and that's the kind of part I'm always striving for (*Current Biography, 1944*).

Regardless, Sturges' velvet satirical touch has never been more provocative then in *Miracle*. The multi-layered film seemingly presents a Capra-like America on the surface, while it manages to subtextually derail every small town value for which this populist stood, including patriotism, marriage, idealized family life, old-fashioned romance, and expurgating corruption with a single simple-minded hero. Moreover, Sturges creates this critical and commercial smash during jingoistic World War II (history's "good" war)—shish kabobbing the very values for which America was fighting. By the time *Miracle* is over, independent film pioneer John Cassavetes' Capra crack seems like stating the obvious, "Maybe there really wasn't an America, maybe it was only Frank Capra."

Miracle's narrative involves four main characters: a single parent curmudgeon of a father (Sturges regular William "Pratfall" Demarest), his two teenage daughters (Betty Hutton and Diana Lynn), and a sweet, bumbling small-town schnook (Bracken) who has *always* had a crush on Hutton's character. The provocative period plot twist early in the story is that patriotically promiscuous Trudy Kockenlocker (older sister Hutton) gets pregnant after a night of community-sponsored parties for young military men going to war. To Trudy's credit (and Hollywood's censorship office demands), the girl thinks she got married first. But between too much alcohol-spiked punch and bumping her head during a night of dancing revelry, Trudy can neither remember what this alleged husband looks like, or even his name. Finally, after thinking hard, an often painful task for her, Trudy guesses the mystery man might be named Private Ratzkiwatzki—a memory moniker further accenting her cartoon character-like mind.

However, Sturges performs instant damage control on Trudy's shaky morals by doing what he does best—penning a script so fast-forward in its action that the viewer is soon more concerned with how to solve Trudy's problem, rather than belaboring why it happened. Moreover, Sturges' gift for pricking a subject while simultaneously softening the satire comes from the writer-director's ability to use Norval as a potential patsy fix for Trudy's dilemma (as the substitute father/husband), without making the audience think even worse of Hutton's character. Sturges so enthusiastically sells the upbeat turnaround ending—predicated upon Trudy's sweet but *so* unlikely appreciation of nerdy Norval—that the film ultimately feels like a celebration of Capra populism.

Trudy's angelic transformation is made more comically palatable by contrasting it with her sister Emmy's (Diana Lynn) Machiavellian ideas about using poor Norval: "He was made … [to play the patsy] like the ox was made to eat and the grape was made to drink …." Thus, the attitude of Trudy's beautiful but wickedly wise younger sister brings out a defensive mothering instinct in Hutton's character towards poor Norval. In the speed-of-light pace of a Sturges film, this soon passes as love for Trudy.

If normally virginal Main Street young women are manipulative and naughty, the populist stereotype can be further satirized by showcasing the strong male as clinically weak. Bracken's Norval more than fills that bill. His character anticipates a later more celebrated satirical take on the American male, which James Ursini's Sturges biography (1973) describes as:

> [Bracken/Norval is a] precursor of the Jerry Lewis characterizations of the '50s and '60s. He is a complete failure—physically handicapped with high blood pressure, rather confused mentally, and cursed with a pusillanimous character… He represents to us [viewers] the weakest and, therefore, most disturbing side of our personality …. (This … may explain why many reject characters like the ones played by Bracken and Lewis so violently. It is a side of us we do not readily like to admit to.)

Betty Hutton between her father (William Demarest) and a maybe husband
(Eddie Bracken) in *The Miracle of Morgan's Creek* (1944).

This analogy between Bracken and Lewis is further strengthened by noting that Lewis later even loosely remade *Miracle* as *Rock-a-Bye Baby* (1958), directed by another gifted satirist—Frank Tashlin.

Sturges does, however, soften the viewer's acceptability of bumbling Bracken in two ways. First, by anchoring the story in a screwball comedy framework, where males are traditionally manipulated by women, weak Norval almost seems like business as usual for this genre. And keep in mind, calling Bracken's figure a foreshadowing of Jerry Lewis does not negate the aforementioned link to Harold Lloyd. There are parallels between Lloyd's nerdy go-getter and Bracken's conscientious antihero. Indeed, Sturges' screwball satirical perspective on Lloyd's persona in *The Sin of Harold Diddlebock* underlines that point.

A second way Sturges makes nondescript Norval more tolerable to the audience is that the movie's only other pivotal male, Demarest's put-upon papa, is another satirical variation on the American male. Though perennially exasperated, Demarest's inspired bluster still makes him no more successful than the milquetoast manner of Bracken's Norval. Demarest is the big mouth, take-charge male who is always willing to get physical ... his Constable Kockenlocker is forever trying to give people the boot ... which only results in some amazing pratfalls. Though he plays a small-town cop, he acts more like an apprentice gangster.

Kockenlocker is also one of many *Miracle* characters to satirize the state of marriage. His gun cleaning scene on the porch when Norval comes to visit for some potential son-in-law advice reminds the audience more of the proverbial less-than-romantic shotgun marriage. Moreover, Kockenlocker is full of negative riffs about the alleged state of marital bliss. For example, when daughter Emmy (whose darkly comic manipulating thoughts on the institution have already been quoted) tells her father she does not want to talk, *widower* Kockenlocker explodes, "A woman doesn't care to talk? The only time a woman doesn't care to talk is when she's dead!" Yet, Sturges' satirical coup d' état upon wed*lock* comes from *Miracle* lawyer Alan Bridge (E.L Johnson), another of the director's regular supporting players:

> The responsibility for recording a marriage has always been up to a woman. If it wasn't for her, marriage would have disappeared long since. No man is going to jeopardize his present or poison his future with a lot of little brats hollering around the house unless he's forced to. It's up to the woman to knock him down, hogtie him, and drag him in front of two witnesses immediately if not sooner. Any time after that is too late.

All this being said, nerdy Norval still has a loving willingness to marry the pregnant-by-someone-else Trudy, after she finally finds affection for the young man. Does this now make him more savior than sap? Based upon the lawyer's "No man is going to jeopardize his ... future ...." rant, for all Norval's foibles, his Trudy to the rescue action now makes him sound downright noble and romantic. The brilliance of Sturges' satire is that he can offer this point as more evidence of Norval's less than manly ways (where the norm is to run from marriage), and yet make a potential positive from it. This writer/director both mocks populism while embracing it in small doses.

Given all these crazy dynamics, *Miracle*'s helter-skelter script pinballs towards a resolution in a manner reminiscent of Robert Benchley's observation, "Insanity runs in my family. In fact, it practically gallops." Moreover, after Sturges' token tribute to Capra-land, where people are inherently good, it is back to the stinging world of satire. And with marital speed of the essence here, it is fitting that the darkly comic Emmy reminds Trudy, "Nobody believes good unless they have to, if they've got a chance to believe something bad." Indeed, one should add, sometimes Sturges goes beyond satire to black humor, in which the point is there is no point. For example, in one of the Constable Kockenlocker's earlier diatribes against marriage, he threatened the mouthy Emmy with one of dark comedy's central themes—death: "Listen, Zipperpuss! Someday they're just gonna find your hair ribbon and an axe someplace. Nothing else! The Mystery of Morgan's Creek!"

Regardless, before Bracken's character can rescue Trudy by way of marriage, they have to address her undocumented first union to phantom hubby Private Ratzkiwatzki. Except Norval's panacea shouts failure from his opening description, "This [idea] is airtight and watertight. It's foolproof, and almost legal." The Bracken scheme involved marrying Hutton under an assumed name (so Trudy's undocumented fly-by-night first marriage could be legally ended by divorce), before they married again using their real names. Unfortunately, Norval signs the wrong moniker on the first marriage certificate, and the comic fuss budget justice of the peace (Porter Hall) gets Norval arrested. The charges range from attempting to corrupt a minor, to impersonating a serviceman (he had donned an amusingly distinctive World War I uniform during World War II—Ratzkiwatzki had been an Army man). Demarest's law officer facilitates a comic escape, and Norval takes it on the lam for several months. Sturges' brief lull before the big finish is pleasingly plot driven, with a nod to the censorship office, too. That is, getting Norval out-of-town for an extended period after the jailbreak allows the story to jump ahead to Trudy's due date, eliminating what was essentially a 1940s verboten—showcasing a woman near term.

More importantly for the iconoclastic Sturges, the calendar movement now makes it Christmas time—*the* season for populism. The genre that Sturges lampoons in *Miracle* is tied to the belief that people inherently do the right thing. But to further hedge that bet, populism often gerrymanders its story around this sacred holiday—knowing many audiences will be more palatable to such feel-good behavior at this time. For instance, Capra uses a Christmas Eve backdrop for the conclusion of both *Meet John Doe* (1941) and *It's a Wonderful Life*.

Along related lines, Capra scripts also frequently draw verbal parallels between their protagonists and Christ, from the metaphorical "crucifying" of Jimmy Stewart's title character in *Mr. Smith Goes to Washington* (1939), to references in *Meet John Doe* to Pontius Pilate and the original Doe who "died 2000 years ago." Capra's 1975 memoir addressed the Christianity factor directly when he stated:

> I think that the gospels are a comedy—good news. I think that the greatest comedy of all is the Divine Comedy— the Resurrection, victory over death. Every Sunday the Catholics [his faith] celebrate the mass, celebrate victory over death. That's what comedy means to me ....

Why belabor Sturges' use of this populist Christmas component? It is important to underline his satirical audacity—comic sacrilege, if you will, at least for the 1940s. Trudy is pregnant by some undocumented ephemeral figure and Norval is asked to step up in order that the "miracle" of the title be fulfilled. There is even a shot of a non-showing pregnant Trudy with a cow, à la the livestock of the Nativity, just before Norvel's return. Sturges is satirizing the backstory of the Virgin Mary—another hard to explain pregnancy, and a soon-to-be husband struggling with these developments ... until a "miracle" is explained to him in a dream. Consequently, with regard to Bracken, instead of Sturges satirizing Capra's tendency to use a male lead as a Christ-like figure, *Miracle* has poor Norval more in the Joseph "the beard" mold—after getting an explanation from a "dream" girl, he is also a bystander to another mysterious phenomenon ... though sometimes also known as an unwed mother.

Sturges' deus ex machina "miracle" involves Trudy giving birth to sextuplets—a brilliant defusing of puncturing the Christmas story, though the satire now takes several new twists. Since Hutton's character has been, to borrow a crack from film critic Eric Jonsson, "thoughtful enough to transcend disgrace with 'sextuplets,'" Sturges will soon demonstrate how hypocrisy is often pronounced "hurrah," if the transgression catches the public fancy. One is also tempted to use a line from Charlie Chaplin's later dark comedy, *Monsieur Verdoux* (1947): "Numbers sanctify." Though the comedian's title character was actually referring to war dead, the same numerical hypocrisy applies here. Small-town blue noses can quickly embrace an unwed mother if she abruptly becomes a *cash cow* by having six baby boys.

This money morality by way of a human litter is best explained in three parts, to better appreciate the full extent of the satire. First, *Miracle* is told through a framing devise, opening with a frantic call from the local newspaper editor (Victor Potel) to the state's Governor McGinty (with Brian Donlevy in a cameo reprising his likeable crooked politician from Sturges' *The Great McGinty*). Something astounding has just occurred in Morgan's Creek, and this segues into the flashback telling of the Trudy/Norval story. (This disjointed narrative is also a basic dark comedy component, which is also pure Sturges.) Once the miracle/secret is out (sextuplets), the viewer is returned to the framing device with the governor, and his comically nefarious party boss who got him elected (Akim Tamiroff, also reprising his role from *McGinty*). Consequently, Sturges is essentially satirizing himself by recycling this duo for both additional film fan laughs and potentially calculated added box office.

The second level of *Miracle*'s satirical hypocrisy thus becomes political. If the opening call to the governor and his party boss was wild, their phone response is even more frenzied. Realizing there is a beaucoop amount of money to be made, McGinty and company do what all unscrupulous political machines do:

> **Editor:** There's only one thing, Mr. Governor—the [invisible] marriage!
>
> **Governor:** What's the matter with the marriage? She's married to Norval Jones, she always has been! The guy married them, didn't he? The boy signed his right name, didn't he?
>
> **Editor:** But he gave his name as Ratzkiwatzki!
>
> **Governor:** He was trying to say Jones, he stuttered!
>
> **Boss:** What are you looking for, a needle from a haystack?
>
> **Editor:** Then now about the first Ratzkiwatzki?
>
> **Governor:** He's annulled!
>
> **Boss:** Shnook!
>
> **Editor:** Who's annulled?
>
> **Governor:** The judge, who do you suppose?
>
> **Boss:** Retroactive!
>
> **Governor:** Will you get Mendoza on the phone? [A fellow fixer?]
>
> **Boss:** I'm getting him.

> **Governor:** He's out of the picture! [No sharing the
>   wealth?]
> **Boss:** Was never in it!

The governor's instant patter about buying land around Morgan's Creek, putting up hotels and so on is just as intense. This brings one to *Miracle*'s third satirical measure of money morality—Canada's Dionne Quintuplets. If the antics of McGinty seem overly agitated, even for a satire, period audiences would immediately have thought of the Canadian cash bonanza produced by the Ontario birth of the Dionne Quintuplets, the first quintuplets known to survive their infancy. *Miracle*'s subtextual political satire link to the five Dionne baby girls is fueled by the fact that the Canadian government soon made them wards of the King/state through the "Dionne Quintuplets' Guardianship Act, 1935."

The Dianne babies were shortly housed in the "Dafoe Hospital and Nursery," named after the doctor credited with ensuring the survival of the premature babies. The state had guessed correctly about North America's fa$ination with the children. What soon became known as "Quintland" would be Ontario's greatest tourist attraction for years, with thousands of people visiting the compound daily for an observation gallery sighting of the girls at play. Besides the millions of dollars this zoo-like setting produced, much more cash was generated by the marketing of the Dionne sisters. Their image soon graced an assortment of items such as plates, post cards, books, various toys and other objects ad infinitum. (This author's Depression era Iowa mother most cherished her Dionne Quintuplets paper dolls.)

Besides Sturges' ability to use this event and its ongoing phenomena as a source of *Miracle* satire about money morality, political wheeler dealing, and hypocrisy in general, the director also saved some satirical scorn for the tempest in a teacup mentality. Sturges does this in an assortment of ways, starting with Trudy's sextuplets being a "world-altering" event. Thus, *Miracle*'s near conclusion features a montage of newspaper headlines, including "Mussolini Resigns" and "Hitler Demands Recount," as well as a direct dig at Ontario's "Quintland"—"Canada Protests." (Of course, Sturges had already conquered Canada in a variation of "numbers sanctify," since sextuplets always trump quintuplets.) Viewers are also treated to visuals of Axis power leaders responding to Trudy's densely populated birthing process, such as Hitler being steamed over America instantly having six potential new soldiers. Plus, Trudy's pregnancy also represents a satirical poke at our "patriot" "love them and leave them" "boys," who seem to be deflowering the very womanhood they signed up to protect. Sturges addresses this more directly in a *Miracle* church sequence deleted by his studio (Paramount). A minister speaking to his congregation says, in part:

> during war, the earth is more fruitfully replenished than during peace. The uniforms, the brass buttons ... all of these have so captured the imaginations ... of all young women from the beginning ....

The final satirization is simply *Miracle*'s happy ending, because like a happy ending in a dark comedy, it is patently absurd ... and subtextually biting—miracles just "do not" occur. Sturges' fellow small town satirist W. C. Fields did the same thing in two of his signature films, *Its' a Gift* (1934), and *The Bank Dick* (1940). In both cases a film ending proverbial "gift/ miracle" saves the day and turns hypocrites into the high-minded. Thus, in the ludicrous spirit of pasting happy onto satirical absurdity, maybe the most fittingly cockimamie review for *Miracle* came from *New York Journal American* (January 20, 1944) critic G. E. Blackford:

> You want to laugh? Go to the N. Y. Paramount [theatre] and see the new picture there ... Even if you don't want to laugh and you do go there, you will laugh. If you don't, it can only be because you're both deaf and blind.

> (Reprinted with permission from *USA Today Magazine*, January, 2015. Copyright © 2015 by "The Society for the Advancement of Education, Inc. All Rights Reserved.")

REASSEMBLING THE DUST:

The Art of Biography

WHILE MY DAY JOB is teaching film studies at Ball State University, my real passion is writing. Though that often involves genre studies, such as my recent cinema criticism text, *Romantic vs. Screwball Comedy: Charting the Difference,* the majority of my books are biographies. I am fascinated by the profiling of lives.

The penchant for biography mirrors a national inclination. During the last decade, the American public has been especially drawn to the chronicling of lives. The interest has been fed by a proliferation of cable television profile programming, following the longtime success story of A&E's "Biography." Moreover, A&E's hit has expanded from once a week to a nightly show. Meanwhile, the newsstands are peppered with profile-related publications, from the mainstream *People* and *Us* to A&E's *Biography Magazine.* The making of film biographies (both for television and theatrical release) has seen a marked increase as well.

Why this interest? There are three key reasons. First, for profiler Frank E. Vandiver, biography at its best is "history made personal." For example, an individual might have little interest in war, but George C. Scott's electrifying title performance in *Patton* (1970) draws the viewer into the myriad of minidramas that constituted the close of World War II in Europe. Along similar line, the viewer need not be a fan of classical music to be swept up by the darkly comic scope of *Amadeus* (1984), the provocative chronical of composer Antonio Salieri's jealousy of the genius of Wolfgang Amadeus Mozart.

"History made personal" works as a small-scale equation, too. For instance, in director John Ford's classical film, *Young Mr. Lincoln* (1939), the attraction is not about Civil War leadership, but, rather, seeing how a soon-to-be great man responds to rite-of-passage universals that impact everyone. Thus, Henry Fonda's moving portrayal of the future president explores the loss of a loved one, the courtship of a spouse, and Lincoln's relationship with his mother.

Second, acclaimed biographer Barbara W. Tuchman reminds us that the genre can also be about the "universal in the particular." That is, a life story can make a complex subject more intellectually manageable. To illustrate, director Warren Beatty's sprawling chronicle of American writer John Reed's embracing of communism, *Reds* (1981), helps make the Russian Revolution easier to comprehend, especially for an American viewer. Along comparable lines, director Elia Kazan's biography of Emiliano Zapata, *Viva Zapata!* (1952), starring Marlon Brando, helps make the Mexican Revolution more understandable. Another aspect about the "universal in the particular" is an extension of "History made personal." Seeing how this focus individual managed human universals can inspire us to succeed and/or warn us about the sacrifices, dangers, temptations…one might encounter. Most importantly, it makes these people real again—not idealized icons stuck in amber.

Third, a good biography can feed an interest in the genre by simply being masterfully informative. For example, I have always been taken with surrealistic paintings of Mexican artist Frida Kahlo, but producer/actress Salma Hayek's extraordinary chronicling of her life in *Frida* (2002) is a revelation. Here was a passionate artist whose work and life were often overshadowed by her tempestuous marriage to social realist painter Diego Riviera, brought to life in an equally passionate film biography by Hayek, who also played the title role.

As the author of 10 print biographies, including forthcoming volumes of Carole Lombard and Irene Dunne, I am attracted to the genre for additional reasons. For the conscientious biographer, it all begins with what author Doris Kearns calls "angles of vision." This is a three-part take on the focus subject.

A biography is normally written because the author has a novel take (angle of vision) on the subject. Thus, in 1983, when I chronicled Charlie Chaplin's life, my revisionist aim was a new perspective on the comedian's signature figure of the Little Tramp. I made a case for his alter ego character being more capable than he was given credit for.

The second angle of the vision component for the biographer involves the public's take on the subject. When doing my first book on the Marx Brother (1987), I had to address the popular mistaken belief that

Bob Fosse's *All That Jazz* (1979) was really about "All His Jazz."

Groucho ad-libbed all his great film lines. Though Groucho did have a gift for comic riffing, his most-classic comments were provided by a who's who of satirical writers, especially S.J. Perelman and George S. Kaufman.

Groucho also provides a segue for the final take on angle of vision— the personal slant of the subject himself. In my second Marx Brothers book

(1994), I keyed on Groucho's conscious decision to alter his approach to comedy as he moved from film to television. The comedian recognized the demands of different medium. The result was a less-frantic, nonsaturation comedy style than his movie norm. His calmer small-screen persona reacted to the craziness of his eccentric "You Bet Your Life" (1950-61) guests, instead of causing chaos, à la his film figure. Groucho's changed persona was just right for the more-intimate medium of television.

Regardless, after the multifaceted angle of vision factor, the good biographer is attracted to the genre because of the detective work component. What would be pure research drudgery for some (novelist Virginia Wolfe once likened it to "donkey work") is merely an entertaining puzzle for the biographer. For my 1984 profile of W.C. Fields, I initially had trouble finding complete descriptions of his stage acts. Then, based upon the comedian's fierce protectiveness over his comedy routines (he once physically attacked comic Ed Wynn for allegedly stealing material), I played a hunch and checked the copyright division of the Library of Congress. Bingo! Fields had indeed copyrighted his stage routines, and I had a newsbreaking plus for my biography.

A final attraction for the chronicling of memorable lives is the search for historical truth. That goal helps explain writer Desmond MacCarthy's pivotal definition of a biographer: "An artist upon oath." The profiler learns that, while he or she might not be sure of finding the "absolute truth," the objective is to get the "best truth" possible. You cannot ask any more of a profession that is all about, as a stand-up comedian once observed, "reassembling the dust."

McCAREY vs. CAPRA:

A Guide to American Film Comedy of the 1930s

THE 1930S REPRESENT A UNIQUE period in American comedy, a period in which two diametrically opposed types of humor vied, on a national level, for preeminence. These two comedy rivals were the anti-hero and the crackerbarrel Yankee. Under the direction of Leo McCarey and Frank Capra, this battle, though neither director probably thought of it as such, was portrayed at its best in American movies of the period.

The comic anti-hero, who tries to create order in a world where order is impossible, had only fully arrived on the American scene a few years earlier. Most often associated with the work of such *New Yorker* writers as James Thurber and Robert Benchly, the anti-hero is a young urban character who appears all the younger because of his utter incompetency at any and every task. His childlike nature is underlined by the fact that he knows no type of employment—every moment is taken up with the frustrations of leisure time. Moreover, he's so frustrated by domestic, daily problems (largely female) that he never approaches the political issues that dominate the Yankee's life. In American humor he would soon grow to be the dominant comedy character.

The Yankee, on the other hand, had been the dominant figure in American humor since the 1830s. He was a rural figure full of wisdom learned through experience. His main interest was talking politics or giving advice. He would remind you of someone's father or grandfather, busy and successful at work he enjoyed but always patient and considerate of everyone's needs. Unlike the anti-hero, when a character in the world of the Yankee found himself in a comic dilemma it was due to his own incompetency. Since the assumption was that the world was rational, the character could right himself by making his own life well-ordered. This proved to be the case in American comic fiction, from the world of Seba Smith's Jack Downing in the 1830s, to that of Will Rogers in the 1930s.

McCarey had been a charter member of the anti-hero group. His teaming and molding of Laurel & Hardy in the late 1920s, paralleling the beginning of the *New Yorker*, had introduced the first full articulation of the comic anti-hero into American film. During the 1930s McCarey continued to focus on the comic anti-hero in his feature length films, from *Part Time Wife* (1930) to *My Favorite Wife* (1940), which he co-wrote and produced.

Capra came to the traditional Yankee somewhat later than McCarey's discovery of the anti-hero. Moreover, American film already had a very popular Yankee in the guise of Will Rogers. In fact, the year before his death (1934) Rogers was the number one box-office draw in United States motion pictures, dramas or comedies.[1]

Rogers' untimely death in 1935 changed all this. Though American fiction would never know another Yankee figure of national significance, the crackerbarrel cinema void was more than filled by Capra, with works such as *Mr. Deeds Goes to Town* (1936) and *Mr. Smith Goes to Washington* (1939).[2] Moreover, they enjoyed the same huge commercial success of the Rogers films.

In the second half of this period (1935-40), then, the crackerbarrel philosopher did not diminish in popularity but more and more he was able to share top billing with the comic anti-hero. Appropriately, Capra was the dominant force behind the crackerbarrel figure during this time (the Academy rewarded him with directing Oscars for two post-1935 films in this genre—*Mr. Deeds* and *You Can't Take it with You* (1938). Moreover, just as appropriately, McCarey received comparable recognition on behalf of the comic anti-hero: he was given the directing Oscar for *The Awful Truth* (1937). No other best director Oscars for comedy were given during this period.

Andrew Sarris has noted that, "There is on film a record of a thirties Oscar ceremony during which Capra and McCarey playfully wrestled on stage for a golden statuette they both coveted. It is perhaps at that very moment that their joint preeminence was officially recognized...."[3] Thus, any examination of American film comedy of the 1930s must focus on a McCarey-Capra comparison. Not only has this natural dichotomy been missed in film scholarship, the opposite course has been followed—"McCarey and Capra seem to go together like ham and eggs,"[4] or "…McCarey [was] Capra's primary rival as a director of sentimental-moralistic comedies."[5]

Certain parallels do exist in some of their work—but the parallels exist only as a result of comparing McCarey's lesser films, outside the anti-hero sub-genre (the vast majority made after the early 1940's) with Capra films of the preceding period. Under these conditions, certain equivalents can be drawn, e.g., both made films which extolled a fundamental belief in the American system and the opportunities it afforded the individual (McCarey's *The Bells of St. Mary's*, 1944 and *Good Sam*, 1948; Capra's *Mr. Deeds* and *Mr. Smith*); and both led moral fights against isms—McCarey's anti-fascist *Once Upon a Honeymoon* (1942) or Capra's *Meet John Doe* (1942) and McCarey's later anti-communist *My Son John* (1952) and *Satan Never Sleeps* (1962).

It is because of this misleading comparison that McCarey seems inferior to Capra, e.g., "Capra's ability to capture this underlying human texture makes his films look particularly good in comparison to Leo McCarey's…."[6] To better understand American film comedy of the '30s, as well as appreciate the work of McCarey, you need to focus on his comic anti-hero films. Once this is done, any comparison of McCarey and Capra will represent a game of distinct differences instead of general parallels. The following pages will compare the comedy characterizations of the two directors '30s work according to a five point criteria: use of time, interest in politics, general capabilities, apparent age, and residency.

McCarey's features of the 1930s continue the anti-hero tradition so nicely portrayed in the Laurel & Hardy shorts—beginning with characteristic number one—an unlimited supply of free time. The best example of this leisure life occurs in *The Awful Truth*. As the film opens, Cary Grant has just returned from "a trip to Florida" (he tells a friend that he stayed in New York and essentially took a break.) But his wife (Irene Dunne) returns home later, with her handsome French singing instructor, and pleads car problems for her overnight tardiness. Grant feels that he's been cuckolded and divorce proceedings begin. The rest of the film deals with the mating habits of the idle rich, as both attempt to establish new relationships before they get back together.

In all situations McCarey has demonstrated his interest in the personal and domestic rather than the professional and political side of his anti-hero. That this was a conscious effort is best illustrated by the difficulty Grant has in playing one particular scene in *The Awful Truth*, when he offers to help his estranged wife out monetarily:

> When Cary came to that scene he stopped and laughed.
> "Where am I supposed to have gotten any money?" he asked.
> "I never work...you never show me doing any sort of a job."
> My reply was that the audience would not be interested in
> how he got the money, but merely in the efforts of the two
> people to straighten out their married life.[7]

While the anti-hero mourns his inability to function in what amounts to a year-round holiday, the Yankee usually maintains a profession, though it is rare that it will interfere with his advice service. Moreover, Yankee examples from fiction, such as Mr. Dooley the bartender, Sam Slick the clock peddler, and Jack Downing the political advisor, not only allow access to a large public, they often demand it. Thus, Clark Gable plays a reporter in *It Happened One Night*, Gary Cooper is a working poet (his poems are sold to a card company) who will eventually become the trustee of a large fortune in *Mr. Deeds*, and Jimmy Stewart is head of a youth organization before he becomes a U.S. Senator in *Mr. Smith*.

The second characteristic of the comic anti-hero is that he is non-political. McCarey's features revolve around marital dilemmas rather than political dilemmas. Moreover, the anti-heroic character has enough trouble getting out of bed in the morning, let alone following world politics. Even the most simplistic task, from Edmund Lowe's golfing sequence in *Part Time Wife* (1930), to the Gloria Swanson-dominated dinner party in *Indiscreet* (1931), represents a monumental task to him. Also, their focus on fun activities precludes any time for politics, or for that matter, the thinking process in general. Consequently, they very much remain day to day, non-intellectual people, with no time reserved for politics or thinking.

The situation is reversed for the Yankee crackerbarrel philosopher. His primary interest is political, and any wife or girlfriend is of secondary interest. This is best exemplified in Capra's *Mr. Smith Goes to Washington*. As his name implies, Jefferson Smith symbolizes the belief in Jeffersonian democracy, the belief in a rural-small town America in need of little federal government. Thus, the Capra country philosopher constantly acts as a brake on the dangers of Hamiltonian big government—Mr. Smith stops corruption in the Senate, while John Doe, in *Meet John Doe*, stops (or at least slows) a Fascist organization from creating a major American third party.

The McCarey protagonist of the thirties upholds the third characteristics of the anti-hero in that he is a totally frustrated figure, keeping well within the tradition of Laurel & Hardy. Any attempt to deal rationally with an irrational world must meet with failure. McCarey's anti-heroes are most frustrated by wives. But whereas Laurel & Hardy often had drill sergeants for wives in the short films, McCarey's features, with broader audience demands (increased costs necessitate larger audiences) and a more complex plot, were more likely to have beautiful wives, from the lovely Leila Hyams of *Part Time Wife* or Gloria Swanson of *Indiscreet,* to the equally lovely Irene Dunne of *The Awful Truth* and *My Favorite Wife.* The continued defeat of the male in these new situations thus became all the more ironic—the McCarey husband was no longer battling a wife that looked like a heavyweight wrestler. But rather, he confronted and lost to what was truly "the little woman." Moreover, with this female beauty seemed to come skill in some leisure time activity (the female in the comic anti-hero story always seems to be able to make adequate use of this free time, while the male only becomes frustrated). These activities take the liberated female out of the house and allow her contacts with other males, e.g., in *The Awful Truth* Grant's initial frustration is both the result of Dunne's possible sexual dalliance when she returns late with her singing instructor, and the fact that she was not at home to greet him after his *Florida trip* in the then "true" tradition of womanhood. (Plus, it is never clear if he might have had his own dalliance while remaining in New York.)

What occurred more frequently, with the increased exposure of the attractive wife to the outside world, was the evaporation of the uniqueness of the husband's last masculinity treachery—those occasional secret flings. This double standard was the last veneer of masculinity for the male. Thus, it was usually the central conflict in McCarey's battle of the sexes in the '30s features.

With that final masculine veneer gone, exchanges in traditional sexual roles occurred. The best single example is in *My Favorite Wife,* when Irene Dunne returns home, after having been missing for seven years in the South Pacific. She has been rescued by the navy and is now dressed in the pants and top of a sailor. When she first meets her young children, one asks, "Are you a lady or a man?" The other adds, "My mother was practically a sailor."

Later in the film, Cary Grant, who by this time has become so frustrated over what to do with two wives that he is hardly coherent, must get some clothes together for Dunne, without revealing her existence to his new wife. Thus, with this second wife there and a psychiatrist who's been called to monitor his strange behavior, Grant chooses a dress from

Frank Capra and Jean Arthur during the production of
Mr. Smith Goes to Washington (1939).

the closet and holds it in front of himself while looking at its effect in the mirror. He then picks out a lady's hat and puts that on, carefully scrutinizing his appearance. Next, he tries another dress in front of the mirror, asking wife number two and the doctor if they think it matches the hat. In answer to their concerned looks he replies that they're not for him but rather "for a friend of mine. He's waiting downstairs." This merely seems to confirm the worst fears of his now wife and her psychiatrist, for the friend downstairs is a man. (He wants Dunne but is afraid to tell wife number two about the situation.)

The Yankee's ability to handle any problem is especially true of his relationship with the anti-hero's biggest frustration—the female. For Capra and the crackerbarrel philosopher of the 19th century American humor, there is no place for the dominant woman. There is a telling scene midway in *Meet John Doe* that demonstrates both these principles. The protagonist, Gary Cooper, admits the rare example of a dream to the girl he's fallen in love with—Barbara Stanwyck. As is usual in a Capra film, the hero has been duped thus far by the female. Yet as Cooper relates his dream, he tells of seeing himself as Stanwyck's father at her wedding, which causes him to spank her in the dream. In his explanation he implies the husband figure in the dream was not good enough (at this point in the film Stanwyck is romantically linked to the nephew of the Fascist leader). Yet, her support for Cooper is ultimately crucial.

Cooper then returns to the dream and states that he next plays both the role of father and the justice and again Stanwyck is to be spanked. Thus, even before he asserts himself, he intuitively senses the problem and embraces the fundamental answer—that of personal initiative through direct action. At this point in the Capra film the woman loses whatever powers of trickery she might have had over the male and becomes secondary to him.

As is to be expected of an approach born of the 19th century, it is generally implied that the Capra woman will dutifully follow her man back into the country once his services are no longer needed in the East. This is what the Jean Arthur character does in both *Mr. Deeds* and *Mr. Smith*. Frustration then, if present for the Yankee, is something of temporary duration embracing political issues of national significance. Domestic dilemmas centering on dominant women do not fulfill any of these requirements, yet ironically, their support is usually what helps the man succeed.

The fourth characteristic of the comic anti-hero finds him to be the perennial child figure of the modern couple. His best friends are children and/or dogs. But not only does he have little companions, the McCarey anti-hero is associated with playthings in all shapes and sizes. In *Ruggles of Red Gap* (1935), during Ruggles' journey back into childhood, Egbert and his friend Jeff have taken Ruggles to an amusement park. While there they ride the merry-go-round. McCarey gives us a different view of each "cowboy" on his pony. Jeff comes around riding as if he's on an unbroken stallion. Egbert comes around in the most relaxed of manners, riding his as if it is a sofa—the most natural child among them. The transition has been made.

When it comes to the association with smaller playthings, the best example comes at the close of *My Favorite Wife,* as well as displaying a child-husband and a mother-wife. The frustrated Grant has joined Dunne at their cabin in the mountains. He is obviously on the verge of making his decision in her favor, but he's too frazzled by this point to know how to express it. Moreover, at bedtime she does not hurt her cause any by being both very attractive as well as forceful in assigning them separate rooms, she in the master bedroom, he sentenced to a bed in the attic.

The effect of Grant's trek to the attic is that of a little boy sent to his room without supper. The outcome is heightened by the nursery surroundings of the attic and the little bed he must sleep in. It is a scaled down version of the children's bedroom in the McCarey Laurel & Hardy short subject *Brats* (1930). Grant gets ready for bed with toys literally hanging from the low ceiling. As he crawls into the squeaky bed, knocking things down, your eyes focus on two specific toys—a doll beside the bed and a toy cannon just underneath. As if to accent the focus, as well as reveal his thoughts, the doll falls and says "mama." With this suggestion, he does, in fact, get up and go to "mama's" room. And in getting up, we see for the first time a second doll in a small bed right beside his bed.

After he has made the long trek back down to Dunne's room, she reinforces the earlier suggestion of the supperless child by asking in the most motherly of ways, "Are you hungry?" Needless to say, the true answer is something of a yes and no but he replies in the most appropriate of little boy styles that he can't sleep. There are no "nice mattresses" in the attic like there are here—referring to the spare bed in Dunne's room. She coyly says then that he can sleep on this one. After his face has sufficiently lit up, like a little boy's at Christmas, she tells him he would be most welcome to take the mattress upstairs.

The crestfallen child then takes the mattress out, but McCarey's camera remains with Dunne, and Grant returns in seconds, complaining that the mattress does not fit. Then, in added befuddlement he quietly states, "I'm stuck. This could go 'till doomsday. I'm stuck but I don't care what people think." After this pointed regression, we once again see them in their separate beds.

Grant must somehow express to Dunne that she truly is "my favorite wife." But because of his long puzzlement over the decision, and this complete childhood regression, which itself could be seen as the actualization of a childish male ego that refuses to admit a mistake, Grant seems to be literally struck dumb—unable even to communicate with normal speech patterns.

When you note this verbal incapacity of Grant's you also remember that " 'Do it visually,'" was McCarey's byword.[8] Grant can be expected to perform some very comically symbolic act to resurrect their marriage. Moreover, whatever symbol is chosen to represent the uniqueness of this day, it should be something commensurate with a red-letter day in childhood. Grant is obviously operating with the mind of a child, and it is only natural that he should communicate as such.

After individual shots of Grant and Dunne, both in their separate beds, the camera remains on Dunne. You then hear Grant's attic bed collapse, followed by another crash, then the squeak of the attic door, and finally jingle bells on the soundtrack. Grant then bursts in dressed as Santa Claus and cries "Merry Christmas." Since Christmas is probably the most anxiously awaited moment of childhood, Grant's happiness over this apparent reconciliation proves to be a most effective communication. Moreover, just as in childhood, Grant plays his game by dressing up as someone else and imagining it is a different time. And, despite the fact that "good-night" is then written across the screen, by ending the film with Grant's Santa Claus entry, the asexual nature of the child (and the comic anti-hero) is maintained.

The concept of the child-husband and mother-wife are essential factors in the husband-wife reconciliation at the close of several McCarey films. Throughout these films, the male has taken on something of an asexual role. As with Laurel & Hardy, extramarital activities are not condoned, though their rejection doesn't match the physical degree of rejection at feminine advances shown by Laurel in *We Faw Down* (1928). The anti-hero of McCarey's features is more apt to be in a state of intense confusion and frustration.

This husband-wife reconciliation thus takes on rather significant consequences in several McCarey films. In *The Awful Truth, My Favorite Wife,* and to a certain extent, *Six of a Kind,* (1934), the child-husband attempts to have himself tucked in by the mother-wife, or be enabled to slip into bed with "mother." It occurs at the film's close, and is symbolic of the new world—the new marriage—that traditionally ends comedy, for at this point the McCarey male-child is finally allowed the suggestion of sexual manhood. But for the viewer, he remains forever the child.[9]

In contrast to the anti-hero as child, the Yankee is a father or grandfather figure. He makes the decisions that run the country as well as the family. And he is at all times a leader. The most logical choices from Capra are the worldly wise Grandpa Vanderhoff of *You Can't Taken It With You* (1938), or Mr. Deeds—the poet of Mandrake Falls. Deeds is especially interesting, because though he is young and initially put off balance by the city, eventually he develops a blueprint for a successful revamping of a depression torn society.

Interestingly, however, Gable's role in *It Happened One Night* (which showcases both Yankee and screwball traits) has him as a refugee from the city, ironically he represents the essential fatherly characteristics of the Yankee crackerbarrel; he's a good, common-sense "parent-teacher." Much as a similar Charlie Chaplin raises Edna Purviance on the road in *The Vagabond* (1916). Gable takes care of Claudette Colbert in similar circumstances in *It Happened One Night*. Without these "fathers" neither girl could have survived. Each has to be taught the most basic of tasks, from Chaplin's lesson on washing the face, to Gable's demonstration of how to dunk a donut. Whereas, the comic anti-hero is totally incompetent in a fully automated house in the city, the Yankee is quite capable of living off the land. So capable, in fact, that he is also able to support something of a dead weight pupil until she has learned the ropes.

All this is not to deny that the homespun philosopher of the Capra film, like the crackerbarrel image of Lincoln at his dry goods store, contains much that is childlike. But again like Lincoln there is always a dark cloud in the distance that will force that child to grow up. Consqeuntly, Deeds slides down bannisters and chases fire engines, Smith does bird calls and gapes at monuments, and Doe plays baseball in the living room and dreams of being a major leaguer—but in each case they will be able to rise to the demands of a crisis. And in each case, as it was with Lincoln, that crisis will have threatened the very existence of the nation.

Lincoln, the man and the legend, is an important figure in the crackerbarrel tradition and of central interest to Capra—especially in *Mr. Smith*, where he serves as a model for the freshman senator. Lincoln is, of course, far from the beginning of this tradition. He is predated by numerous characters in American fiction, as well as such flesh and blood Yankees as Ben Franklin, Davy Crockett, and Daniel Boone. But because of the unique attributes of the man and the severe situation he served under, he has become something of a patron saint of America.

Fifth, the McCarey comic anti-hero in these features continues to reside in the city. McCarey demonstrates that the city decreases masculinity. Midway in *My Favorite Wife* Grant finds out that Dunne had not been shipwrecked for seven years all by herself. When he does some investigating as to who this Robinson Crusoe companion was, he finds that it is the very masculine Randolph Scott.

Grant's first sight of him is on the high diving board at the Pacific Country Club. Scott, attired in wall to wall muscles and a standard swimming suit, then executes a most difficult dive, while one of his poolside admirers asks of Grant—"Is that Johnny Weissmuller?" Alongside this, Grant feels rather anemic. Moreover, events will soon sketch an even worse picture of him.

Scott plans to return to the shipwreck island, and he wants Dunne to come with him. Precisely as this is being explained to Grant, his second wife (who has just found out about Dunne) attacks him. He cowers before her but she manages to land a solid right to the nose. Then, while Grant holds a hanky to his nose, Scott unloads the devastating, "In the law of the jungle, when a man finds his mate he doesn't have to think it out." But at this point, the only "mate" acting forcibly is Dunne, and she is bossing Grant around in a motherly medical manner, telling him to hold his head way back to stop the nosebleed. Moreover, Grant is still frustratingly undecided about how to "think" himself out of his two-wife dilemma. Most appropriate of all, this has just followed Grant's scene with the "matching" dresses and hat. He has little in common with Randolph Scott.

Whereas the anti-hero is city based, the Yankee is from the country or the small town. And though he often enters cities and cures their problems—Jack Downing or Jefferson Smith handling Washington, D.C.—he always longs to return to the pastoral setting. This is the case for the vast majority of Capra's films—Deeds is very anxious to return to Mandrake Falls, Smith wants nothing more than to get back to his woods and the Boy Rangers, and Doe is continually tempted by the Colonel (Walter Brennen) to wander across the wilds of America.

To the Yankee figure, a product of Jeffersonian democracy, the city by nature was evil. Little that he saw there changed his mind, though under some circumstances it could be entertaining. Mark Twain liked to think of Congress as that "asylum for the criminally insane," because then he could go down and view the "inmates." Capra's Colonel loved to expound on the dangers of helots (those people who "try to sell you stuff"). After a lengthy line on the demands of urban materialism (cars lead to license plates and then to insurance…), he would confidently conclude with, "Then you're a helot yourself." But generally for the Yankee, and most particularly for the Capra Yankee, the rural-urban dichotomy took on the qualities of a war.

In this war, the cities were a target constantly under attack. Often personified by a giant industrial-political boss (generally played by Capra's stock villain, Edward Arnold), they were becoming totally immune to human values. This was a result of both monopoly control of all mass media and the growing callousness of the urban dweller. The expanding bureaucracy of Hamiltonian government was rarely seen in terms of comic anti-hero frustration. Instead, it was something totally evil, to be disbanded as foreign to American soil, just as the city has no true place in Jeffersonian democracy.

This is most obvious when dealing with the Gable figure in *It Happened One Night* (the sometime screwball, sometime Yankee film), because he is the one Capra protagonist of the period that is supposedly a city person (though he is seldom seen in an urban setting and his cross-country abilities rank him with the best of Yankees). In later Capra films, the cynical urban reporter is always won over by the conscientious though naïve Yankee figure. In *Meet John Doe* this becomes more complex; reporter Barbara Stanwyck is moved by what is essentially not Doe but rather a recycled image of her "Yankee" styled father, through his diary.

The Gable of *It Happened One Night* is forced to fluctuate between cynical reporter and Yankee figure. Runaway heiress Colbert, because she constitutes the other half of the love relationship, should represent the characteristics of the Yankee. But other than an independent spirit, she is the antithesis of all that is Yankee. Thus, Gable must be both pitcher and catcher for the rural point of view. (Colbert best represents the screwball nature of *It Happened One Night*.)

This is only made somewhat palatable by Gable's rather sketchy tale of an island he saw once, an island he now wants to return to because of the corruptness of the world. And in true Capra fashion, Colbert is to follow him back. It is through this dream island monologue that a certain promise is held out to the viewers, the vast majority of them urban: you too can reach the world of the Yankee, because in each of us there is a bit of a dream island, of the ideal.

Whereas the Yankee approach to the urban-rural dichotomy is one of total war, the comic anti-hero is not overly concerned with it. He is genuinely frustrated with his life in the city, and sometimes he throws barbs at the country for what he feels is unwarranted competition. McCarey's unmuscled, jealous Grant of *My Favorite Wife* baits "savage" Randolph Scott occasionally with lines like, "Do you ride in cabs or just trot alongside?" But generally speaking, the comic (urban based) anti-hero is not overly antagonistic toward the country.

The McCarey figure lived in the city because by then this was where the majority of Americans lived. Urbanization was an accepted lifestyle for him; he did not question the political repercussions to Jeffersonian democracy—it was the property tax he questioned, or the chuckholes on main street. It must be remembered that though the comic anti-hero lives in the city, he is also a victim of the city. In comparison, the Yankee excels in his home environment—the country—and is constantly threatened by victimization in the city. Moreover, this threatened victimization is likely to involve fundamental political rights, rather than the victimization the anti-hero feels in putting an antenna on his roof to get the pro fight on channel seven.

The Capra Yankee believes he can answer these exterior political threats, and then safely retreat to the country. The McCarey anti-hero knows he can never retreat from the largely internal damage already done by city living (the mental frenzy of frustration). There can be no escape to the country, for the anti-hero finds things just as frustrating there.

The 1930's, then, represent a unique period in American comedy, a period in which the anti-hero and the Yankee opposed each other on a national level, for preeminence. McCarey and Capra were responsible for the creation of what is now considered the standard film stereotype of each comic vision, with McCarey refining the anti-hero first used in the Laurel & Hardy shorts, and Capra making Mr. Deeds and Mr. Smith the quintessential embodiments of what, by then, was a hundred-year-old tradition in American humor.

McCarey and Capra had difficulty adapting their comedy approaches to the war years of the '40s. After their initial film efforts in that decade (*My Favorite Wife*, 1940 and *Meet John Doe*, 1941) they both put their comic protagonists in situations they were incapable of handling. In each instance these "new" films—McCarey's *Once Upon a Honeymoon* (1942), and Capra's *It's a Wonderful Life* (1946)—represent a distinct break with the anti-hero and crackerbarrel patterns that have been delineated thus far.

McCarey attempted to put his anti-hero in a political situation (Nazi Europe), have him comment on its realistic ugliness in something approaching rational terms, and at times even become heroic. It was no doubt an honest effort—a war effort—but it was and is impossible for the anti-hero by his very nature.

As McCarey's anti-hero was suffering difficulty, so was the Capra Yankee. However, where McCarey's anti-hero had managed to get by in earlier non-political days but was now floundering in the war years, the Capra Yankee was suffering a different problem; things were beginning to go so fast that he was not able to keep up. He did not have those time-honored precedents to fall back on. These new crises had no precedents. Moreover, unlike earlier Yankees, who might initially make mistakes and then rectify them in later, wiser years, the then contemporary Yankee began to face decisions that did not always offer a tomorrow.

But where Capra and Yankee humor in general would recede from the national scene, McCarey's anti-hero creation would be continued by others and eventually become the dominant American comedy type. Thus, the '30s competition of these two men represented both an ending—the final culmination of a century-long tradition in American humor, and a beginning—the first articulation of what would soon become the national model.

Even with its '30s popularity, however, the Yankee had already become something of an anachronism. Depression audiences attended films at a time when the American economic-political system was being severely tested. It was quite natural that any screen Yankee they confronted (who in effect represents the system) would come forward to bolster it. Thus, Will Rogers would be number one at the box office in 1934, always extolling crackerbarrel wisdom. Yet, even Rogers' screen Yankee seems to hedge on then current problems, because his setting was often an earlier time, when crackerbarrel wisdom was seldom questioned, when things seemed so much simpler.

Capra's Yankees, while not retreating to the past, still reinforce the contemporary ('30s) complexities that had driven the other Yankees back. This reinforcement is displayed through the generally compromised victories of Capra's Yankees after *Mr. Deed Goes to Town*. Crackerbarrel author (Judge Priest stories) and actor Irvin Cobb probably sums it up best for all these methodical Yankees when he states, near the end of his life (1941), his preference for an earlier time—"Living was pitched to a less feverish, a less hurried, a less killing pace than the pace by which we since have learned to live."[10]

McCarey, on the other hand, had articulated a comedy figure (the anti-hero) tied to the most frustrating of contemporary settings.

When the depression struck, a comedy character based upon perennial frustration was to seem all the more appropriate. Thus, while McCarey would not take his anti-hero beyond the depression period (he would move toward works of religious faith, such as *The Bells of St. Mary's* 1945), a new tradition in American comedy had begun. Others would follow McCarey's anti-hero example.

Though there are no easy explanations as to why this anti-heroic tendency continued, the changes in American culture caused by the depression and World War II certainly contributed greatly to the growth and eventual dominance of this new strain and stress in American humor. Different cultural conditions and needs, in short, made audiences more sympathetic to the anti-hero, and correspondingly rendered the Yankee figure more and more obsolete.

(Originally appeared in the *Journal of Popular Film and Television*, vol. 7, no. 1, 1978; Wes D. Gehring copyright.)

Notes

1. Richard Gertner, ed., *International Motion Picture Almanac 1976* (New Work: Quigley Publishing Company, Inc., 1976), 51. Will Rogers was a bigger box-office draw than such contemporary comic rivals as Mae West, W.C. Fields and the Marx Brothers. In fact, Fields and the Marx Brothers represented specialized tastes in the '30s, because they never made Quigley Publication's annual poll of top ten money-makers. West's best box-office years were 1933's eighth place finish—Rogers was second, and 1934's fifth place—Rogers was first. All figures were drawn from Quigley Publication's annual poll of United States theatre exhibitors.

2. It is important to note that Capra not only followed some opportunist inclination when he filled the void left by Roger's death. At the very beginning of Capra's career (when he worked a short time for Hal Roach) Rogers, also on contract, had taken the young man under his wing. Capra writes quite warmly about this period in his autobiography— *The Name Above the Title* (New York: Macmillan Company, 1971), 39-40. And Capra was no doubt influenced by him, especially when parallels can be drawn between an early Rogers work like *Going to Congress* (1924) and Capra's later *Mr. Smith* or *Meet John Doe.*

3. Andrew Sarris, *The American Cinema: Directors and Directions, 1929-1968* (New York: E.P. Dutton & Co., Inc., 1968), 100.
4. *Ibid.*
5. General Mast, *The Comic Mind: Comedy and Movies* (Indianapolis: Bobbs-Merrill Co., Inc. 1973), 264.
6. Mast, 264.
7. Leo McCarey, "Comedy and a Touch of the Cuckoo," *Extension,* Nov. 1944, 6.
8. Pete Martin, "Going His Way," *Saturday Evening Post,* 30, Nov. 1946, 70.
9. In the McCarey written *Bells of St. Mary's* he has the priest remark, "We should never get too far away from our childhood."
10. Irvin Cobb, *The Autobiography of Irvin S. Cobb: Exit Laughing,* (Garden City, N.Y.: Garden City Publishing Co., Inc., 1941), 545.

BOB FOSSE'S

Jazzy Black Humor

SINCE THE 1970S, genre-crossing dark comedies frequently have masqueraded behind other categories, such as the nominal Western *Little Big Man* (1970), or the titular neo-film noir *Chinatown* (1974). This is, while these movies embrace the twisted trio of black humor themes—the omnipresence of death, the absurdity of the world, and man as beast—one's knee-jerk response is to categorize them elsewhere. Moreover, even these genre cloaks break their own category conventions, adding to the attraction of dark comedy. For instance, in the Cavalry vs. the Indian world of *Little Big Man*, one now roots for the Native Americans. The token femme fatale in *Chinatown* (Faye Dunaway) actually is an innocent victim, and Jack Nicholson's prerequisite gumshoe is a prosperous detective whose métier involves divorce cases in stunning California sunlight. Where is the down-and-out Philip Marlowe, or Sam Spade, who lives in those murderous German Expressionistic nights come to Los Angeles?

Still, the 1970s' best example of these more complex genre-crossing dark comedies is Bob Fosse's *All That Jazz* (1979), in which the term "subterfuge" might serve as a subtitle. Ostensibly a musical, this tale follows the life and death of stage and screen director Joe Gideon (Roy Scheider). A musical comedy about death is hardly Fred Astaire and Ginger Rogers territory. Moreover, unlike the long takes and shots the choreographing Astaire used in their films, in order to prove the duo's artistry (excessive editing might make viewers question the team's talent), Fosse assumed the opposite perspective. As early as the "Hey Big Spender" number in *Sweet Charity* (1969), Fosse was creating dance through editing now called the "montage musical." This is best showcased in *All That Jazz* in the open audition sequence of "On Broadway," when Fosse's editing morphs several hopeful dancers into a single leaping and spinning figure.

Another anti-genre smokescreen for *All That Jazz* is how Fosse performs a topsyturvy maneuver on the art house film, the non-traditional genre that asks raised-issue questions, such as is there a God, or why are we here? Yet, there is none of the macabre, deep dish symbolism of Ingmar Bergman's *The Seventh Seal* (1957), in which a disillusioned knight (Max von Sydow) plays chess with a black-garbed death (Bengt Ekerot) so that the returning Crusader might buy time to make sense of God's silence.

In contrast, Fosse's figure of death is a flirtatiously sexy woman in white (Jessica Lange), who periodically comes to tempt Gideon closer and closer to the end of life. Yet, Scheider's character has no real raised issue questions, except maybe why God does not like musical comedy. No, Gideon, like most of us, is too busy with life's lived issues, in this case, trying to stage a new Broadway play while simultaneously completing the editing of an otherwise finished film. Plus, death does not appear randomly, as in the case with Bergman's film. Gideon, closely based upon Fosse's real life, is a workaholic hedonist. (Fosse would suffer his first heart attack in 1974 while also trying to juggle a play and a film concurrently.) Consequently, as will be the case for many of us, Gideon is his own executioner. Thus, death comes not as an arbitrary scary stranger, à la *The Seventh Seal*, but rather

Fosse's alter ego, Joe Gideon (Roy Scheider), and the lovely Angelique, angel of death (Jessica Lange), in *All That Jazz* (1979).

as someone with whom he is only too familiar. (Fosse never changed his lifestyle and died of another heart attack in 1987).

A final *All That Jazz* anti-genre deception involves what French New Wave director Francois Truffaut labeled "profile films." These are not pure biographies, yet they are galvanized by real lives. A prime example would be *Limelight* (1952), by the Fosse-influenced Charlie Chaplin, an impact apparent as early as the Tramp-like gait to "Who's Got the Pain" number in *Damn Yankees* (1958). Regardless, when an artist goes the autobiographical profile film route, he invariably makes his alter ego sympathetic. Thus, the *Limelight* Chaplin plays Calvero, an unappreciated 1914 clown at a time—the Communist witch hunts of Sen. Joe McCarthy (R.-Wis.)—when much of America abhorred the creator of the Tramp. Moreover, after Calvero's moving comeback finale, which simultaneously launches his young protégé, he poignantly dies in the wings as the grand show and/or life goes on.

In contrast, while Gideon, like Calvero, also suffers a fatal heart attack, Fosse goes out of his way to make his surrogate less than sympathetic. While the director and Scheider keep Gideon from being totally unlikable, his film-closing death production occurs only in his mind. There is neither a brief public pay-it-forward to make modest amends for an often wasted life, nor a mentored apprentice continuing tradition. Instead, Gideon's hallucinated "all that jazz" death production merely is what might have been. His invisible exit also reflects an equally unsympathetic craft. Thus, as he is zipped into his body bag, Ethel Merman ironically belts out her theme song, "There's No Business Like Show Business," on the soundtrack. (Black comedy routinely uses music which does *not* reinforce the visual.)

Dark humor has come a long ways from the pioneeringly direct dark comedy of Chaplin's *Monsieur Verdoux* (1947), or Preston Sturges' *Unfaithfully Yours* (1948), in which one immediately gets down to the basics of death, absurdity, and beastly behavior. These later, more complex black comedies have changed the "art is where you get it right" axiom to a Kurt Vonnegut dictum, which is best paraphrased as: Bring chaos to order, then everyone will understand that there is no order in the world, and we must adapt ourselves to the requirements of chaos instead.

DANCING TO
SCREWBALL

ONCE AGAIN TURNER CLASSIC MOVIES (TCM) will be offering a free online summer class for film aficionados. The subject this year will be classic musicals. My home university (Ball State) is again largely orchestrating the project, and thankfully I will be involved as one of the teacher scholars. My perspective on some of the pictures will be linking connections between comedy and music. This column keys on one such film—Fred Astaire and Ginger Rogers' *Top Hat* (1935). This was the fourth of ten movies in which the duo appeared, nine for RKO (1933-1939), and a 1949 MGM finale, *The Barkleys of Broadway*.

Top Hat is now considered their premier picture and was easily their most commercially successful. Indeed, though 1930s box office numbers are often open to debate, *Top Hat* is normally credited with being second only to *Mutiny on the Bounty* as the industry's most commercially successful 1935 picture. Astaire and Rogers were not a team in their first film, *Flying Down to Rio* (1933). However, RKO producer Pandro S. Berman saw a special music and comic spark between the two and decided to team them. (All the Astaire and Rogers RKO musicals were made during Berman's production regime).

Fortuitously for my perspective on the TCM series, I had extensively interviewed Berman when I was a young professor. I was in Hollywood doing research on a book about Berman's 1930s heyday, and he was gracious enough to invite me to a long, leisurely lunch at the Hillcrest Country Club—established early in Hollywood history when Jewish artists were banned from other similar organizations. (Berman shared that back in the day when one club offered to wave the rule, if Groucho Marx did not use the pool, he cracked, "My daughter's only half Jewish; could she wade up to her waist?")

Astaire & Rogers films were first cousins to screwball comedy, such as Gregory La Cava's *My Man Godfrey*, with William Powell and the decade's official screwball heroine, Carole Lombard.

Regardless, Berman was especially expansive on Astaire and Rogers. His most insightful comment was that the team's pictures were meant as screwball comedies set to song and dance. This was an especially acute comment, given that this paralleled the birth of the genre. Though we have always had farce, screwball comedy largely came about because of stricter film censorship, beginning with the establishment of 1934's Production Code Administration (PCA).

A later description of the genre, which equally applied to the Astaire and Rogers films, was that the movies needed to be "sex comedies without the sex." Given the Depression, moreover, escapist screwball comedy and the Astaire and Rogers pictures were usually set in ritzy upscale settings in which money was not a concern. Fittingly, for both these qualifiers, a popular description of Astaire and Rogers was that he gave her class, while she gifted him with sex appeal. Ironically, given that screwball comedy and the Astaire and Rogers films end with a love match, the couples often struggle with romance.

Consequently, when Astaire comes to London to star in a play produced by his close friend Horace (Edward Everett Horton; this could also double as the story's thin plot), the dancer is randomly encouraged to marry. A *solo* Astaire immediately responds with a delightful song and dance set to Irving Berlin's "No Strings (I'm Fancy Free)." Performed in a hotel room directly above Ginger Rogers, his uninhibited dancing makes an enemy as she attempts to sleep.

Screwball comedy often further negates the concept of marriage by having supporting players in less than romantic couplings. *Top Hat* showcases this perfectly with Horace's comic passionless union to Madge (Helen Broderick). Regardless, having Rogers initially angry with Astaire is often also a screwball ploy referenced as a "comedy of remarriage"— building a plot on getting a couple together. This quickly begins for Astaire and Rogers with a Berlin title which says it all—"Isn't This a Lovely Day (to be Caught in the Rain)." Taking shelter in a bandstand, their routine of flirtation is equal parts comic and romantic, moving from mocking imitations to a sense of equality demonstrated by playful hopping steps to top spin barrages.

This is soon followed by arguably Astaire's greatest tap *solo*, Berlin's "Top Hat, White Tie and Tails." Again, this elaborate number, his first with his signature cane, is full of comedy. Highlighted by his ability to change tempos, it includes miming a series of emotions, from caution (about love?), to cocky confidence. Astaire so threw himself into the number he atypically included some improvisation—a phenomenon at the core of screwball comedy. In fact, Berman admired artists capable of extemporizing, such as his friend Gregory LaCava's often improvised seminal screwball comedy, *My Man Godfrey* (1936).

There is more, but by the time Astaire and Rogers dance to Berlin's "Cheek to Cheek," with the composer being very impressed by Astaire navigating a song whose melody, like love, kept climbing, the starring couple had completely negated "No Strings ...." Like a normal screwball comedy, a rocky start had ended in love. Oh, and the connection between that genre and *Top Hat* was not hurt by the fact that two supporting players, Horton and Eric Blore, often also appeared in screwball comedies. In truth, Horton played support in two excellent examples of the genre, George Cukor's *Holiday* and Ernst Lubitsch's *Bluebeard's Eighth Wife* (both 1938). Moreover, Rogers was no stranger here either, with her *Vivacious Lady* (1938) practically being a template for the genre—her title character showgirl was perfectly teamed with Jimmy Stewart's absentminded professor. And Rogers' later *Monkey Business* (1952), another screwball comedy with an absentminded professor (Cary Grant), had the added fun of affectionately spoofing her dancing background.

In the 1930s "musical comedy" could be said to have embraced a broader spectrum. After all, Bob Hope and Shirley Ross sang the Oscar winning song "Thanks for the Memory" in *The Big Broadcast of 1938*, and it soon became his theme song.

DECODING THE DETAILS

SIGNATURE SCENES:

Generating Insight & Discussion

WHAT IS THE SIGNATURE SCENE of that film you just saw, and/ or your favorite film? Such sequences provide added perception into the picture as a whole. However, these seminal excerpts often differ among viewers, and one might even change your signature scene upon a subsequent reviewing of a picture. What follows are four such segments from films gone by.

The most riveting *Godfather* (1972) scene involves the staging of Al Pacino's revenge killing of the men responsible for the attempted murder of his father, Don Corleone (Marlon Brando). Up until this point in the picture, Pacino has been a "civilian," with the Don not wanting his son to be a part of the Mafia. However, with his father near death, Pacino decides to change the course of his life. He helps orchestrate an alleged olive branch meal with the rival mob boss and crooked police commissioner who ordered the hit on his father. The neutral site sit-down is a small Italian restaurant somewhere in New York City. As a civilian, Pacino's figure is not seen as a threat by his two rivals, although he is patted down for a weapon upon arriving at the cafe. During the meal, Pacino excuses himself to go to the restroom, where a revolver has been hidden. As with many New York businesses, the restaurant is built over the subway. When Pacino exits the restroom, a train suddenly is underfoot. Its close proximity gently shakes the building while producing a roar that briefly makes speech impossible, but this bit of New York realism is an inspired metaphor for the physical shock that must be going through Pacino's system, as he contemplates the double murder he is about to execute coupled with the abandonment, forever, of a normal life.

In another train-related scene, Robert Downey Jr.'s title character in the biography film *Chaplin* (1992) has returned to his native England for

After the restaurant revenge shooting, *Godfather* (1972) title character Marlon Brando is replaced by his son (Al Pacino, seated).

the premier of *The Kid* (1921). The comedian is anxious to reconnect with the love of his life, actress Hetty Kelly (Moira Kelly), but in a casual conversation with a former mentor, Charlie Chaplin discovers she has died. Almost simultaneously, the train enters a tunnel, with the resulting flickering lights and heightened locomotive sounds no doubt mirroring the sudden shellshock Downey's character would be feeling. As the train approaches London's Victoria Station filled with thousands of adoring fans, only Chaplin's assistant realizes the tragic sadness of the situation. When he asks the comedian what they should do, cinema's most celebrated funnyman says simply, "Smile." At the same time, on the soundtrack, one hears a haunting instrumental rendition of Chaplin's signature composition, "Smile," as the unspoken lyrics counsel: "Smile, though your heart is breaking...."

The cliff jumping scene in *Butch Cassidy and the Sundance Kid* (1969) is a darkly comic capsulization of the entire movie. With the pair surrounded by a "super posse," Butch (Paul Newman) has to convince a hesitant Sundance (Robert Redford) to jump. Eventually, Sundance reveals the reason behind his reluctance: he cannot swim. With this, Butch is convulsed with laughter, eventually replying, "Why, you crazy... the fall'll probably kill you!" After this bit of illogic, they both jump.

The film essentially is a Western parody, predicated upon what the stereotypical *High Noon* cowboy never does—run away. The cliff scene is the movie's most entertaining example of this practicality. Yet, the death-threatening absurdity of such an escape also plays into the film's darkly comic take on the pure nonsense of life. The scene also provides insight into the creative process of its Academy Award-winning screenwriter, William Goldman. In 1980s correspondence with the writer, he revealed his fondness for the cliff-jumping segment of the classic adventure film, *Gunga Din* (1939, which also has parody overtones). Goldman suggested a link between the *Butch Cassidy* jumping scene with the "Cliffs of Insanity" segment from his 1973 novel, *The Princess Bride* (which he adapted to the screen in 1987). Again, *Bride* is an affectionate spoof of romantic fairy tales. Goldman's homage to *Gunga Din* in one of his letters underlines its "great influence" on *Butch Cassidy*, "The camaraderie, the sadness of good men dying, the joy of what film can do... nothing has ever moved me as much as a kid as 'Gunga Din.' It is, still, my favorite [film]."

Several film historians, including Gerald Mast, have suggested the single greatest movie scene is the close of Chaplin's *City Lights* (1931). The picture chronicles how the Tramp has fallen in love with a beautiful blind girl (Virginia Cherrill), prompting him to move the proverbial heaven and Earth to acquire the necessary cash for a sight-producing operation.

Cherrill's character thinks her benefactor is a handsome young millionaire. Thus, when they meet by chance sometime after the successful surgery, the Tramp is overjoyed that she can see—and overwhelmed about what that means for them. However, all the girl can see is a laughable hobo apparently smitten by her beauty. Worse yet, she gives him a coin out of pity. This is a brilliant stroke by Chaplin, since this act—she has touched his hand before—allows the former blind girl to realize the Tramp is the one. Yet, the shock when she realizes this is her benefactor, and the final poignant image of his face, are the picture of pathos—the difficult smile that somehow acknowledges that this romance certainly is at an end. As critic James Agee wrote, "It is enough to shrivel the heart." Chaplin provides the ultimate life lesson: do the right thing, even when that means losing the love of your life.

MOVIES WITHOUT ENDINGS:

Artist Comfort vs. Chaos

IN RECENT YEARS, films with ambiguous or open-ended conclusions seemingly have been on the rise. Examples would include Sofia Coppola's *Lost in Translation* (2003), Darren Aronofsky's *The Wrestler* (2008), and Christopher Nolan's *Inception* (2010). In each case, it is up to the viewer to decide just what happens next. "Lost" appears to end with no hope for the May-December relationship of Bill Murray and Scarlet Johansson. Both feel a real soulmate connection for each other, yet they are locked into unhappy relationships—but when they part Murray whispers something into her ear, and the potential for romance rebounds. Maybe he has suggested a scenario straight out of *An Affair to Remember* (1957), where the equally unavailable to each other Cary Grant and Deborah Kerr decide to meet again in six months, if they feel their random shipboard romance really is love.

In *The Wrestler*, Mickey Rourke's title character has sacrificed everything for a pro-wrestling career, but after years of physical and steroid abuse, his health is ruined; a return to the ring constitutes a potential death sentence. Thus, Rourke attempts to establish a relationship with a neglected now-grown daughter. Plus, he awkwardly tries to connect romantically with a lovely but aging exotic dancer (Marisa Tomei), whose based-upon-a-body "entertainment" career, like Rourke's, rapidly is approaching an expiration date. The wrestler's new life shows promise, but then misunderstandings, mistakes, and money needs tempt him into a comeback bout. The movie goes to black just as he returns to the ring and begins to execute his most physically demanding wrestling move. Will it kill him, or will he survive and somehow get a second chance with the two women in his life?

Inception is a complex story of dreams within dreams: Leo DiCaprio performs futuristic espionage by entering the subconscious minds of corporate leaders in order to plant and extract pivotal information. However, his noirish character is haunted by nightmare images of his late wife (Marion Cotillard). His guilt over her suicide death (for which he is wanted for murder) fuels her periodic surprise appearances—and sometimes nearly sabotages his elaborately constructed multiple dream states. DiCaprio puts his now-compromised abilities to one final test, which, if successful, will clear his name and allow him access to his children. Yet, there are risks that he will not be able to survive this last three-layered labyrinth of dreams.

The nature of this dreamscape work necessitates that DiCpario and his team each carry a totem, a small object whose basic properties allow them to differentiate between reality and a subconscious state. DiCaprio's totem is a spinning top. In a dream it would spin perpetually, ultimately signaling death. If it wobbles and falls, DiCaprio safely is back to reality—such as it is. "Inception" ends with DiCaprio succeeding and returning to his children, but Nolan closes with a shot of the spinning top. Is this happy ending real?

There is nothing inherently new about ambiguous endings. As a middle schooler I remember a once popular homework assignment—provide an ending for Frank R. Stockton's celebrated open-ended short story, "The Lady, or the Tiger" (1882). An evil ruler creates a perverse form of justice for offenders. The accused is placed in an arena with only two exits. Behind one door is a lovely maiden, and behind the other a tiger. If the door he picks has the woman, he is innocent, but he must marry the lady. If he chooses the tiger door, a guilty verdict and death would be almost simultaneous. The story twist occurs when the king discovers his daughter loves a commoner. Naturally, the young man ends up in the arena, and anxiously looks at the princess for a hint of which door to choose. She knows but, either way, the girl loses her lover. Finally, the princess indicates a door, and there Stockton's story ends. Was it the lady or the tiger?

Though ambiguous conclusions are more common today, early cinema had them, too. Indeed, the sequence often called film's greatest single scene—the ending of Charlie Chaplin's *City Lights* (1931), where the once-blind flower girl (Virginia Cherrill) finally sees her romantically frustrated benefactor (Chaplin's alter ego Tramp)—is a key example. Expecting a handsome young man of means, will she accept Chaplin's vagabond character? Including *City Lights* as a pivotal instance of this phenomenon merely underscores ambiguity's popularity today, as classic cinema study always has "read" the scene as one of rejection.

Of course, maybe decades from now, equally polemical shifts will have occurred in how to interpret the endings of *Lost*, *The Wrestler*, and *Inception*.

Charlie Chaplin's Tramp pondering the formerly blind young women's decision
about *their* future, *City Lights* (1931).

Ultimately, the beauty of realism's ambiguous nature frees viewers from rigid spoon-fed conclusions. Recognizing that angles of vision are changing constantly in art and life is the final component in a true education, and a safety valve against what an earlier generation called "future shock."

Remember, while filmmakers labor long over creating the perfect final-cut movie, every individual's life is in perpetual rough-cut mode, with a sudden ambiguous ending the fate of many. While art traditionally has given us a chance to create a brief sense of order in life's chaos, today's greater appreciation of open-ended movies could be interpreted as an increased sense of heightened interactive maturity. It is your call to make.

LIVED ISSUES vs. RAISED ISSUES:

Jokers Wild

LET US DEMONSTRATE THE LINKS between mainstream genres (such as romantic comedy, horror, science fiction, etc.) and art house movies (like Ingmar Bergman's *The Seventh Seal*, 1957, in which a disillusioned knight returning from the Crusades plays a chess game with Death). While this might not seem as intrinsically interesting as, say, the public's often perverse fascination with the self-destructive artist (a James Dean or Heath Ledger), all of these things, including the "die young and leave a good looking corpse" type, are interconnected.

Traditionally, a pop culture genre deals with "lived issues." Will Michael Douglas straighten out his love life in *Wonder Boys* (2000), or will Robert Redford hit the pennant-winning home run in *The Natural* (1984), or how can Will Smith save the world yet again *in I Am Legend* (2007)? Art house movies are about intangible "raised issues," often a combination of "Why am I here?" and "Is there a God?" (à la that *The Seventh Seal* picture), and a "seize the day" mantra, whether the "day" is late (the elderly professor of Bergman's *Wild Strawberries*, 1957) or just beginning (the students of *Dead Poets Society*, 1989).

At some level, everyone can relate to the "lived issue" phenomenon, looking for love, coming through in the clutch, and maybe pulling a Walter Mitty daydream about sacrificing one's self for the good of humanity (even if *Legend* simply morphed into a big budget zombie movie). These "lived issue" films are entertaining mind candy that act as a necessary balm, buffer, or boost to human morale.

In contrast, despite that wonderfully hoary axiom, "The unexamined life is not worth living," the "raised issue" self-conscious art film is leperlike to many audiences. Of course, this is inherently disturbing stuff.

These thinking films are open-ended; unlike John Ford's classic Western, *Stagecoach* (1939), the cavalry never rides to the rescue in any deep dish saga. Worse, haunting questions posed early are never answered, not even when Googled.

One might draw a comic comparison between classic art house movies and standard genres from Woody Allen's *Love and Death* (1975,

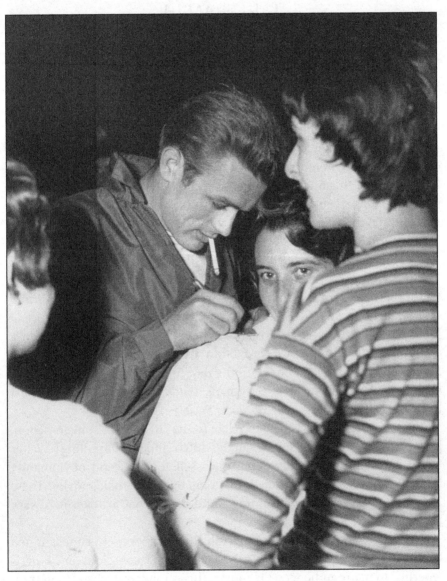

James Dean signing autographs during the production of *Rebel Without a Cause* (1955).

which could be described as Bob Hope trapped in *The Seventh Seal*). Yet, whereas God always has laryngitis in Bergmanland, Allen forever is peppering the *Silence* (1963, Bergman) with pertinent quips: "the mind [coffee house cinema] embraces all the nobler aspirations, like poetry [and] philosophy, but the body [the multiplex movie] has all the fun."

So, why would one want to avoid the fun film crowd in order to dabble with death and the chaos of life? Well, there is a balm-buffer-boost here, too—the discovery that you neither are alone in your fears nor unique in your pain. Oscar Wilde observed in 1891's *The Picture of Dorian Gray*, "To become a spectator of one's own life is to escape the suffering of life." Granted, that is easy to say if one can transform the ravages of age and debauchery onto a poor picture in the closet, but doesn't a lack of serious self-reflection leave one unprepared for real life? As the blacklisted writer Dalton Trumbo said of the McCarthy era, "Where there is fear, there is hysteria." Even if the *Dorian Gray*-inspired "spectator of one's life" cannot always alter things, there is a certain theater in your head about being self-aware. Comedian George Carlin likened it to "watching one corner of your mind work from another corner of your mind."

The thought-provoking film also offers a respite of order from the chaotic world. As Allen's playwright observed in *Annie Hall* (1977), "Art is where you get it right." One can draw personal insight and comfort from studying and creating such structured patterns in life, or even gain a feeling of payback for inequities suffered—you briefly impose order on the fractured cosmos. Directors make movies, my grandmothers made quilts—same principle. Ah, but there's the rub. The longevity of deep dish art sometimes comes from hiding in plain sight, like grandma's quilt. For every *The Single Man* (2009), there are dozens of mainstream movies interwoven with cerebral subtexts. Indeed, there are such works disguised as Westerns, *The Shootist* (1976); musicals, *All That Jazz* (1979); sci-fi, *District 9* (2009), etc. To paraphrase *New Yorker* Anthony Lane's praise of this subterfuge, "They could make an adventure out of a sermon."

Where, however, do those aforementioned martyr movie star types like Dean or Ledger fit into the wrinkled brow equation? Biographers, critics, and artists themselves often fuel the connection by romanticizing the creative process, blurring the line between public persona and private person. In Dean's case, he erased the line. When he died in a sports car accident—seemingly emblematic of his title character—just days before the opening of what became his signature film, *Rebel Without a Cause* (1955), a now forever young Dean became the freeze-frame symbol of the frustrated, alienated, low-on-self-esteem teen. Between the tragedy and the timing, the public deified Dean for what seemed like an artistically sacrificial death. Had his inspired performance not been italicized by an early exit, he might have—following Marlon Brando—become lost in the Method acting stampede.

"Raised issues" are embedded in many "lived issue" pictures, but whereas death frequently is part of the scripted art house story, sometimes the mall movie only seems to resonate with subtext if the Joker dies in real life, too (à la Ledger's passing before the 2008 release of *The Dark Knight*, in which he played the Joker).

(Reprinted with permission from *USA Today Magazine*, May, 2010. Copyright © 2010 by "The Society for the Advancement of Education, Inc. All Rights Reserved.")

ANALYZING THOSE MOVIES:

Within Movies

WHAT SEEMS TO BE casual references to movies within movies usually are anything but. These self-referential moments, which will be limited here to actual film footage introduced into the narrative, tell the viewer something about a central character or add an ironically insightful subtext to the picture.

As one example, a mainstream movie starting point might be the breakfast scene in *Field of Dreams* (1989). Kevin Costner's novice farmer has just begun hearing the "voice" that will inspire him to build a baseball diamond. This act of fantasy film redemption results in the return of "Shoeless" Joe Jackson and other Capraesque scenes of feel-good populism. Initially, however, Costner's character simply fears he is crazy. In fact, at one point Patsy Cline's "Crazy" is heard on the soundtrack, but the in-film movie reference to his anxiety occurs when he finds his daughter (Gaby Hoffman) watching *Harvey* (1950) on television. In this picture, adapted from Mary Chase's play, Jimmy Stewart is the delightfully daft drinker Elwood P. Dowd, whose constant companion is an invisible six-foot-tall pooka (bunny) named Harvey whose comments are heard only by him. Costner quickly disparages said movie to his daughter, and young Hoffman misses the rest of her breakfast entertainment.

In contrast to this amusing twist on Costner's anxiety level, an in-movie sequence from Woody Allen's *Hannah and Her Sisters* (1986) actually saves the comedian's screen character. Allen's standard hypochondriac-neurotic New Yorker is feeling suicidal and blindly wanders into a movie revival house in Greenwich Village. He comes in on the *Duck Soup* (1933) sequence in which the Marx Brothers simultaneously are satirizing war and early sound musicals with a number entitled "This Country's Going to

War." Allen has called it "probably the best talking comedy ever made," and the American Film Institute cites it as one of the country's three funniest movies (joining *Some Like It Hot*, 1959, and *Tootsie*, 1982). Fittingly, after Allen's *Hannah* character sees the inspired multifaceted funny scene, he decides to embrace life again. A comic catharsis of "Marxist" proportions, or the Groucho-Harpo-Chico-Zeppo artists of your choice, help one weather anything.

The in-film film reference also can reveal darker contrasting insights about characters. For instance, in Arthur Penn's *Bonnie and Clyde* (1967), when the title characters go to the movies after a botched robbery, their reactions are a study in contrast. Bonnie (Faye Dunaway) is engrossed in the Depression-era escapism of the "We're in the Money" number from Mervyn LeRoy's *Gold Diggers of 1933* (1933), but Clyde (Warren Beatty) cryingly struggles with the fact that he has just killed a man. Paradoxically, the next morning, Clyde offers to put Bonnie on a bus home, since her identity is not yet known and things now are going to get "rough." Yet, he is the one who has wilted under pressure. In fact, moments before his exit offer, Bonnie is singing a refrain from the aforementioned song, "We've got a lot of what it takes to get along," while primping in front of the mirror and admiring her coin necklace—which apes the jewelry worn by the chorus line of *Gold Diggers*. She never has been more in her element. It is Clyde who does not have "what it takes."

In contrast, Curtis Hanson's *Wonder Boys* (2000), adapted from Michael Chabon's novel, has one of the title characters, Tobe Maguire's gifted college student, watching a television broadcast of Oscar Wilde's haunting novel, *The Picture of Dorian Gray* (Albert Lewin's 1945 screen adaptation), while getting stoned. The Wilde sequence, like the Academy Award-winning Bob Dylan song ("Things Have Changed") in *Wonder Boys*, suggests that, when one embraces everything—even with a "safety net" portrait in the closet—self-destruction is the result. Maguire and his fellow wonder boy, Michael Douglas' mentoring professor, must embrace reality by making choices, or face Gray's sad demise. Yet, since *Wonder Boys* ultimately is a comedy, the channel-surfing Maguire next turns to Judy Garland and Mickey Rooney auditioning a number ("Good-Morning") that soon will make them *Babes in Arms* (1939). The subtext is clear; the *Wonder Boys* also have a chance to reach their own literary Broadway (Douglas for the second time), if only they can focus half of the entertainment energy of Garland and Rooney. Happily, this is the film clip destiny awaiting Douglas and Maguire.

Unlike the previous examples, the highlighted sequences in Michael Mann's *Public Enemies* (2009) are anchored in a macabre—and poignant—piece of pop culture history. Mann re-creates the fatal, yet somewhat fitting, last decision of John Dillinger's life—attending a theatrical screening of W.S. Van Dyke's gangster film, *Manhattan Melodrama* (1934, with Clark Gable). Before exiting the movie and dying in a hail of FBI bullets, Dillinger (played by Johnny Depp) is seen deeply immersed in two *Melodrama* sequences. The first involves Gable turning down an offer

When *Play It Again, Sam* (1972) was not using Bogie footage from *Casablanca* (1942), Jerry Lacy was made to seem as if this icon had stepped off the screen.

from his friend the governor (William Powell) to commute the death sentence: "Say, you think you're doing me a favor by keeping me locked up in this filthy trap for the rest of my life? No thanks. Come on, warden, let's go." With cutaways to an approving Dillinger and the developing FBI ambush being set up outside Chicago's Biograph Theater, the second *Melodrama* clip has Gable briefly stopping on his walk to the electric chair in order to respond to a supportive aside by another death row inmate. Though gracious, Gable's gangster will accept no sympathy: "Die the way you live—all of a sudden; that's the way to go. Don't drag it out. Living like that doesn't mean a thing." With the same attitude, Depp's Dillinger then unknowingly walks to his own "execution."

In Richard Attenborough's biography film *Chaplin* (1992), Robert Downey Jr. is so inspiringly dead-on as the title character that the actor convincingly is able to re-create some of the comedian's set pieces, but the film's tour de force close, where Chaplin receives a Special Academy Award at the 1972 Oscar ceremony, has Attenborough revisiting that night by showing actual film footage of several signature Chaplin scenes. These sequences include the Tramp's brilliant doubling as a fun house mechanical figure in *The Circus* (1928), and the emotionally gripping rooftop rescue of Jackie Coogan in *The Kid* (1921). Downey so successfully has gotten into the oversized shoes of the *Little Fellow* that these real clips simply reinforce his performance.

Along similar biographical lines, in a fictionalized "profile film," to use a phrase from critic-turned-filmmaker Francois Truffaut, movie clips can be employed to enhance the creation of a composite cinema "individual." For instance, Don Siegal opens the *The Shootist* (1976) with a montage of movie moments from title character John Wayne's elegiac Western career, including *Stagecoach* (1939) and *Rio Bravo* (1959). The tribute-like introduction doubles as a mini-biography of the actor's *Shootist* cowboy, giving the viewer a fascinating back-story to the actor's final variation of his iconic man of the West.

Though I have just chronicled my favorite in-film movie references that double as pointed commentaries on said pictures, there are countless other variations of this phenomenon that bear noting. For example, some parody movies couple spoofing the conventions of a specifically targeted genre or film with recycled footage from these movies. In Woody Allen's *Play It Again, Sam* (1972), the ghost of Humphrey Bogart tutors the comedian on dating and, as the title suggests, this necessitates utilizing several Bogart clips from *Casablanca* (1942).

In *Sam*, Allen only deals directly with Bogie's ghost (Jerry Lacy) but, in Carl Reiner's spoof of film noir, *Dead Men Don't Wear Plaid* (1982), new Steve Martin footage is cut into various vintage clips. Thus, Martin's detective seems to be interacting with a who's who of the genre, including Bogart, Alan Ladd, and Dick Powell. On a more modest level, in Marty Feldman's underrated *The Last Remake of Beau Geste* (1977, which he cowrote and directed), the pop-eyed comedian has a scene in which, through the magic of special effects, he appears to be sharing screen time with a movie legend—Gary Cooper's title character in the original *Beau Geste* (1939).

On the other end of the movie within a movie spectrum, from the multiplicity of a "Sam" or "Plaid," are the almost subliminal clips. Though too brief to qualify as a capsulization of a movie theme, as exemplified by most of the sequences cited, even these snipets rarely are random. To illustrate, in Martin McDonagh's stunning dark comedy *In Bruges* (2008), there is a short, seemingly throwaway scene in which the most sympathetic of hit men (Brendan Gleeson) is watching a movie on late-night television. The viewer only sees a few seconds from the opening of Orson Welles' noir classic, *Touch of Evil* (1958), but how appropriate—a hit man is watching another hit man plant a bomb.

In Anton Corbijn's more somber tale of a hit man, *The American* (2010), George Clooney's assassin title character is seen briefly in an Italian café in which a big screen television is playing the Sergio Leone spaghetti Western, *Once Upon a Time in the West* (1968). The fleeting images focus upon a hired killer (Henry Fonda), but this film within a film placement is not just a compound hit-man reference. In each movie, an iconically American screen star (Fonda and Clooney), normally synonymous with positive values, is cast against type as a ruthless assassin. Leone's darkly comic Italian sensibility permeates his revisionist American Westerns. In *The American*, Clooney's strong silent figure, literally a "man with no name" (á la Clint Eastwood's roles for Leone), finds himself in a series of shootout situations (largely in Italy) which would not be out of place in a Western.

In yet another of Barry Levinson's brilliant Baltimore tales, *Liberty Heights* (1999), Bebe Neuwirth is watching television while her youngest son (Ben Foster) is getting ready to go out with a friend. One glimpses just a few moments of her favorite movie—the carnival sequence from Alfred Hitchcock's *Strangers on a Train* (1951), in which a young woman is murdered. As this fact registers with the attentive viewer, Neuwirth tells her screen teen he is staying home. Though a coming-of-age comedy, Foster's character will have his life threatened later in the movie.

So, although critics sometimes are accused of "reading" too much into a film, there often is a great deal hidden in plain sight.

MIRROR, MIRROR IN MY MOVIE...

MIRROR MOVIES ARE FASCINATING. These are films in which reflected surfaces highlight a pivotal sequence. For instance, there is the Marx Brothers' "mirror scene" from director Leo McCarey's *Duck Soup* (1933), in which Harpo doubles as Groucho's nightgown-attired reflection. (Maybe even more famous is Harpo's 1955 television appearance on *I Love Lucy*, in which he and Lucille Ball re-create the *Soup* sequence—with the key variation merely being that the common costume now is Harpo's, as opposed to the look-alike Groucho's of the film.)

A student of McCarey can, of course, draw upon many memorable mirror scenes. The most significant example, after *Duck Soup*, comes at the close of his watershed romantic comedy, *An Affair to Remember* (1957). Cary Grant's character has brought a special sentimental Christmas gift to an almost lover (Deborah Kerr). The present is a shawl belonging to his beloved grandmother (Cathleen Nesbitt), which Kerr had admired greatly. When Kerr had failed to make an earlier lovers' rendezvous at the top of the Empire State Building, a scene forever referenced in later romantic comedies (see especially Nora Ephron's *Sleepless in Seattle*, 1993), Grant assumes she no longer cares. He does not know Kerr's character had been injured seriously on the way to their meeting. Since she now is an invalid, Kerr never had gotten in touch with Grant, fearing a potential pity partner.

After their nonrendezvous, Grant's playboy figure is motivated to pursue his neglected talent for painting, with his best canvas being a likeness of Kerr in the aforementioned shawl. The later death of Grant's grandmother is the catalyst for him to surprise Kerr at home with his gift. (Kerr's condition remains a secret, because he is ushered into her presence by a maid, and Kerr remains seated upon her living room couch.) However, Grant's awkward small talk banter eventually leads to a surprising admission: he had allowed his art dealer to give the portrait of Kerr to a woman who repeatedly visited the exhibit simply to gaze upon the painting.

As Grant slowly fleshes out the fact that said lady was handicapped, he has an epiphany—is Kerr the woman? Is that why she missed the rendezvous? Grant distractedly starts to search the apartment for the portrait. He soon has his answer. McCarey frames a transfixed Grant in the doorway of Kerr's bedroom. As the emotion generated by Grant's bittersweet expression sweeps over the viewer, McCarey artfully ups the sentimental ante by slightly panning the camera to the right. While the emoting Grant remains in the film frame, the audience now sees a reflection of the Kerr painting in a bedroom mirror. It is truly a multiple-tissue moment.

These two McCarey scenes chronicle a mirror movies truism: basic genre conventions are reinforced. For instance, the *Duck Soup* example is consistent with the surrealistic absurdity at the heart of clown comedy, especially when it involves the Marx Brothers. The *An Affair to Remember* sequence is an exercise in the emotionally melodramatic "will love triumph?" closing equation common to romantic comedy.

Yet another entertaining genre use of the mirror occurs in McCarey's screwball comedy *The Awful Truth* (1937). This film type also answers to the name "bedroom farce," and that is precisely the focus of its mirror scene. Grant's character has stopped by the apartment of his estranged wife (Irene Dunne). Both of them would like to get back together, but a potential problem is that Dunne's handsome French music instructor (Alex D'Arcy) currently is hiding in her bedroom. It is all innocent; D'Arcy had stopped by first and simply hid when the jealousy-prone Grant arrived. Dunne manages to weather the potential storm, that is until Grant prepares to leave and mistakenly gets D'Arcy's derby—which is swimmingly too big. (This haberdashery distress is reminiscent of those times when the McCarey-teamed Laurel & Hardy accidentally put on each other's chapeau.)

The Awful Truth mirror scene that follows involves a merry myriad of Dunne explanations and suggestions on making Grant's suddenly oversized derby fit. The comic "topper" is watching Grant try to tuck his ears inside of it. As with most farce, even mirror tricks cannot keep that extra-man-in-the-bedroom secret.

Groucho (right) and Chico relax on the *Duck Soup* (1933) set during rehearsals for the mirror sequence. Note that Groucho is wearing the nightgown attire which will be worn during the scene.

While these McCarey mirror sequences have been funny or heartwarming, this director never worked in the genre of film noir—the French criticism moniker for murder mysteries and tough guy detectives, almost always shot in black-and-white. If *Duck Soup* arguably is cinema's best comic mirror sequence, one could posit that Orson Welles' noir classic *The Lady From Shanghai* (1947), with the riveting hall of mirrors climax, takes the cake for drama. Rita Hayworth and her cinema husband (Everett Sloane; Welles was her real-life husband at the time) commence shooting at each other in a mirrored fun house, but with all those multiple-mirrored Hayworths and Sloanes, the almost theatre of absurd violence quickly becomes a mesmerizing murder match of visual elimination—until many shattered images produce two real victims.

This *Shanghai* sequence probably was inspired by Charlie Chaplin's more true to the name "fun house" mirror scenes in *The Circus* (1928), in which the Tramp eludes various forms of apprehension by way of his sudden comic cloning. While neither mirrors nor Tramps are killed in the process, Chaplin, like Welles and McCarey, uses mirrors to question reality. In contrast, Peter Bogdanovich's biography film *Mask* (1985) takes a carnival distortion mirror poignantly to peek at normalcy. That is, a teenage boy (Eric Stoltz) whose face has been disfigured by a rare disease, has a brief glance at what might have been, courtesy of a now not-so-crazy mirror.

Ultimately, many mirror movies are like an ironic reading of life. If an individual has been blessed with a long life, is there not an element of surrealism in watching one's mirrored image change over time? Like Groucho seeing his reflection as Harpo, passing years create similar-looking imposters for all of us. Thus, like most art, these mirror movie scenes often are lies that tell the truth.

MOVIE DOORS:

And the Meaning Behind Them

THE USE OF DOORS and doorways in art is fascinating. My interest in this subtext possibly was fueled by growing up in the hometown (Cedar Rapids, Iowa) of American regionalist painter Marvin Cone, whose work often featured this subject matter. While Cone's paintings never achieved the fame of his close friend and fellow Iowa artist Grant Wood, there always seemed to be a haunting quality to the multiple meanings "behind" his doors.

I have transferred this interest in the subtextual "reading" of the subject to memorable movies. For instance, in D.W. Griffith's controversial classic, *The Birth of a Nation* (1915), the culmination of the epic's first part is the Little Colonel (Henry B. Walthall) returning from the Civil War. As he is greeted by family in the doorway of his home, it is almost as if the house itself embraces the veteran.

Charlie Chaplin was a great student of Griffith's film career, and a variation of the Little Colonel scene surfaces poignantly as the finale to the comedian's *The Kid* (1921). Chaplin's Tramp thinks he has forever lost his beloved surrogate son (title character Jackie Coogan) when the once-abandoned child he has raised since birth is missing. The authorities had been hounding the Tramp about his right to the child. Thus, when the boy is suddenly gone, and the police pick up Chaplin, the Tramp assumes the worst. Instead, Chaplin's iconic "Little Fellow" is ushered to the doorway of a pleasantly oversized bungalow. The door opens and the kid and his biological mother (Edna Purviance), now reunited, welcome Chaplin to a new home and life in a manner reminiscent of Griffith's starting-over signature scene from *Birth*.

Fast-forward to John Ford's watershed Western, *The Searchers* (1956), showcasing arguably the most influential doorway scene in cinema history. Ford, sometimes described as the sound era D.W. Griffith (but

Julie Harris' (right) child-like heroine in *The Haunting* (1963), with Claire Bloom.

with a sense of humor), does an emotional one-eighty from the mood of the two previous examples. That is, after an epic chronicling of the title characters' (John Wayne and Jeffrey Hunter) long Odyssey-like search for a once-small child (Lana Wood) abducted by Native Americans, the pivotal doorway finale shuts Wayne out.

Ethan's (Wayne) obsession to find his niece is not an altruistic quest. This racist former Confederate soldier, probably suffering from post-traumatic stress, initially plans to kill a child he perceived to have been contaminated by her long contact with Native Americans. Ethan's young companion on this relentless mission (Hunter) equally is driven to protect the girl, but by the time the rescue finally occurs, after a nearly decade-long search, Ethan's attitude towards the now young woman (Natalie Wood, Lana's older sister) has softened.

Still, the homecoming of the girl and "the searchers" does not integrate Ethan. Everyone, including the welcoming family, enter the home—except Wayne. Forever the outsider, he lingers briefly in the final film frame door frame, and, as he turns to leave, the door closes on Wayne and the West. Unlike the warm return to normalcy for the Little Colonel or the doorway offering the Tramp a first home and a second chance, in *The Searchers* it neither is appropriate nor fitting that Ethan's savage antihero pass through a portal symbolic of civilization. Wayne's wanderer never will find a traditional home or haven.

Just as Chaplin was inspired by Griffith, Ford's doorway close to *The Searchers* had a profound impact upon Francis Ford Coppola's *The Godfather* (1972). Near the end of the movie, after Michael Corleone (Al Pacino) has consolidated his Mafia power, he needs to compartmentalize and close off his private life. His second marriage, to an outspoken non-Sicilian WASP (Diane Keaton) is starting to create marital fissures. After one final well-played lie to her, Pacino returns to his throne room-like study and his ring-kissing subordinates. Symbolically, the study door then closes on Keaton's Kay. Visually, the scene is strikingly similar to the conclusion of *The Searchers*, in that another character is barred from a "family" situation.

The Ford and Coppola scenes do differ, however, in one significant way. As noted earlier, Wayne's Ethan is not suited for civilization. Though he decided to spare the girl at the eleventh hour, his apocalyptically bloody rescue involved scalping the Indian husband who held her captive. Fittingly, Wayne's character and the story itself were the inspiration for Martin Scorsese's cold-blooded *Taxi Driver* (1976), where the Ethan figure (Robert De Niro's Travis) is played in an even more paranoid and searingly sick manner. In contrast, Keaton's *Godfather* character represents normal human decency—which is being barred, via the door closing, from the savage family world of Michael's Mafia don.

These are seminal door-related scenes, drawn from four different genres—war, personality comedy, a Western, and a gangster picture—but, if any genre has a corner on this subject, it would be horror movies, which are most effective when the signature door neither is opened nor closed. As Stephen King writes in his nonfiction text, *Danse Macabre*, "[Horror is] used to almost quintessential effect in Robert Wise's film *The Haunting* [1963], whereas in 'The Monkey's Paw,' we are never allowed to see what is behind the door."

The viewer's imagination inevitably is more frightening than anything a filmmaker might create. Maybe the most disturbing such door-remaining-closed horror scenes occur in *The Leopard Man* (1943), from RKO's master of the macabre, Val Lewton. The sequence involves a young Mexican girl being terrorized by something on the way home from the store. Ironically, she is caught and clawed to death as she vainly tries to get someone to open her own locked home door, but the viewer only hears the horror from the other side of the door. Thus, the frightening shock of an imagined monster is intensified by the unseen grizzly death of a young innocent. Lewton then tops this double unseen whammy of horror by something gut-wrenchingly visual—under the still-closed door trickles a rivulet of blood.

In life, one never knows whether it is an opportunity at the door or just another salesman; in art, though, the possibilities often are much more dramatic.

CINEMA PERIODS OF SELF-REFLECTING ISOLATION

THE FIRST MOVIE I REMEMBER seeing in a theatre was John Sturges' adaptation of Hemingway's novella, *The Old Man and the Sea* (1958, with Spencer Tracy in the title role). Fittingly, I saw this parable about an aging fisherman's ongoing battle against the elements with my grandfather, who, as a farmer/survivor of the Depression, also knew a great deal about battling the elements. Moreover, Hemingway's fisherman was shadowed by a young boy, the role I had assumed in my grandfather's life. How could this movie not have made an impression upon me?

Still, many other things about the film resonate with me, starting with the old man's central mantra (at the core of all Hemingway's work), "A man can be destroyed but not defeated." Maybe even my lifelong love of the Yankees began with this work, since the stoicism of the fisherman is inspired by a pinstripe legend: "I must have confidence and must be worthy of the great DiMaggio who does all things perfectly even with the pain of the bone spur in his heel."

Interestingly, as a movie historian I now realize the picture gifted me with another legacy—a fascination for films where characters spend prolonged periods in self-reflecting isolation. The catalyst might range from a quest to a battle for survival. Not surprisingly, such cerebral sequences represent a special challenge to be cinematic. Consequently, after Hemingway's *Old Man* hooks his giant marlin and is towed further and further out to sea, director Sturges utilizes some standard movie devices to tell this singular story. For example, there are Tracy voiceovers from a work which led to a Nobel Prize for Literature (1954). Sturges also makes effective use of periodic cutaways. These startling transitions are often of lions in Africa—a frequent subject of the sometimes drowsing fisherman. There is even a brief monologue with a bird. Most significantly,

281

however, Tracy's character is given a non-traditional character at which to voice his questions about life ---the great fish pulling him into the Gulf Stream.

Prolonged sequences of such cinematic self-reflection are not the norm, yet they are hardly rare. Another favorite of mine would be Billy Wilder's depiction of the first solo nonstop transatlantic flight in *The Spirit of St. Louis* (1957, with Jimmy Stewart as Charles Lindbergh). Like Tracy, Stewart gives a tour de force performance, ably assisted by Wilder's filmmaking, including Stewart voiceovers inspired by Lindbergh's Pulitzer Prize-winning memoir (1954) of the same name. In addition, there are several flashbacks, which further flesh out Lindbergh's past, ranging from his barnstorming flying circus days, to an amusingly slapstick first attempt to solo. Stewart also has a non-human sidekick with whom to philosophize—a stowaway fly! Ironically, however, audiences probably related most to this American hero when he resorts to some basic physical shtick in fighting sleepiness during his 33-hour flight, such as the common comic pop-eyed expression of someone opening his orbs *wide* to stay awake.

Of course, the literary father of many movies about solitary self-reflection would be the *Adventures of Robinson Crusoe* (1719), by Daniel Defoe, an author who doubled as the inventor of the adventure novel. His defining character came to represent the capable and practical-minded protagonist. Crusoe was better able to understand himself and appreciate the human condition by the peaceful, rational principles he was forced to formulate after being shipwrecked upon a seemingly deserted island.

There are countless screen adaptations of this work, with maybe the most provocative being Luis Buñuel's Mexican production of the same name (1952, with a dog companion). More typical, however, are the contemporary variations upon the story, such as Robert Zemeckis' epic *Castaway* (2000, with Tom Hanks stuck on another deserted island). With no narration, little music, and a volleyball named "Wilson" to which to talk, Hanks makes us care about his survival and just how fragile are our notions of life, sanity and civilization.

More desperate than even a shipwrecked solo exile, however, is Danny Boyle's *127 Hours* (2010), an adaptation of Aron Ralston's real-life memoir *Between a Rock and a Hard Place*. As the latter title playfully suggests, a Ralston (James Franco) hiking accident in an isolated Utah canyon places him in a sort of Wile E. Coyote existentialistic cartoon—jarring loose a boulder, his fall results in said stone pinning his right arm against a rock wall in a deep chasm. Yet, with no rescuing animator, the young man must eventually amputate his own arm to free himself.

As if challenged to redefine Defoe and the adventure novel, Boyle's goal was to create "an action movie with a guy who can't move." The director does this by pushing the cinema tricks envelope with flashbacks, hallucinations, and something new—flash forwards (what might have

Spencer Tracy in *The Old Man and the Sea* (1958).

been … if the hero lived). Appropriately, for our most recent example, Ralston's reflections are directed at his video camera. Paradoxically, like the other noted protagonists, Ralston/Franco's ultimate self-reflective insight is the norm … with a negative twist. That is, he realizes everything he has done in life has led him to this situation. However, unlike the positive perseverance of the fisherman, the planned goal orientation of Lindbergh, and the inherent practicality of all the Crusoe clones, Ralston's situation was the result of a lifetime of taking foolish chances.

Happily, however, Ralston does possess the others' great ingenuity and survives. Moreover, as he learns his lesson, I can imagine my grandfather saying, "This was the most valuable reflective transition of all."

DELIGHTFUL DISTRACTIONS:

The Accidental Article

MARK TWAIN ONCE OBSERVED, "The older I get, the more clearly I recall events… that never occurred." As a frequent author of biographies, I often run into this problem when conducting interviews. On balance, it still is paramount to track down as many older historical witnesses as possible, and then play the proverbial 20 Questions game. Yet, the most accurate and refreshing perspectives on any given subject usually are found in articles and interviews that appeared as close as possible to one's focus topic. Thus, a good share of my research has me trolling old documents on microfilm.

The beauty—and distracting danger—of such duty is that one uncovers oodles of fascinating material that have nothing to do with the subject at hand. The problem is compounded further, if, as in my case, your writing covers a broad spectrum of subjects, from almost anything related to film and comedy, to an equal obsession with baseball and biography. For example, I am currently writing a biography of Will Cuppy (1884-1949), a popular humorist and mystery fiction critic for the now-defunct *New York Herald Tribune*, my favorite Gotham newspaper of yesteryear.

Naturally, I once again have been entertainingly derailed by unrelated material. Yet, here is the good news: sometimes new material congeals together just begging to be written about. For instance, Hollywood's transition to sound always has held great interest to me, and my recent metaphorical excavations for Cuppy material from the early 1930s has uncovered a wealth of fresh takes on the birth of the "talkies." What follows are just a few of these formerly lost period insights.

First, Mack Sennett, the father of American slapstick film (starting with his signature "Keystone Kops"), blamed the demise of live action

Ruth Gordon, with Bud Cort, in her later dark comedy cult classic,
Harold and Maude (1971).

physical comedy upon both sound and the animated cartoons, "A nimble rodent [Mickey Mouse] has become the world's hero. Mickey must always remain a scraggly mustachioed villain whose mischief will never be undone." In other words, how can any mere human comic top the anything goes antics available to Mickey and his animated friends?

Of course, there were horrors to be faced by the stage stars entering sound films. Here is a most-vivid description from the legendary Tallulah Bankhead, the witty, raspy-voiced beauty best remembered in film for her role in Alfred Hitchcock's *Lifeboat* (1944): "Acting fear... possessed me the first time I faced the dead, opaque eyes of a battery of cameras with a microphone overhead. I was absolutely terrified. My greatest difficulty was the lack of a real flesh and blood audience. I had no means of sensing just how things were going... I felt as though I were the veriest amateur, with all my stage training and experience counting for naught."

In contrast, popular stage and screen star Leslie Howard, later immortalized as Ashley Wilkes in *Gone With the Wind* (1939), made an easy transition to early sound films. Yet, he returned to the stage, feeling movies "have enormous undeveloped potentialities but to achieve their... most perfect development, they must dispense with sound, which is only a gratuitous and unwarranted mechanical addition to an otherwise adequate form of expression." This sounds as if he had just huddled with Charlie Chaplin, who still strongly was resisting any suggestion that his beloved Tramp ever would speak.

In delightful contrast to all of these perspectives, young stage actress Ruth Gordon, a future Academy Award recipient for *Rosemary's Baby* (1968), but today remembered as a cult favorite as Bud Cort's senior lover in *Harold and Maude* (1971), had this to say about early talkies: "[I] adored acting in front of the camera. I love the absolute quiet, when that [shooting] bell rings and the little red [silence] light goes on. You do your stuff and there's no one out front [in a theatre setting] to cough, or come in late, or drop programs on the floor; it is just heavenly silence... and after all, in the last analysis, you act for yourself, always. You work it out..."

These period quotes are reminders of my favorite euphemism for the goal of a good biographer, "Bring 'em back alive!" Such lively visceral comments during a topsy-turvy time in Hollywood underscore the organized chaos passing for history's now more-staid description, "the transition to sound," Despite the cutting edge spontaneity of these formerly forgotten pieces of time, most of them were accurate barometers for the speakers.

Bankhead's greatest future successes would be back on stage, away from the "dead, opaque eyes" of Hollywood cameras. The Mouse definitely killed Sennett's career. Film cheerleader Gordon also would go on to be a seminal cinema writer, too, such as co-scripting *Adam's Rib* (1949, the best of the Katharine Hepburn-Spencer Tracy teamings). Only Howard seemed to do a 180-degree perspective change on pictures, since he soon came to represent the perfect civilized English intellectual to American screen audiences, be it in a gangster film like *The Petrified Forest* (1936, which made Humphrey Bogart a star), or George Bernard Shaw's farce *Pygmalion* (1938). Yet, maybe the consistency of his original respect for the high art of silent cinema drove him only to embrace the best of sound film's potential.

Thus ends my exercise in microfilm distractions. Like Robert Frost's poem "The Road Not Taken," sometimes such rerouting "has made all the difference."

(Reprinted with permission from *USA Today Magazine*, July, 2013. Copyright© 2013 by "The Society for the Advancement of Education.")

THE LIGHTER SIDE

RED SKELTON:

The Gift of Laughter

Delivered as the keynote address at Ball State University, September 18, 1986, when the university conferred an honorary Doctorate of Humanities upon Red Skeleton.

WHEN I WAS ASKED TO DO THIS, many emotions went through my mind—joy that I would be able to take part in this celebration of one of my longtime comedy heroes, and fear (always a strong tradition in my family) that I might stumble on my way to the stage. But then I figured a pratfall—intended or otherwise—would hardly be out of place for the event at hand. In fact, as Red Skelton himself has chronicled, it was an unintended pratfall at the age of ten that marked the beginning of his comedy career.

I was also made somewhat nervous by the description of what I was supposed to say. I was told my comments should be "somewhere between footnotes and funny." Yes, there's nothing like good, clear directions, I always say ("Somewhere between footnotes and funny" rather reminds me of the first draft of my dissertation). I pondered this directive at length and finally decided that if my remarks ended up being less than what I intended, I could always claim I was just following instructions.

Anyway, preparing these comments really proved quite easy. Like many other television viewers of the 1950s and '60s, I grew up doing imitations of Red Skelton's cast of comedy characters. My favorite was his Mean Widdle Kid, whose delightful punchline always had him deciding in favor of mischief with—"I Dood It."

In fact, "I Dood It" became a national catchphrase after it was introduced on early 1940s radio. During World War II Colonel James

Skelton during the author's keynote address.

Doolittle's famous raid on Tokyo was widely reported by the press with the headline "Doolittle Dood It." And the comedian himself starred in a 1943 film entitled *I Dood It*. The Mean Widdle Kid and "I Dood It" are still funny today, but then—so are the whole cast of Red Skelton characters.

Indeed, probably the most fascinating thing about Red Skelton's gift of humor, besides the sheer joy of laughter it provides, is the diversity of his comedy types. His characters represent a cross-section of American humor. Mr. Skelton is America's greatest living mime, and when he combines his talents in this ancient art with his Freddie the Freeloader character, he has a character reminiscent of Chaplin's Charlie the Tramp— with whom critics have long compared him. Freddie is Red Skelton's most celebrated comedy alter ego and the showcase of the comedian's greatest gift. Freddie is also one of comedy's Everyman figures, whose appeal is universal.

Conversely, Mr. Skelton's San Fernando Red (the politician), though also very popular, is the mirror opposite of Freddie. He is the classic American huckster, the smooth-talking con man, the comic enemy and opposite of the Everyman Freddie—just as his comedy is focused on the verbal instead of the visual. San Fernando Red is a parody of all that is slick. Johnny Carson has paid Mr. Skelton the ultimate compliment by basing one of his own characters on San Fernando Red—Mr. Carson's tea-time movie host, Art Fern.

Contrasting again, Mr. Skelton's Clem Kadiddlehopper is the archetype of the country bumpkin—an affectionate parody of the rural rustic. Here was a character more crackers than crackerbarrel. That the comedian is a native Hoosier probably did not hurt the development of this figure. Of course, as we all know, in recent years Indiana has become completely sophisticated, and the bumpkin is extinct.

Mr. Skeleton's Mean Widdle Kid represents the smart-aleck youngster who has become such a central part of American humor since the 1940s, when the Kid and Edgar Bergen's Charlie McCarthy did so much to popularize the type.

Whereas these characters are all of a mainstream comedy nature, Mr. Skelton's seagull comedy team of Gertrude and Heathcliff gave us a truly unconventional showcase of humor years before the Theatre of the Absurd descended upon the scene. Of course, the fact that these two birds had many of the same problems you and I faced endeared them to us all the more. For example, my favorite Gertrude and Heathcliff dialogue had them discussing how nervous breakdowns were hereditary—"You get them from your children."

If I were allowed to have footnotes, I would add that some of this unlikely comedy team's best material is available in a book written by Mr. Skelton entitled, appropriately enough, *Gertrude & Heathcliff*, which comes complete with delightful illustrations by the comedian. However, because of the restrictions I agreed to, you'll just have to disregard what I just said.

Of course, there were countless other Red Skelton characters, favorites being Sheriff Deadeye (who was anything but a deadeye—unless the target was his own foot) and boxer Cauliflower McPugg (who added his own touch of the absurd by forever ducking whenever an imaginary flock of birds flew overhead).

To all these characters and more Mr. Skelton brought his supreme timing, his gift for slapstick, and a vulnerability that makes him one of America's greatest comic antiheroes—still the dominant comedy type of today and the character whose actions forever comically unravel—a situation most movingly demonstrated by the celebrated Freddie the Freeloader's Christmas plan to escape the cold. Freddie's plan simply entailed ordering a large restaurant meal for which he would be unable to pay—which would lead to a warm term in jail. Ironically, however, because it is Christmas, Freddie receives forgiveness instead of incarceration. Thus, even on that rare occasion when Freddie is granted a kindness, it comically backfires.

Before Mr. Skelton's long-running and award-winning television show (and paralleling his successful radio career), he also showcased a number of other comic antiheroes in a series of very popular motion pictures. Probably the best of these was *The Southern Yankee* (1948). This Civil War comedy finds him alternating between bravery and the more natural impulse of the moment—fear—as he graduates from bellhop to fumbling spy.

His movie antiheroes also surfaced in more traditional and contemporary settings, such as the delightfully comic frustrations of his title character in *The Fuller Brush Man* (1948). The public so loved his door-to-door comedy in this film that another famous redhead—Lucy—followed his lead and starred in *The Fuller Brush Girl* (1950).

Film stardom and his own radio program, *Red Skelton's Scrapbook of Satire*, had actually been made possible by his earlier comic antihero film, *Whistling in the Dark* (1941), in which a radio detective tries to survive one of his own productions. He also appeared in two sequels: *Whistling in Dixie* (1942) and *Whistling in Brooklyn* (1943). Mr. Skelton's achievements in this Whistling trilogy were recently underlined when the generally very funny Gene Wilder failed in this past summer's *Haunted Honeymoon*, a film whose story line was reminiscent of the *Whistling* films.

Besides his many memorable characters, there have been several classic comedy routines independent of these Red Skelton figures. The first and most legendary was his doughnut-dunking pantomime, which became an early trademark for him. Precipitated by a theatre manager who wanted something new in Mr. Skelton's act, the result was a hilarious look at the various ways in which people dunk their doughnuts. There was, however, a serious drawback to this socko routine. Each performance required him to eat twelve doughnuts, one each in twelve different ways. And the major vaudeville circuit upon which Red Skelton was touring had him doing the twelve-doughnut sketch three times a day. This continued for three years and thirty-five pounds. (I was tempted to make some comment here about "big time" vaudeville, but remembering my instructions, I deleted it.) Other pivotal Red Skelton sketches must include his "Guzzler's Gin" routine, his Civil War veteran watching a Fourth of July parade, and the hungry man mistaken for an actor and placed before a table full of food.

As great as these comedy accomplishments are, Red Skelton's humor is in no way limited to character or sketch situations. He is also delightfully effective playing himself as storyteller and general stand-up comedian. Even as a very young performer, he showed signs of greatness in the manner in which he handled a drunken heckler: "You know, sir, you show possibilities of developing into a total stranger." Such comedy calmness was also present in the company of the most prominent—Mr. Skelton once interrupted a presidential toast at a White House birthday party for Franklin D. Roosevelt with the warning: "Careful what you drink, Mr. President; I once got rolled in a joint like this."

His importance in the world of laughter has been underlined by the numerous comedy guests who have praised his gift. Most significant were the toasts of W.C. Fields and Groucho Marx. The mustached Marx Brother, whose comedy was so dependent upon someone to play off (especially the punning Chico, or the archetypal high-society matron Margaret Dumont), was bowled over by Red Skelton's self-contained troupe of characters, whose costume changes were limited to minor alterations on the most moldable of old hats. Thus, Groucho frequently praised Mr. Skelton.

Yet, more unusual still were the kind words of W.C. Fields. Whereas Groucho was never one to hold back praise if he thought it deserved (his cynical image notwithstanding), Fields was as apt to give away his praise as his liquor. In fact, probably his most famous pronouncement upon a rival comedian was his jealous description of Charlie Chaplin as a "damn ballet dancer." Consequently, when Fields, late in life, told a friend that if anyone ever played his life on film it should be Red Skelton, there were few higher accolades a comedian could receive.

Unlike Chaplin's aspiration to play Hamlet, or Mark Twain's belief that his rather maudlin biography of *Joan of Arc* would be his greatest work, Mr. Skelton has thankfully never second-guessed the importance of his comedy. Indeed, he has been so happy making other people happy that he has even made a shambles of the old axiom—one mustn't laugh in the telling of a story. Red Skelton's comedy joy is also ours, and this shared laughter underlines the most appropriate humor moral: comedy is contagious. Thus, he has graced the world with more than sixty years of humor in nearly every entertainment medium known to man. Of course, he also found time along the way to become an accomplished composer, painter, and author... truly, a twentieth-century Renaissance man—in clown make-up.

Still, it is those sixty plus years of laughter we celebrate tonight, a man who once described the performer's only reward as "the echo of the applause and laughter of the children." Although many have been his awards, none will express more heartfelt appreciation than is expressed tonight for a native son. It would seem most appropriate, then, to end with Red Skelton's own longtime television close—only this time addressed to him—"May God Bless."

An Addendum:

> [It was a real rush to make a favorite clown laugh who had so often made me do the same as a child. And in later research I discovered that many class clown Baby boomers like myself (including Steve Martin) had borrowed Skelton's children friendly comedy for recess material.]

> (Originally appeared in Ball State University's *Forum*, Summer 1989; Wes D. Gehring copyright.)

SMOKE 'EM IF
YOU GOT 'EM

AS A FILM PROFESSOR and writer constantly doing research, uunplanned essays keep finding me. That is, one keeps coming across related subject matter that is not your original focus. Since my studies often key on the first half of the twentieth century, lately I have been buried in mainstream newspaper and magazine articles from the late 1920s, to the early 1940s. What has really jumped out at me currently has been the elaborate cigarette ads involving movie stars.

Since this is a well-worn niche of my research territory, it is not as if I had previously been unaware of them. However, for whatever reason the detailed endorsements of what my great grandpa McIntyre used to call "coffin nails," decades before the American Surgeon General declared them a cancer risk (1964), has caught my attention.

Naturally, movies themselves have long rightfully taken it on the chin for getting people hooked on cigarettes. For example, there still seems to be some sort of chic trench coat noir aura about a cigarette dangling from Humphrey Bogart's lips. Indeed, the American Film Institute (AFI) picked him as the twentieth century's number one male movie star.

Oddly enough, arguably the two most iconic cigarette movies both occurred in 1942. The first to open was Bette Davis' ultimate worldly romance *Now, Voyager*, which closes with her former lover (Paul Henreid) lighting two cigarettes, and then with stylistic eroticism, taking one from his lips and passing it to her. A month later cigarettes helped add sacrificial passion to Bogie's repertoire in *Casablanca*, with Henreid part of a wartime triangle involving Ingrid Bergman.

As a personal addendum, and the perfect example of the axiom that "one writes to discover who they are," it had not occurred to this aging Baby boomer until just now that the two movie posters in my first dorm room had a macho tobacco connection. One was the image of 1939's *Gone*

With the Wind Clark Gable as Rhett Butler at a poker table, a small cigar clenched in his teeth. The second poster was of Sean Connery as James Bond at a high stakes gaming table in *Dr. No* (1962), just as his cigarette is lit. (I might also have had gambling issues?) Regardless, as with the movie history significance of Bogart, Gable was considered Hollywood's "King" during its golden age. Plus, Connery was Bond—*the* Bond.

Be that as it may, the print cigarette endorsement I kept encountering were often so long and detailed that the copy further belied what one always assumed—the validation represented well-paid ghosting. For example, a 1937 *New York Times* Lucky Strike testimonial from Spencer Tracy stated, "*Captain Courageous*, my new MGM picture, runs about two hours. But if all the film taken were shown, it would run three solid days and nights. Many scenes were taken on the open ocean. Naturally raising my voice PUT A STRAIN on my throat. In one scene I had to yell for most of two days. Yet, I could always take a Lucky without worrying about my throat… Maybe it's a better tobacco. Well, anyway, I like them plenty, and so do most other people around MGM."

In a later 1937 *New York Times* Lucky ad, President Franklin Delano Roosevelt's favorite actress, Myrna Loy (most synonymous with MGM's "Thin Man" series), observed, "It's always easy for me to get a Lucky from Joan Crawford or Clark Gable, or even from most of the newcomers to the studio." From many endorsement choices, Loy was showcased for several reasons. First, her popularity was such that at the same time Gable was labeled Hollywood's King, she was named Movie Land's "Queen." Second, her FDR link is appropriate, since he is the president possibly most associated with cigarettes, given the many Depression era confidence-boosting pictures of him smoking by way of a cigarette holder tilted upward.

A third link is Loy's MGM status. The American Tobacco company (producer of Lucky Strike) paid some movie stars as much as $10,000 a year (well-over $100,000 in today's currency) to endorse Luckies. The company wanted to control the film industry, and MGM was *the* studio. The only misleading item in the research is suggesting it was a sound era phenomenon. Silent film *Photoplay* magazines are equally full of such ads, though other cigarette brands are more common. For instance, a 1928 *Photoplay* Old Gold blurb has Charlie Chaplin pitching, "One cigarette test was like shooting a scene successfully after a series of failures. It just 'clicked' and I named it my choice…. It seems that Rin Tin Tin and Strongheart [another canine film star] are the only film stars that don't

The Tramp smoking away (circa 1915).

smoke them." Though no doubt also a paid endorsement, at least my favorite comedian's blurb is funny.

Moreover, speaking of comedians, there was at least one 1930s iconoclastic cigarette star in Hollywood. W. C. Fields' mid-decade ill health had stalled his screen career, but he was able to rebound by way of very lucrative radio work with ventriloquist Edgar Bergen and his smart aleck dummy Charlie McCarthy. (Do not try to make sense of a hit ventriloquist *on radio*.) In researching a book on Fields, I discovered he was being paid $7,500 a week by the all-powerful sponsoring Luckies. Yet, despite that salary, Fields could not help playing a fifth columnist after the sponsor moved him to another popular radio program "Your Hit Parade." For his comedy sketch material, he created a fictitious son, Chester Fields (à la Chesterfield cigarettes). It was weeks before the less than happy Lucky Strike people caught on.

PSYCHO SPOOFED

One of Hitchcock's favorite stories concerned a man being led to the gallows who expressed concern over the rickety construction of the trap door, asking, "Is that thing safe?" Hitchcock's goal therefore, was to be both darkly comic *and* "to provide the public with beneficial shocks [presumably, those which are not fatal]."

– Alfred Hitchcock

THANKS TO *PSYCHO*, Alfred Hitchcock, the man who single-handedly revived the nightlight business and made nerve medicine a growth industry, is considered the father of the modern horror film. *Psycho* demonstrated you need not go to Transylvania for things which go bump in the night; you could just as easily be scared out of your mind (such as it is) by that nice boy or girl next door. *Psycho* was also called a "dirty" movie (no, not that kind) because after Janet Leigh's unfortunate decision to take a shower, people refused to go near running water for months.

Hitchcock himself merely thought of it as a "humorous film," a "fun picture," which gives you some idea of why his dinner parties were never too large. Repeated viewings of *Psycho* reveal, however, some comically macabre lines -- like "title character" Norman Bates observing, "Mother, what's the phrase? She isn't quite herself today." Darn straight; she's stuffed and tucked away in, you should excuse the expression, the fruit cellar. (What Hitchcock says about the movie is actually pretty funny, but we won't go into that here. However, anyone who named his dog Phillip of Magnesia, as he did, was not always a laugh riot with which to deal.)

Hitchcock himself had been a strict mama's boy reared with oodles of Catholic guilt. Yes, if he had been reared in another faith, say

Episcopalian (which is like Catholic "Lite," with one-third the guilt), he probably would not have been as great an artist. Hitchcock later joked about the still lingering guilt which had been drummed into him as a child. For instance, when asked what his tombstone epitaph should be, he replied: "This is what we do to bad little boys." Moreover, the director's mother was the original Iron Maiden, who forever responded in the calm, measured way made famous by the French Revolution.

Anyway, as with all Hitchcock films, it is hard to get into the first few minutes since you're too busy looking for his famous cameo appearance. But once you spot him outside blonde Janet Leigh's place of business (Alfred had a thing for blondes; it's in all his bios), you're ready for some plot analysis. Oh, just a little analysis. Leigh's character, Marion *Crane*, living in *Phoenix* (There's a hidden bird motif in *Pyscho*, but if it's hidden, what good is it?), is about to meet a psychopathic *bird* taxidermist. She has just stolen $40,000 from someone lower than pond scum. Thus, we can hardly hold it against her, especially since she needs it to start a new life with her financially pinched sweetie. Of course, the viewer wonders if this guy isn't completely off his nut for refusing to marry Crane merely because of a cash flow problem. This is especially so since Alfred "voyeuristic" Hitchcock has portrayed her in such a sexy manner early in the film. (Initial surveys found she had made male viewers' teeth sweat.)

The stolen money is Hitchcock's most famous example of a red herring—making something insignificant momentarily seem important. In simple language, always a rarity in film study, it jump starts the story. And among Hitchcock fans, which includes everyone this side of Mars, the red herring is referred to as a "MacGuffin:"

> The term MacGuffin is allegedly derived from an old nonsense joke about two men traveling by train (Hitchcock's favorite means of transportation) in Scotland. One man notices a goofy-looking package in the overhead luggage rack and asks what it is.
>
> "It's a MacGuffin," replies the other.
>
> "What's that?"
>
> "It's a contrivance for catching lions in the Scottish Highlands."
>
> "But the Scottish Highlands don't have any lions!"
>
> "Well, then, I guess that's no MacGuffin!"

Crane leaves town to meet her lover and as night falls, she drives into a terrible storm. She cannot see her hands in front of her face, not that there is much pleasure in that. The viewer who is alert to such things knows the storm is either a symbol of her internal moral dilemma over the MacGuffin (the stolen money, you putz) or a low pressure front from Kalamazoo. Regardless, storms are frightfully dramatic, just ask any meteorologist.

Alfred Hitchcock getting in touch with his feminine side on the set of *Psycho* (1960).

The film cuts to the next morning. Crane had pulled off onto the shoulder during the storm and had fallen asleep in her car. She is now awakened in the middle of nowhere by a highway patrolman the size of a Buick, wearing those irritating mirrored sunglasses and tapping on her window (more voyeurism). This is not the most pleasant wake-up call, especially when it looks like this guy has been reared by Nazis. (If this is God's country, He can have it.) Moreover, Mount Rushmore with a badge is not only scary, he gives deadly advice, as in suggesting Crane try an area motel. In another life this was probably the same guy who directed Custer toward Little Big Horn.

Hitchcock often portrays law enforcement types as scary. According to an army of Freudian biographers, little Alfred was once locked up in the neighborhood slammer for twenty minutes on some nothing infraction, like dealing jelly doughnuts. It seems his father thought it would be an amusing way to teach the boy respect for the law. Evidently, old man Hitchcock was into dark humor, too. But I digress. (Actually, digressions are a major part of academic life.)

Crane drives on and on. It seems her lover lives somewhere on the other side of the planet. Halfway there she changes cars. One is never sure if this was a cover for her crime or if she had just worn out the first car. Was the entire Sunbelt without plane service at this time?

Facing a second night on the road, Crane decides to stop at the Bates Motel. Big mistake. Ask anyone. She must have misunderstood those Bates "half-off" signs. After registering, she has a long talk with Norman, who seems to be such a nice boy. So much for first impressions. Norman tells her, "I think we're all in our private traps." But little does Crane know this trap should have a sign over it saying, "booby hatch." He also tells her, "We all go a little mad sometimes." Unfortunately, she thought he was speaking metaphorically.

Crane soon discovers her lover's town is merely minutes away. Now, just between you and me and your favorite hiding place during thunderstorms, wouldn't you think she would jump into her car and make tracks to her boyfriend? But no, she sticks around for some unknown reason (dare we say the good of Hitchcock's plot?). Of course, the director was never into logic. As Casey Stengel would say, "Look it up."

That night as she undresses for a shower, Bates peeks at her through a hole in the wall. The picture which normally covers the hole is of *Susanna and the Elders*—the Biblical story of a woman overtaken in her bath by voyeurs whose passions were aroused as they spied on her. You can say what you want about Hitchcock—especially now that he's dead—but the man was a terror, so to speak, on detail.

Hitchcock's voyeurism here, as we join Norman in peeking through the window, will implicate the viewer in the forthcoming crime. You know, the shower murder. Must the author keep track of everything? Let's not argue. As a footnote, always big in academic settings (actually required), even Hitchcock's anti-exercise philosophy was tied to voyeurism. He once observed, "My exertion is all from the neck up. I watch. Consequently, a real workout for the director would be something like shaving … which, of course, necessitates more watching.

Anyhow, the male viewer does not mind another peek at the disrobing Crane. Hitchcock has done this twice before, and nothing happened, other than hubba-hubba Crane making every male viewer's interest in cinema "study" increase. But this time is different. We identify with the peeking Norman, shortly before he, dressed as his mother, kills Crane. He was funny that way.

Moving to the shower scene. Frequently called by film critics the most—you should pardon the expression—well-cut segment in movie history, let's be brief. Many critics are still in therapy from the first time they saw it. Film texts note the knife never actually touches Crane's body (yeah, right, tell that to my heart). The slashing effect is done through editing. Less than a minute in length, the expensive sequence took a week to shoot, not to mention the water and towel bills. Two cameramen drowned.

Part of the shock involved in the shower scene is the fact that Crane has just decided to return the money and go straight. Thus, the shower would initially seem to represent (WARNING: symbolism just ahead) a sort of cleansing or baptism… a new start. Plus, scary things are supposed to happen in the dark, nasty places—not your cozy, warm, well-lit shower.

But knowing all these horror film rules, Hitchcock still goes ahead and knocks off Crane, with Bernard Herrmann's piercing, scream-like score necessitating local dogs be re-housebroken. However, the biggest shower shock was Alfred killing off the *star*—only one-third of the way into the film, for crying out loud. That kind of thing still isn't done. You identify with her, feeling secure nothing will happen. After all, Leigh has top billing… and she's cute. Following this sudden exit, many viewers nearly lost meals they had had in the '50s.

Next comes the spic and span scene, where Norman comes in to discover what "Mother" has done (the silly goose still doesn't realize he periodically becomes Mother). Well, he cleans up what his other half has done, but this is one case where cleanliness is not next to Godliness, unless we're talking Old Testament bipolar God and, say, turning Lot's wife into a pillar of salt.

Now that Norman has cleaned up that nasty old bathroom it is time for a short aside about Hitchcock's sophomoric fascination with toilets. It was just this side of "hello, perversity." He was titillated by objects connected with private bodily functions, as well as showing things on screen which the period censorship code found radically subversive. You know, like flushing a toilet—long a telltale sign of political unrest. Thus, *Psycho* was the first mainstream film in which he could showcase a working privy in all its erotic glory. And the director was as pleased as you can legally get about what polite society calls the comfort station but which, in lieu of his British citizenship, we will call the throne room. As a crapper footnote to this subject, Hitchcock's favorite gift item for special friends was the noiseless toilet, which always makes a certain statement under the Christmas tree. There is, however, no truth to the 1960s rumor that Hitchcock's favorite song was "Smoking in the Boy's Room."

Now, if you haven't made the connection that Norman is Mother Bates, there is a tendency to identify with him. Besides needing some focus character after the shower scene, Norman is sympathetic. Wouldn't you hate it if you always had to clean up after your mother's murders? Here you have had a hard day of changing sheets at the motel—not to mention stuffing birds for the office—and now you have to mop up all that blood in the next room. In a rare moment of sympathy for the *Psycho* audience, Hitchcock decided against shooting in color, feeling this would be too much for the viewer. Thus is recorded a rare instance of this director misreading the modern audience. Personally, I think he was just saving some money. Plus, since he loved ice cream, and liquid chocolate doubled for blood in black and white movies, you pick an answer.

Viewer connection to Norman is best displayed in the next scene, where Crane's body is in the trunk of her car and the dutiful son is watching it sink into the ever-handy swamp on the back forty. Suddenly, the car stops submerging and you panic just like Norman does; it's never good to have murder evidence sticking out of your neighborhood bog. (Or at least that was the case when this project started).

Then the car resumes its descent and we, like Norman, can breathe easily again. Of course, one feels a bit perverse about having rooted for the sinking car, but time passes and you continue to eat your popcorn. The postscript to the scene is that unbeknownst to Norman, he has also sunk the stolen money. Crane had hidden the cash in a newspaper, which also gets placed in the trunk as more evidence of her presence which needs to be disposed of. And Alfred "red herring" Hitchcock has manipulated us once again. (My first wife always remembered this phrase as "pink salmon." I sensed you wanted to know.)

Hitchcock called such cinema exploitation "pure filmmaking." Translation: the man definitely liked jerking his audience around. Of course, we shouldn't feel too badly. Hitch was harder on his actors, since he knew the ultimate performance was really in his editing. Any of us could have just as effectively played Leigh's character in the shower... not that people would be standing in line to sub. However, Hitchcock forever denied having said, "Actors are cattle." He corrected the actual quote to: "Actors should merely be treated like cattle." Regardless, Hitchcock's direction was minimal. One of his actors explained, "If Hitchcock liked what you did, he said nothing. If he didn't he looked like he was going to throw up." Voyeurs are like that.

As a sexual addendum (always a popular addition), actor Anthony Perkins' ability to play both mother and son so effectively was probably assisted by his bisexual nature. Indeed, an AC-DC sexual preference was something Alfred "repressed sexuality" Hitchcock looked for in performers. He felt they had to be part feminine and part masculine to get inside their characters. Subjectively for him went beyond gender... which can be painful. For more information on this, or some lovely French postcards, simply phone Hollywood's favorite erotic bakery— affectionately called "Get Your Buns in Here." Operators are standing by (they cannot afford chairs).

Returning now to our normally scheduled plot synopsis, the rest of the film is about Crane's lover (who looks nothing like an ambassador (President Reagan later appointed him our Mexican Ambassador) and sister trying to discover what happened to her. This portion of the story is often a bit fuzzy because many of us hid under our chairs during the shower sequence and it took several days to pry us out—part fear and part all those old Jujubes on the floor.

Actually, most viewers only hid under their seats for half an hour. Unfortunately, many came up just about the time the detective (Martin Balsam) was going up the steps in Norman's creepy old house. Before you could say, "You fool, you fool," there was another mess to clean up. *Psycho*'s shock scenes occur every thirty minutes, almost as methodically as Englishman Hitchcock took tea breaks. The director adds one of his dark jokes here—the "private eye" is fatally stabbed in the eye. Of course, it could have been worse; Hitchcock might have called him a "dick."

The rest of the film represents another descent, but we're not talking bog here. This one is psychological—an exploration of major fruitcake Norman, who limited himself to two personalities because he never wanted a big family. On the subject of learning more, the audience is on the fence (which is more comfortable than being under those seats). Hitchcock has been so successful at linking us to Bates, from hot-to-trot voyeurism to rooting for sinking cars, that there is a certain fear on our part that suggests maybe we're all capable of something like this.

Why does it come as no surprise that two of Hitchcock's favorite books as a youngster were *The Strange Case of Dr. Jekyll and Mr. Hyde* and *The Picture of Dorian Gray*? (You were expecting maybe *Rebecca of Sunnybrook Farm*?) Young Hitchcock probably did not spend an over abundance of time in the sandbox… unless he was burying something. Regardless, the double or dual personality theme is very important to him, especially in *Psycho*, where Norman, via Mother Bates, is (like that old gag about the excited Siamese twins) "beside himself."

Alfred further contributes to this disturbing dual personality effect as Crane's good-guy lover and sicko Norman look so much alike. Thus, when we have a confrontation late in the film, facing each other across Bates' office counter, you want to shout, "Stop the projector! Let's play Twister!" (Sorry about that.) The two characters seem interchangeable, and that's scary.

While the men fight, Crane's sister goes to Norman's house—not a terribly bright idea, but it gets the old blood pressure soaring again, especially since another 30 minutes are about up. Her exploration of Norman's domain uncovers more Freudian levels than Sigmund's toolbox. Crammed with Victorian décor, the dump literally oozes sexual repression. (As an adult Hitch introduced himself as "Just Hitch, no cock.")

When Norman comes to the house, Crane's sister hides in the basement—another major league boner. Has this person never seen a scary movie? Downstairs she spots the seated backside of Norman's mummified mommy. But just as she starts to turn the chair (luckily it is a swivel style), Norman, dressed as murdering Ma, comes zipping down the stairs with his trusty knife.

Well, Sis throws up her arms, as you are want to do when a psychotic killer dressed as an old woman comes at you with a blade as large as a horse's leg. One of Sis's arms bumps the dangling overhead light, and its swinging casts eerie—make that downright disturbing—light in and out of Ma Bates' empty eye sockets. Sis's scream, often bolstered by the screams of chicken audience members everywhere, merges with Bernard Herrmann's ever chilling score (it's those shrieking violin strings again). But quicker than you can say "I can't handle another murder today!," Crane's lover comes to the rescue and Norman is out of the motel business.

The boringly complacent explanation by the court psychiatrist at the film's close is not so much to enlighten the viewer as to seemingly give him or her a few moments in which to get composed, put eyes back in the head, and resume normal breathing before getting up. Of course, Doc does explain why Norman did his taxidermy thing on Ma Bates. It seems Norman lost a sense of security with her death: can't live with her, can't live without her. You know, the down side of murder. Consequently, he wanted to keep her memory alive, which shows a nice spirit by Norman, though unfortunately, the timing for this change of heart was not ideal for Ma Bates.

Regardless, there is no rest for the voyeuristic audience. Just as this clinical overview starts to lull one into a sense if security, Hitchcock jerks us back to watching Norman (who has now forever become Mother) in his little padded cell. And as we play Peeping Tom one last time, checking out the now permanent mad stare of Mother (another Hitchcock example of death taking possession of the living), we hear her thought: "They're probably watching me now [meaning asylum security—but then again, maybe "she" knows we're tuned in, too]… I hope they are watching! [You got it, sweetie.]" Hitchcock then superimposes a skull on "her" face (always a comforting image) and the film closes on Crane's car being pulled from the bog. Because viewers have at sometimes invariably related to Norman, there is a tendency to feel as slimy as the swamp car.

Despite being forever spoofed, with just this side of a zillion copycat films from Hollywood, where all things are created sequel, *Psycho* continues to have the power to manipulate audiences, especially the heebie-jeebie fears which come from thinking about our own dark sides. So don't let anyone ever tell you *Psycho* is just a horror film. That would be like describing Charles Manson and friends as just another dysfunctional family.

(Originally appeared in *Film Classic Reclassified*, 2001; Wes D. Gehring copyright.)

THE WIZARD OF OZ
SPOOFED

People still believe "There's no place like home," which, to paraphrase Robert Benchley, proves why democracy can never be a success.

IF REDONE TODAY, *Oz*'s conclusion would probably include a high speed car chase on the Yellow Brick Road and/or some gratuitous sex (like Munchkins doing it) and violence (maybe graphic film footage of the house squishing the first witch). But musical fantasy does demand suspension of disbelief. For instance, when the Wicked Witch of the West zooms by on her souped up broomstick, no one in the audience jumps up and says, "cut the crap-ola; witches can't fly, unless they go coach like the rest of us."

Along the same lines, you just have to accept that some teenager would burst into song on the family pig lot. This is not to say it couldn't happen. But a recent random survey of people who have warbled on pig farms found "Over the Rainbow" selected only once. The "Oscar Meyer Weiner Song" usually clocked in at number one.

Like most fantasies, the key to *The Wizard of Oz* is the sense of home. Indeed, Dorothy even manages to fly to Oz in the family dump. Now while she was somewhat assisted by a tornado, it's a fitting development for the genre. (Genre is a la-de-da French term sometimes thought to mean "use the small fork," but when referred to in films it means types, like Western, musicals … Please finish this out on your own.) Regardless, another example of fantasy's forever-going-home is that nearly everyone Dorothy knew in Kansas pops up in Oz. Sure they might be sporting a fur coat and tail or a tin jumpsuit, but they're the same folks. It's all there in the credits.

311

While Dorothy hangs out a lot with a scarecrow, a cowardly lion, and a tin man (not recommended for children at home), the pivotal *Oz* characters in terms of fantasy are: the Wicked Witch (a regular bad day in Bosnia), Glinda the Good Witch, and Dorothy. (Apologies to Toto fans). That is, most of these anything goes fantasies have a super villain, a super mentor, a super child, though copyright restrictions have kept

Dorothy (Judy Garland) and company in *The Wizard of Oz*, with (left to right) Jack Haley, Bert Lahr, Ray Bolger, and up top, Frank Morgan.

them from wearing tights and a cape. Comparing it to *Star Wars*, Glinda is a combination Obi-Wan Kenobi and Yoda (though naturally her voice is higher and she's into those floating bubble entrances and exits). The Wicked Witch could be equated with Darth Vader, despite there being no known footage of him on a broom.

Of course everything revolves around Judy Garland's Dorothy. A full-bosomed and mature-looking sixteen-year-old, Judy Garland was probably not exactly what *Oz* author Frank Baum had in mind for his *child* hero. Neither did Hollywood's resident Wicked Witch, er uh, Warlock, Louis B. Mayer—head of the studio (the one with the lion) making *The Wizard of Oz*. He originally wanted Shirley Temple for the part, but the Good Ship Lollipop girl's studio told Mayer, "In your dreams, fat boy," or words to that effect. Poor Mayer, he was only *stuck* with a soon-to-be superstar. The down side was for Judy. For a time Garland had to prance around in a blonde wig and frilly dress à la Temple. Mayer was bound and determined she should look Temple childlike, so he had her bosom bound, too, or at least girdled and strapped. Plus, wanting his Dorothy to look wide-eyed and gaunt (being whirled about by a tornado often does that), he subjected Garland to alternate days of fasting. The near major league boo-boo of not casting Judy is only rivaled by the initial decision that the song "Over the Rainbow" was just too darn long and should be cut from the film! Yes, you heard right. Moreover, it was only reluctantly added later when the powers that be … make that the dumb powers that be, decided they didn't have time to film another number. Thank goodness for time constraints.

Like many fantasy films, the *Wizard of Oz* also functions as a coming of age movie. Just think of Judy's Dorothy as a rebel without an attitude. As Professor Marvel (and soon to be the Wizard of Oz) described Dorothy's running away, "They don't appreciate you … You want to see other lands – big cities, big mountains, big oceans." You'll note, however, that there's never any mention of flying monkeys . . .something that frequently makes one rethink those running away plans. One should add that W. C. Fields turned down the Professor Marvel role. Maybe he did drink too much! If he had taken the part, the flying monkey sequences could have been played as an attack of the DTs. Because as Fields once observed, "It's hard to tell where Hollywood ends and the DTs begin."

Be that as it may, as with many would-be fantasy rebels, Dorothy spends most of the time trying to get back home. Actually, this represents the greatest suspension of disbelief—that she would pick old fuddy-duddy black and white Kansas over Technicolor Oz—with its zany flora and fauna, from talking trees to those cute midget Munchkins. Dorothy had obviously never driven across Kansas in the summer time. It's so flat you can watch your dog run away … for days. But put this question to anyone, "Would you like to vacation 'over the rainbow' in Oz's Emerald City (not to mention your own poppy field), or be sentenced to two weeks in Topeka, Kansas?" If this is a tough decision for you, chances are, like Dorothy, you've recently been smacked in the noggin by some airborne house shutters. (Ah, Kansas, where they think a good time is an extra hour of church!)

The film's most understated line, "Toto, I have a feeling we're not in Kansas anymore!" is rebelliously ironic, since at the movie's close one discovers it has been a dream and she has never left home. Don't you hate it when films end with that "it's only a dream" crap? It takes away from Dorothy's adventure. Here she has this great swashbuckling quest of a story to tell and everyone says, "yeah, yeah you were just snoozing." Besides, a dream with that large a cast (over 9,000, honest!) would have surely short circuited most noodles, whether they were sleeping or not. And they never pulled any of this "it's only a dream" baloney on Peter Pan.

In Baum's original story Oz was no dream, which also suggests this guy could really party. But if you have to have the dream cop-out close (there's always some spoilsport), there is a historical parallel of interest. The same year *The Wizard of Oz* was published (1900), Freud's *Interpretation of Dreams* appeared. And since that time numerous psychiatrists, those talent scouts for mental institutions, have used *The Wizard of Oz* as a metaphor for everything from the traumas of growing up, to the dangers of landing your house in a new time zone.

Freud thought of the writer juggling concepts as really like a child playing with his or her toys, which just goes to show maybe it was Freud who should have been on the couch. Still, classic children's literature has as much for the adult as for the shrimp, though as Groucho reminds us, it would be a better world if the adults had to eat the spinach. Regardless, Baum's Oz is the reminder that the most powerful "Wizard" can end up being a fake from Omaha (cities may vary from person to person), and that we often painstakingly search for things we already have (this does not apply to lost car keys).

Oz's original celebrated upbeat ending is tied to the fact that traditional Dorothy is just pleased, after her lawless spree, not to be serving major time in some Oz slammer. Her infractions included:

wearing stolen shoes, carrying a concealed dog, melting a witch without a permit, inciting Munchkins to riot, trafficking in (or actually trafficking through) poppies, crash landing a farmhouse on a prominent citizen, appropriating apples, loitering with little people, excessive perkiness, conspiracy to swipe a broom, extorting wishes from a broken-down wizard, and repeating "There's no place like home" one time too many. Fleeing to Kansas, Dorothy was undoubtedly aware that the state did not allow extradition to Oz, or any other dreamy place. Staying in Kansas was punishment enough.

For Judy Garland fans, which includes most of the civilized world (and even parts of Trenton, New Jersey), *Oz* also holds a special poignancy, given her less than happy later life. People often equate Dorothy's innocence with that of the young Garland; this can result in a good cry, if there is such a thing, and strange looks from any nearby little people, as in children, not Munchkins. So to avoid possible embarrassment, as the film comes to its moving conclusion, distract yourself with thoughts of either flying monkeys, or that old comic definition of a fantasy: a yarn told to pacify a suspicious spouse. But whatever you do, get off the couch for a while. Even if there's no place like home, people are beginning to think you don't have a life.

(This abridged version originally appeared in *Film Classics Reclassified*, 2001; Wes D. Gehring copyright.)

HE ADORES THE CITY
SO NICE THEY
NAMED IT TWICE

[Since so much of my research has taken place in my favorite city—New York—it seems only fitting that I close this collection with an essay about my dearest visit to a personal Eighth Wonder of the World.]

HEY, I HAVE A CONFESSION TO MAKE. Oh, let's not get too excited here; this is nothing to make your teeth sweat. My shrink, the last person I talk to before I talk to myself, just thinks I should open up more. And I mean that in a strictly "non-flasher" manner.

My confession? I love New York. There, I've said it. And I don't care who knows it. You've heard all the jokes, like it is "the city that never sleeps… because people are guarding their hubcaps and chaining down their valuables."

But after a recent trip to New York, I remain the city's biggest fan. There are so many inspired distractions, many of them legal. And the culture! Avant-garde film, ballet, theatre… Why, just outside my hotel there was a guy who could play "Lady of Spain" on his head, not to mention a dynamite, blindfolded rendition of "My Way."

This trip, however, had a special twist; I took my daughters, 11-year-old Emily and 16-year-old Sarah. (Yes, former readers of my "Comedy Corner" column, "Baby Sarah" is nearly college age. Just a minute while I get my heart medicine.)

Anyway, for years they have heard about my New York research trips and have forever dropped subtle hints like, "Take us, please!" Recently, it dawned on me that time was running out, especially since Sarah seems to be spending more and more time with some guy named Rick, though that might be just some alias. (The fellow I have tailing him reports back to me a week from Tuesday.)

Despite never having a bad experience in New York, I was a little anxious about taking my girls. As the standard Nervous Nelly Dad, I kept seeing images of Mel Gibson in *Ransom*.

This was brought home to me by my normally tough-nut Emily. Remember, this is the shrimp that won a *USA Today* "Kids Say the Darnedest Things"-style contest at 5 with a response to my innocent comment, "Want to go steady?"—"I'm your daughter; what do you want to do, end up like Woody Allen?" Anyhow, normally Little Miss Moxie asked me while the trip was still in the planning stage, "You wouldn't mind if I held your hand—sometimes?"

Having raised the girls to honor the Beatles above all others, with the possible exception of Charlie Chaplin, the hit of the trip was visiting Central Park's tribute to John Lennon, "Strawberry Fields," where they had me take just under 6,000 photos.

I had told them that people often leave remembrances on the "Imagine" (his greatest song) sidewalk mosaic, so the girls decided on flowers and an apple—the latter being the logo for the Beatles record label. The apple created a buzz among the tourists, with Sarah finding herself momentarily surrounded by a group of little old ladies politely drilling her about the significance of "this fruit."

Of course, there were also the more mainstream required stops, such as a visit to the Empire State Building. This year, for added safety, there was a periodic strip search (always a favorite for me) before going out on the observation platform.

Ironically, however, the day we were there, King Kong had managed to get by security. But he seemed quite amicable and posed for pictures. (He's much shorter in person and claims Fay Wray and he were "just friends.")

Since my NYC trips normally involve research, our itinerary included a brief stop at the pivotal, for me, Lincoln Center Special Collection Library. The girls were impressed by the casual, almost jaunty security: "Yo, youse behave or we break your legs."

Yes, there is nothing like simple communication. Compliance is nearly 100 percent, though there is the occasional scream. But it is nothing you cannot work through. These are people who probably once had food fights with the food still in the cans.

I also took the girls to the center of American wit during the 1920s: the Algonquin Hotel's Round Table. Here celebrated humorists like Robert Benchley and Dorothy Parker traded dark humor, like her suggestions for her tombstone epitaph: "This is on me," or "If you can read this, you are standing too close."

Woody Allen and Diane Keaton in *Manhattan* (1979).

Yes, the walls seemed to be talking, but then that often happens when one drinks. When Benchley was warned that alcohol consumption was slow death, he observed, "Who's in a hurry?"

Any negatives? Only one. The evening we were to take a boat cruise out to the Statue of Liberty territory, Sarah took ill. In a scenario titled "Parental Nightmare" (with illustrations by that artist who did the painting *The Scream*), I stood at a pier ticket window trying to get a refund while 20 paces away Sarah was feeding the fish and a disappointed Emily was yelling in my ear, "Just send her back to the hotel in a taxi." One can't blame the city for Sarah's upset tummy, though the three of us had knocked down a lot of New York cheesecake.

Thus, I continue to strongly recommend this place. And if you have any thoughts on the subject, I'd be surprised… uh, er, I mean, swell. We can share wild cab ride stories or discuss that zany fixture on Columbus Circle who specializes in heated arguments with himself.

(Originally appeared in the *Muncie Star Press*, August 11, 1997; Wes D. Gehring copyright.)